3-30-65 (61-17061) Sparks

T. Butler King of Georgia

T. BUTLER KING

T. Butler King of Georgia

BY EDWARD M. STEEL, JR.

UNIVERSITY OF GEORGIA PRESS *Athens*

EDWARD M. STEEL, Jr., a native of Tennessee, is a member of the History Department at West Virginia University. He was graduated *cum laude* from Harvard in 1940. During World War II he served as a bomber pilot in the Eighth Air Force in Europe. After the war he taught English for two years at Virginia Polytechnic Institute, and then began graduate study in history at the University of North Carolina. While there he was a Fellow of the Institute for Research in the Social Sciences. He received his M.A. in 1950 and his Ph.D. in 1953. He has also taught at Millsaps College and Limestone College.

Contents

Preface

STUDENTS of the past frequently focus their attention on the most outstanding political and military leaders, to the exclusion of those men in public and private life whose roles were less than heroic. Yet the lives of these supporting actors can contribute to our knowledge; they may even restore a perspective otherwise lost. Thomas Butler King achieved prominence in several fields of activity. As a cotton planter, Whig politician, railroad promoter, and Confederate propagandist, he kept in the forefront of the economic and political scene. Although he was a spokesman for the cotton planters of Georgia, his greatest legislative triumphs promoted the maritime interests of the nation. He began to extol railroads when they were novelties, and in the middle years of the century he was an ardent supporter of a transcontinental line. As a propagandist for the Confederacy he had no superior.

This study is an attempt to follow King's career and assess his leadership. It was begun at the suggestion and under the guidance of Dr. Fletcher M. Green, for whose supervision and counsel I wish to express my gratitude. I take this opportunity to extend my thanks to Dr. Isaac Copeland, Nashville, Tennessee; and Dr. Milton S. Heath, Chapel Hill, North Carolina, for reading portions of the manuscript and suggesting improvements. The late Mrs. Margaret Davis Cate, Sea Island, Georgia, very kindly gave me access to otherwise unobtainable material in her possession relating to Thomas Butler King, as did Dr. Alexander Heard, Nashville, Tennessee.

For the many courtesies afforded me over the course of several years, I wish to express my appreciation to members of the staffs of the following institutions and organizations; Bancroft Library, University of California, Berkeley, California; Buffalo Historical Society, Buffalo, New York; Bureau of Railway Economics, Washington, D. C.; California State Library, Sacramento, California; Duke University Library, Durham, North Carolina; Georgia Historical Society, Savannah, Georgia; Library of the Georgia State College for Women, Milledgeville, Georgia; Henry E. Huntington Memorial Library, San Marino, California; Library of Congress, Washington, D. C.; Louisville Free Public Library, Louisville, Kentucky; National Archives, Washington, D. C.; Edwin Smith Historical Museum, Westfield, Massachusetts; Southern Historical Collection, University of North Carolina, Chapel Hill, North Carolina; Library of the University of North Carolina; Library of West Virginia University, Morgantown, West Virginia.

EDWARD M. STEEL, JR.
Morgantown, West Virginia

· I ·

A Fortunate Young Man

TOWARD THE close of the year 1839, a vigorous man in his late thirties left his plantation on Saint Simons Island, Georgia, to attend the meeting of Congress in Washington. In appearance, Thomas Butler King was accounted handsome, with his pale complexion, cleanly modeled face, and piercing gray eyes. His chin was firm and his lips met in a stern line, but his manners were affable. In activities, as well as appearance, he fitted the stereotype, already firmly fixed, of the aristocratic Southern planter. Although trained for the bar, he did not practice his profession; instead, he devoted his energies to his planting operations, to his varied business interests, and to public affairs. During the past eight years he had enjoyed repeated successes in state politics, and the voters of Georgia had now elected him to represent them in Congress.

Representative though he might be of his state and class, Thomas Butler King was not a native Georgian. He was born August 27, 1800, in Palmer, Massachusetts, the son of Daniel and Hannah Lord King.[1] Both his parents came of old New England stock, but his mother's forebears were the earlier settlers and the more eminent. Hannah Lord was one of the fourth generation of descendants of William Lord of Saybrook, Connecticut. As merchants, soldiers, and landholders, members of the Lord family played respectable roles in the affairs of their colony from 1635 until the Revolution. By the middle of the eighteenth century they had settled near Old Lyme, Connecticut, and were known as the "River Lords" because of their valley landholdings.[2]

Daniel King's family were comparative newcomers to New England. John King, an Englishman, in 1716 settled in the frontier

1

district of Massachusetts known as the Elbow Tract. He and his
children, with other settlers, soon formed a small community
known variously as King's Row, Kingsfield, or Kingstown. Because
of disputes over land titles the area remained unorganized as a
district until 1752, when it received the official designation of the
township of Palmer. Before the land titles were settled the patri-
arch of the community died. His son Thomas became a leader in
the community and in turn reared a family that included a son
named Daniel. Corporal Daniel King was among the Palmer min-
utemen who answered the Lexington alarm of April 19, 1775.[3]

To the union of Daniel King and Hannah Lord were born six
sons, and of these Thomas Butler King was the fourth. By the time
Thomas Butler was fifteen, both his parents had died, and he was
making his home with relatives in the Wyoming Valley of Pennsylvania. His brother Henry, some ten years his senior, had established himself as a lawyer in Allentown, Pennsylvania, while other
relatives, the Butler family, also lived in the Wyoming Valley.
King's aunt, Anne Lord, had married General Zebulon Butler, the
leader of the Connecticut pioneers who settled in the isolated
Wyoming section of northern Pennsylvania, and whose Pennamite
Wars so disturbed the public peace during and after the American
Revolution.[4]

Of King's youth and schooling little can be stated with certainty.
He attended the Westfield Academy in Westfield, Massachusetts,
one of the many secondary schools that sprang up in New England around the turn of the century.[5] Westfield differed from
many of the academies of the day in that it was a public, not a
private institution. Furthermore, the authorities embraced some
novel educational ideas, for the school was coeducational and corporal punishment was prohibited.[6] After attending the academy
King continued his education in Pennsylvania. He studied law
under Judge Garrick Mallery, a prominent lawyer and jurist
in Wilkes-Barre, and with his brother Henry in Allentown.[7]

The facts available relating to the first twenty years of King's
life afford few clues to the influences that formed his character. Of
his parents, nothing is known save that his father was a soldier in
the Revolution, while his mother is reported to have been a
woman of strong personality. His Pennsylvania background is
equally obscure, but it might be conjectured that General Butler's record of leadership assured his family of a firm position in
the community. King's schooling at Westfield Academy gave him
an opportunity to study at an institution of more than local repu-

tation. From Mallery, his preceptor in the law, he might be expected to have imbibed some of the conservative principles of the Litchfield Law School, of which Garrick Mallery was a graduate. What facts there are suggest that King's background was characterized by stability, that in both Massachusetts and Pennsylvania his family occupied positions of responsibility and leadership, and that during his youth he did not lack for opportunities to develop his mind and talents.

The times in which King passed his minority were anything but stable. In Europe the Napoleonic Wars had ended and the map was redrawn at Paris and Vienna. On the western side of the Atlantic the post-revolutionary generation grew up and fought a war of its own with England. King was about to enter his teens when the War of 1812 broke out. He was still in his teens when the Second Bank of the United States was chartered and Calhoun's Bonus Bill was vetoed. He studied law during the period when John Marshall's decisions were molding the Supreme Court into a powerful arm of the government. Before King's majority the nation had acquired the Louisiana Purchase and the Floridas. The population and political power of the country were moving to the west and south: Ohio, Louisiana, Indiana, Mississippi, Illinois, Alabama, Maine, and Missouri were added to the Union. The admission of Missouri brought before Congress the question of slavery in the territories, but a compromise quieted temporarily that "firebell in the night." Cotton production doubled and redoubled in the two decades. Old states as well as new increased in settled area and population.

During this era of expansion New England exported population, for in an agricultural economy the Northeast could not compete with the more fertile states of the West and South.[8] The dispersal of the King family illustrated this significant movement. Of the six brothers, only the eldest remained in Massachusetts. The others followed their brother Henry to Pennsylvania and from there moved to Georgia. The first to venture south was Stephen Clay King, who in 1820 married Miss Mary Fort, daughter of a wealthy cotton planter of Wayne County, Georgia. Through his own efforts and his marriage he became a large-scale planter. Within three years David and Thomas Butler joined their brother in Georgia, where David became a planter and Thomas Butler began the practice of law. Later their younger brother Andrew also made the southward move, and eventually all six King brothers held land or resided in Georgia.[9] Stephen and Thomas Butler were destined to become leading members of the coastal planter society of Glynn County.

Glynn is next to the southernmost of the counties that form the seacoast of Georgia. Topographically, it occupies the lowest of a series of terraces that ascend from the coast to the central uplands of the state. A number of rivers break the coast into segments with their deltas; the largest river is the Altamaha, which bounds Glynn County on the north. One of the principal geographic features of the seaboard is the chain of islands that raise a low barrier between the Atlantic and the mainland. This natural breakwater forms a protected sea lane from Florida to South Carolina. Since the mainland seldom rises more than a few feet above sea level, the demarcation between land, sea, and islands is indistinct. It is a country of pine barrens and swamps, interspersed with alluvial river lands, difficult of access except by boat.[10] Sidney Lanier saw in the area a peculiar beauty compounded of gloomy woods, sandy beaches, marsh land, and sea. The dominant feature he celebrated in one of his best-known poems, "The Marshes of Glynn":

> How ample, the marsh and the sea and the sky!
> A league and a league of marsh-grass, waist high,
>   broad in the blade,
> Green, and all of a height, and unflecked with a
>   light or a shade,
> Stretch leisurely off, in a pleasant plain,
> To the terminal blue of the main.

On the coastal islands of Georgia and the nearby mainland a society based on plantation slavery flourished in the early part of the nineteenth century. This was the country of Pierce Butler, husband of the renowned Fanny Kemble, and of Thomas Spalding of Sapelo.[11] They, and planters like them, took advantage of the climate and geography to develop their large plantations devoted to the cultivation of rice and Sea Island cotton. The rivers, tidal creeks, and inland waterway furnished convenient highways for the transportation of the plantation crops. However, the shallow coastal waters forced the use of light draft vessels; south of Charleston the only harbor deep enough for large seagoing vessels was at Brunswick, the county seat of Glynn County.[12] Geographically and economically the relatively narrow tidewater area constituted a distinct region of the state, recognized as the province of the aristocratic large planters.[13]

On December 2, 1824, Thomas Butler King married Anna Matilda Page of Retreat Plantation, Saint Simons Island, Georgia.

The bride was the only daughter of William Page, a South Caro-
linian who in 1804 had bought Retreat Plantation at the southern
end of the island. To this original holding Page added several adjoining areas, including Newfield Plantation. By these purchases
and others he became one of the large landholders of Glynn County, and he quickly assumed a station commensurate with his land
ownership. He acted as treasurer of the island planters who subscribed for the building of a church, Commissioner of the Town
and Commons of Frederica, Treasurer of the Glynn County Academy Commissioners, Justice of the Inferior Court, and Major of
the Seventh Battalion of Georgia militia. In addition, he served
as trustee for two estates and carried on other fiduciary business.[14]
Anna Page was born to wealth and trained to responsibility. During her father's absences from home she took over the management
of his affairs, even to the extent of ordering lumber and supervising building on the plantation.[15] Upon her marriage, her husband
automatically was enrolled among the foremost planters of the
area.

Within two years after the marriage of their daughter, both of
Anna King's parents died, leaving an estate valued at nearly
$125,000. About one third of this sum represented an investment
in 140 slaves; another third was the estimated value of real property. The remaining third consisted of personal property and included $21,000 of stock in the Bank of the United States, the
Planters' Bank of Savannah, and the Bank of Darien. By will, all
real and personal property on Saint Simons and fifty slaves were
left in trust for Anna Matilda Page King and her children. There
were three minor bequests, and the residue of the estate went to
the legal heirs. As either heir or husband, therefore, King now
had power over a large property, exclusive of his own holdings.

Anna and Thomas Butler King made their home at Retreat, on
the southwestern tip of Saint Simons Island. The plantation house
faced the beach, looking across the sound toward Jekyl Island. It
was a simple, frame building, to which the Kings added a two-
story wing to house their growing family. Nearby were the de-
tached kitchen and outbuildings, with the gardens—formal, flower,
and kitchen—and groves of orange and olive trees surrounding the
area on three sides. Behind these stood the slave hospital, the barn
and farm buildings, and the overseer's house some two hundred
yards from the main dwelling. A hundred yards farther east a row
of frame slave quarters faced the beach. Shell walks and roads gave
access to the buildings, gardens, and the boat landing. The prin-

cipal road ran north past the slave quarters at Newfield and continued toward the town of Frederica. Most of the buildings were of frame construction, but the greenhouse, hospital, and barn were built of tabby, a mixture of lime, shells, sand, and gravel often used for permanent construction in that locality. Although the plantation house was plain, Retreat had a certain grandeur that proceeded from the site, the extensive grounds, the rich furnishings, and the numerous slaves.[17]

Like other low-country planting families the Kings also owned a residence in the sandhills. Some twenty-five miles southwest of Brunswick lay the summer resort of Waynesville, to which the planters of Glynn, Wayne, and Camden counties repaired to escape the miasma. Here in 1831 Thomas Butler King purchased 150 acres and built a rather elaborate cottage which he called "Monticello." The houses at the resort were scattered along sandy lanes that meandered through the pine forest near a medicinal spring. The summer colonists maintained a clubhouse for social gatherings and an open-air meeting ground for religious services. A summer at Waynesville not only took the families away from the malarial airs of the coast, but also replaced the isolation of the plantation with community living. For the planters, the nearness of Waynesville enabled them to maintain close communication with their overseers, a convenience denied them if they took their families to the more fashionable springs of Virginia or to Saratoga.[18]

Year by year the King family grew. First came William Page and Hannah Page, named for Anna's parents; then Thomas Butler, Junior, and Henry, known to the family by his middle name, Lord. Three other boys and three more girls rounded out the family board: Floyd and Mallery and Cuyler, Georgia, Florence, and Virginia. As King's family increased by almost yearly additions, so too did his landholdings. Besides enlarging and improving his wife's property, he extended his operations to the rice-growing area of the mainland in 1830 when he bought for $12,000 part of the Middleton Barony, comprising some 4,700 acres on the Satilla River. Six years later he offered to purchase the rest of the Middleton Barony for $7,000. His planting ventures were so successful that he planned to finance this purchase and a similar one of 800 adjoining acres out of two years' profits. On this mainland plantation, King began building a third dwelling house, Waverly.[19]

In the first thirty-five years the pattern of Thomas Butler King's life was one of change and success. Born in a small inland Massachusetts village, he exchanged his New England background for the wider horizons of the Wyoming Valley of Pennsylvania. As a young lawyer he migrated to Georgia and contracted a fortunate marriage. By his thirty-fifth birthday he was the father of a large and growing family, the master of 355 slaves, and a planter with extensive landholdings. Large as they were, King's planting interests did not occupy his attention exclusively. During the 1830's he became increasingly involved in public affairs. In politics he won repeated victories at the polls, and in the field of economic development he became a figure of more than local importance.

· II ·

Promoter of the Port of Brunswick

ON THE MAINLAND across from Retreat stood the village of Brunswick, which became the focus of Thomas Butler King's activities for half a decade. Exactly when he first became interested in the town it is difficult to determine. By 1826 he had enough faith in its economic possibilities to become one of ten local residents who secured a charter for building a canal there. However, nearly ten years passed before he became a driving force behind the development of the area. There was a direct connection, too, between his political career and the promotion of the port of Brunswick. Since some of these connections are quite clear and others can only be inferred, it may be helpful to look first at the economic affairs and then to examine the political events in King's life, dealing with them separately even though they were contemporaneous.

King's planting interests on Saint Simons and the mainland gave him a logical reason for seeking to improve the village and port of Brunswick. In the 1820's it was a small place, with two stores, a post office, and about ten or a dozen buildings.[1] Officially established as a town during the colonial era, Brunswick was resurveyed after the Revolution, but it did not quickly realize the expectations of its planners, who laid out a town that might rival Savannah with its parks and squares.[2] It was situated on a deep tidal creek called Turtle River that extended some twenty miles inland and afforded deepwater anchorage for vessels. To the east and north Turtle River opened into Saint Simons Sound, a protected body of water with inland links north to Charleston, South Carolina, and south to the Saint Mary's River in Florida. Direct access to the Atlantic from the sound was provided by the mile-wide channel between Saint Simons Island on the north and Jekyl Island on the south. On the bar some five miles out toward sea the depth of the channel mouth at low tide was 18 feet, ample for sea-going vessels. In 1836 a naval commission had "no hesitation in preferring Brunswick" to all other possible sites for a naval base south of Chesapeake Bay.[3] It was true that the nearest navigable river was the Altamaha, twelve miles to the north across swampy lowlands, but enterprising promoters noted the ease with which a canal might be built which would divert the river traffic to the superior harbor at Brunswick.[4]

Thomas Butler King was one of a group of local residents who in 1826 obtained from the legislature a charter for the Brunswick Canal Company.[5] Once in possession of their charter, however, the incorporators did little. They seemed content to leave the management of the project in the hands of William B. Davis, an enthusiastic but inept promoter. Even when the state supplied aid in the form of a gang of slaves and equipment to open a road through the swamps, Davis made very little progress. Eventually, the legislature ordered the sale of the state-owned slaves, and Davis's mismanagement of the gang on Railroad Creek came to light. He had been plagued by misbehavior, illness, death, and runaways among his charges. Contrary to agreement he had charged the state $500 for his services as superintendent, and he had sold one of the slaves committed to his care, instead of turning him over to the agent appointed to handle the disposal of state property. The legislature passed a resolution of censure and recommended the prosecution of Davis, but he had sold his holdings and had left Brunswick.[6] Yet at the very time that Davis was falling into disgrace, the Brunswick development received an endorsement from a governmental commission.

Three residents of the interior part of Georgia, appointed by the governor to survey transportation opportunities, made an enthusiastic report on Brunswick in 1833. Reviewing the commerce of the state, they regarded the Altamaha, not the Savannah, as the principal river for carrying the traffic of upper Georgia. "Savannah, we fear, [so ran their report] is prostrated by the completion of the Charleston rail-road to Augusta."[7] They examined the harbor at Brunswick and investigated the healthfulness of the area. After recounting the plans for a railroad or a canal between the Altamaha and Turtle River, they concluded that it was "highly advisable for the State to render aid in opening Brunswick to the

interior."[8] Brunswick was thus brought forward as a rival to Savannah for the expanding market of central Georgia. At stake was
not only the fixing of the terminus of projected works of internal
improvements, but also the form and amount of state participation in those works.[9]

It was at this juncture that Thomas Butler King began to
gather into his hands the control of Davis's old Brunswick enterprise. Until now the project had been primarily a local one. Some
elements of state aid had been added by the use of the government
slaves to open a road to Railroad Creek and by the appointment
of the governor's commission. King made a strong bid for increased
aid by the state. Equally important, he enlisted the support of
out-of-state capital. Under his direction the original canal proposal became only the starting point for a more ambitious development. A railroad, a bank, and a real estate company were added
to the canal to attract distant capitalists to Brunswick.

Since he had been elected to a term in the legislature as a senator from Glynn County, King was in a position not only to influence his fellow legislators on the potentialities of Brunswick, but
also to guide favorable laws through the Assembly. In 1834 he
secured the passage of a charter for the Brunswick Canal and Railroad Company, in which he, his brother Stephen, and William
Wigg Hazzard replaced Davis and Dart as incorporators. The new
charter included all the rights and privileges of the one it replaced,
and the power of the company was expanded and clarified. A
peculiar feature of the new charter was the provision that the
operations of the company in canal digging and railroad building
should be separated, that different books should be kept on the
operations, and that investors should have the option of subscrib-
ing to either or both of the projects. In effect, therefore, the new
charter set up two separate but related corporations. By another
act of the legislature the state proposed to subscribe $50,000 to the
company when the organization was completed and other stockholders had paid the assessments on their subscriptions.[10]

King also took a step to convert some of the hitherto fruitless
publicity into concrete plans for a canal. He engaged Loammi
Baldwin, an engineer famous for his work on the Union Canal of
Pennsylvania, to survey the route of the canal and submit specifications and cost estimates of the contemplated work.[11] The lack of
such a survey previously is a measure of the vague and impractical
leadership from which the company had suffered before King
stepped to the fore. Finished plans and reliable estimates would

be indispensable if King was to secure financial backing for the project. Consequently, his assumption of the expense of the survey may be regarded as a contribution of prime importance toward the beginning of the Brunswick canal.[12]

In 1835 the legislature granted Thomas Butler King, Stephen Clay King, and Isaac Abrahams a charter for the Brunswick and Florida Railroad Company. This company, capitalized at $2,000,-000, was given the right to build a railroad between Brunswick and any point on the Florida-Georgia boundary. Work was to commence within two years and to be completed within ten years, and the company was given a twenty-five-year monopoly on its route. By further action of the legislature the Brunswick and Florida Railroad acquired the right to perfect title to all ungranted lands within one hundred yards of its route.[13]

Still a third corporate organization was added to the already ambitious program of the promoters with the chartering of the Bank of Brunswick. The two King brothers, with nine associates, were authorized to form this corporation, capitalized at $200,000. Note issue was limited to three times the amount of paid stock. Although the Bank of Brunswick was separate from both the canal company and the railroad company, the close relationship of the three corporations was revealed by a curious clause regarding increased capitalization. On the completion of the canal, the bank was to be permitted to increase its capital to $1,000,000, and on the completion of the Brunswick and Florida Railroad a further increase to $3,000,000 was to be permitted. By the terms of the charter the United States Bank of Pennsylvania was forbidden to hold stock in the Bank of Brunswick.[14]

Although the charters which King controlled had potential values, they differed only in detail from countless similar projects that were seeking capital for fulfillment. Owners of risk capital customarily require the promise of extraordinary profits before they undertake a venture. In his bid for outside capital King was able to supply this needed element by resorting to an old American institution, land speculation. Fortunately, his brother Stephen Clay King was the joint owner of a large tract adjoining the townsite of Brunswick.[15] By action of the legislature in 1835, one third of the Brunswick town common lying along the Turtle River was surveyed into lots and sold for the benefit of the school and academy funds.[16] King himself acquired title to numerous lots and to 700 acres previously regarded as town commons.[17] If any of the plans for developing Brunswick were fulfilled, the value of lands

within the town and nearby would be greatly enhanced. Armed
with his charters, his survey, and control of lands in Brunswick,
King was well equipped to appeal to the pocketbooks of investors
when in 1836 he journeyed to Boston in search of capital.

The opportunities King presented were quickly seized by Boston financiers. The capital for the completion of the canal was
promised, and arrangements were made for the railroad reconnais-
sance and survey. In addition, the Boston investors organized the
Brunswick Land Company, which bought Stephen King's land
adjoining Brunswick and set about acquiring other real estate in
and near the town. Steps were taken to buy Blythe Island, lying
in Turtle River just across from the town, in the hope that the
federal government would purchase it for a naval establishment.[18]

Unlike the Bostonians, who wished to push the canal to completion and reap quick profits from their land company, King placed
his faith in the railroad as the most important of the schemes.
While he used his place in the state Senate to secure further privileges for all of the Brunswick companies, he devoted his most intense efforts to the Brunswick and Florida Railroad. He completed
the initial organization of the corporation and supplied encouragement to the surveying crews which were reconnoitering the
route. When the surveyors had difficulty securing funds from the
treasurer of the joint companies, he advanced his own money to
enable them to proceed rapidly. After five months of field work
the engineers returned to Boston, paid off their crews with promissory notes, and began to prepare profiles and topographic reports.[19]

The Panic of 1837, which struck the country just as the engineers returned to Boston, caught them and their sponsors by surprise. The reversal of financial affairs that followed hit particularly
hard at the Brunswick companies, for neither had advanced to the
point where any returns could be realized. The close relationship
of the different projects now threatened to disrupt all plans. In an
attempt to minimize their liabilities, the Boston investors abandoned the railroad scheme. Unable to raise funds for the engineers,
they insisted that King was personally responsible for the expenses.
Since the land company had only a potential value, stockholders
were urged to pay delinquent subscriptions so that all efforts
might be concentrated upon the canal project which would en-
hance the land value. King was called on not only to assume the
debt for the railroad survey, but also to pay his share of the assess-

ments to meet outstanding obligations and to maintain the credit of the canal company.[20]

An acrimonious dispute now arose between King and his Boston associates. They charged him with responsibility for 5,500 shares of stock, four times the amount he would acknowledge. He agreed to take over the subscriptions of his brother Stephen and those of Joseph M. White, Delegate in Congress from Florida Territory, but denied any further charges. "I subscribed for no other friends nor persons, nor do I know who you thus call my friends and presume to charge me with their stock," he wrote.[21] Moreover, he pointed out, he had spent his time on the business of the companies, to the neglect of his planting interests. He had even advanced money from his private account to meet sudden demands for capital. He promised to pay his assessments as soon as his crop was sold and called on other subscribers to meet their obligations as well.

More serious differences disturbed King's relations with his Boston associates. He disagreed emphatically with their decision to abandon the railroad in favor of the completion of the canal. Instead of contracting operations, he favored pushing the railroad vigorously and using his recently acquired charter for the Bank of Brunswick to finance all operations. He suggested the consolidation of the land company with the railroad company and the pursuance of a bold policy.

... my object being to create a *great Boston interest* at Brunswick, and in this Rail Road. The interest of the land or city company is inseparably connected with the construction of the Rail Road, *that* being the great *enterprise* which must and will give a value to the city property, greater than can be readily estimated. The canal it is true will unquestionably produce a rich harvest, but the Rail Road vastly greater.[22]

In the same letter King announced his intention to promote the railroad vigorously and to secure further aid from the state.

The Boston investors rejected King's proposals. While they admitted his services to the company and realized the potential value of the bank charter, they insisted that the surveying parties be paid by the delinquent stockholders. The Boston directors recommended that the treasurer collect the debts owed to the railroad company, pay the engineers, and distribute the residue on a *pro rata* basis among stockholders. King was requested to keep the charter alive until a more propitious time.[23]

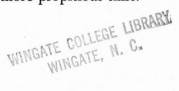

Since King and the Bostonians could not agree on the policy that should be followed, the operations of the railroad and the canal companies entered a new phase. The work on the canal went forward, with the number of workers being reduced from month to month in an attempt to minimize the effect of layoffs on public opinion. Despite the dearth of capital and troublesome right-of-way problems, the contractors continued their work through 1838 and into the summer of 1839. Hopefully, the Boston agent reported to King that "we are not now in want of means . . . we shall go on with the canal."[24]

The Brunswick and Florida Railroad followed a different course. King determined to continue the project in spite of the withdrawal of his Boston colleagues. In February 1838 he once more journeyed north in search of capital, this time to Philadelphia. In most respects his proposition to Philadelphia capitalists resembled the one that he had made in Boston. Since the railroad company had never been formally organized, he still retained control of the charter. In addition, he offered to investors the lands in Brunswick that he controlled. He also offered the control of the Bank of Brunswick, whose charter he had procured in 1836. However, no financial backing resulted from this journey, and King returned to his plantation.[25]

Rebuffed in both Boston and Philadelphia, King turned to the planters of his own area for support. During May, June, and July of 1838 he conducted a series of public meetings in Georgia, Alabama, and Florida, attempting to induce inhabitants in the vicinity of the proposed road to subscribe for stock. The subscription method of financing among planters was an inflationary credit arrangement, involving little actual cash. As outlined by King, it would require the planter to pay his subscription by depositing his notes, and the amount of the notes was to be limited to one half an appraised valuation of the subscriber's real estate, by which the notes were to be secured.[26] The investor who lived near the route and owned slaves would be able to retire his notes by working his slaves on the line in the off season. If all went well he would thereby acquire transportation for his crop, increased value for his land, and stock in the railroad. The response to King's efforts was gratifying. He secured subscriptions for $1,500,000, and he and his agents had no doubt that in many cases the amounts could be increased. King wrote a triumphant letter to one of his Boston friends, recounting his successes and future plans for the railroad.[27]

Under the impetus of King's energetic promotion, plans for the railroad went forward promptly. In a move to inspire public confidence, King induced Moncure Robinson, one of the country's best-known railway engineers, to become chief engineer of the railroad.[28] King also paid off a debt to Henry Curtis, one of the field engineers of the previous survey, by employing him as assistant engineer.[29] Plans were mapped for sale of stock in the north, and for the floating of a bond issue on the London market, part of the payment to be made in iron rails. As senator from Glynn County, King also endeavored to procure state aid for the railroad from the legislature.[30]

Stimulated by the revived railroad plan, the whole Brunswick development regained some of its vigor. The treasurer of the new company wrote from Boston:

I observe here, a very considerable elevation in the spirits of the Brunswick stockholders. . . . This arises, in the main, from the flourishing prospect of our railroad; but partly also from the very decided revival of business. . . .[31]

Stockholders began to pay assessments that were in arrears and to show interest in the new company. Moncure Robinson's acceptance of the position of chief engineer aided the promoters in their efforts to sell stock. So, too, did the connection of General James Hamilton, former governor of South Carolina, who was preparing to go to England to market the company's bonds. Hamilton looked to Boston subscribers to use their influence with the House of Baring in London to effect bond sales.[32] Even more encouraging were the stock purchases that New York financiers began to make. A firm of that city declared its intention to open a commercial house in Brunswick and to run two vessels to the port monthly.[33] The Bank of Brunswick, which had opened its doors the preceding November, continued to maintain specie payment.[34] Ship clearances from Brunswick reached a peak never before attained.[35]

In the spring of 1839 Thomas Butler King had good cause to be pleased with the events of the past five years. He had taken up the old Brunswick project of Davis, had initiated new schemes, and had used his place in the legislature to advance them. Largely through his efforts, money and labor had been poured into Brunswick, which could now boast of an increased population, a hotel, a newspaper, and a bank. The canal, now nearing completion, had employed the labor of several hundred men for three years. The railroad survey was completed, and construction could get under way in the fall. Formidable difficulties had been surmounted through energetic promotion that had required long travels. The cost in time and money had been great and he had neglected his planting interests, but the financial harvest could not now be far away. Another harvest had already been reaped in the fall of 1838, when the voters of Georgia elected him to represent them in Congress. A wider arena now opened before him, as he looked toward service in the House of Representatives in Washington. The management of the Brunswick development would have to be left in other hands, while he moved on to the national scene.

Despite his involvement in politics and business, King remained essentially a planter, dependent on the vagaries of the weather and the cotton market. His railroad, because of the method of financing, was also directly geared to the economy of the agricultural community. In the late 1830's cotton-growing was a feeble staff for anyone to lean on. In the middle of the decade cotton prices on the world market began a downward trend that was to last for ten years.[36] The Panic of 1837 had struck hard at the cotton grower, although the total effect was not immediately apparent. Through the inflationary policies of the Bank of the United States of Pennsylvania, the satellite banks to the south and southwest were able to maintain a semblance of normal operation. When banks generally began to resume specie payment in 1838, cotton prices rose again slightly, seeming to presage the return of prosperity. This apparent recovery was merely the prelude to a more complete collapse. When the Bank of the United States of Pennsylvania suspended specie payment for the second time, on October 9, 1839, the inflated credit system of the cotton South collapsed.[37] Few escaped the general ruin, least of all the large planters on whose subscription the Brunswick and Florida railroad was based. It is hardly surprising, therefore, that the company did not outlast the year 1839. Even the money to pay for Robinson's survey failed to be supplied, and the engineer withheld his report on the grounds that his contract had not been fulfilled.[38] With the suspension of specie payment in October, any thought of beginning the railroad would have been absurd.

The collapse of all the Brunswick development schemes was even more rapid than their rise. The canal and the railroad came to a halt in 1839. The Bank of Brunswick and the *Brunswick Advocate* both suspended operations. Mayor Andrew King laid aside his official duties and made plans to move to Cuba to manage a sugar plantation.[39] The harbor fell into disuse, only one ship clearing the port in 1842. The hoped-for purchase of Blythe Island for a naval base did not materialize, although recommended by a naval commission. A statistical survey published in 1849 dismissed the bright hopes of the previous decade with the comment that "Brunswick no longer attracts public attention."[40]

For King, the full meaning of this financial debacle would not be ascertained until after a general accounting; the disappointment of his hopes was more immediate. Throughout his connection with the Brunswick development schemes he had displayed energy, optimism, and determination. His optimism had led him to pile one under-capitalized company upon another and in their management he had misinterpreted the trends of the economy. His persistence had overcome many difficulties, but lacked the final justification of success. Faulty as his judgment proved in some regards, he nevertheless showed his appreciation of a force that was to revolutionize transportation in the next half-century. The building of the Brunswick and Florida and the Atlantic and Gulf railroads two decades later justified his faith in the route of his railroad, if not in his method of financing. Of his ability to inspire followers there could be no doubt. He was successful alike with urban capitalists in the North, with fellow planters of southeastern Georgia, and with political colleagues in the state Senate. His later successes in politics showed that he retained the confidence of those who were closest to the scene. The political career that developed while he was displaying his talents as a promoter requires further elaboration.

· III ·

Apprentice Days

WHILE HE LED the movement to promote Brunswick as a port, Thomas Butler King also engaged in a career in public life. He served five terms in the legislature as a senator from Glynn County, attended the constitutional convention of 1833, and campaigned for a seat in Congress in 1836 and 1838. During the latter half of the decade he represented his state and section in the commercial conventions that met in Augusta, Charleston, and Macon. By his speeches and actions in these various bodies, he was to reveal his basic political and economic convictions.

Georgia politics in the 1820's was a struggle primarily between personal factions.[1] John Clark led the Clark party to victory as governor in 1819 and 1820; George Michael Troup and his followers triumphed in the elections of 1823 and 1825. The recurrent battles of these forces were bitter, and their victories were seldom decisive. Although interests and issues are hard to define, the Troup forces were generally thought to represent the tidewater in alliance with the expanding plantation area of central Georgia, while the Clark party spoke for the small farmer elements in the less fertile and less thickly populated areas of the piny woods, wiregrass, and frontier regions. Both parties claimed to support state aid to internal improvements, but neither could boast of its record. Both parties agreed that the federal government ought to extinguish the Indian title to unsettled land on the frontier. Both parties supported Andrew Jackson in the election of 1828.

Although Georgia politics could be explained largely in terms of personal leadership until 1828, the years that follow lack any such touchstone. One observer has characterized the course of the

Troup faction for the period from 1828 to 1833 in the following words:

It was dragged from personalism into internal improvements, suffered a diversion on the tariff of 1828, drifted into the Central Bank issue of 1829, blundered through the Cherokee crisis, and side-stepped through a maze of irregular patterns in the nullification scare of 1830-1832.[2]

In the following six years, Troup party leaders gathered about them a new grouping of elements known as the State Rights party. They guided a disciplined organization that included anti-Jacksonians in national politics and supporters of economy and conservatism on the state level. Until 1838 the party scored no general victories, but the groups developed a corps of capable leaders, made inroads on the strength of their Union opponents, and fought the majority Unionists on state and national issues. By the end of the decade these almost equally balanced parties were approximately aligned with the national Whig and Democratic parties, but they contained factions that found the national alliances uncomfortable. It was a transitional era, and the shifting contests of the 1830's often confounded contemporary observers; the passage of time has hardly clarified the picture.

Thomas Butler King first held elective office as a senator from Glynn County in the legislature of 1832. Of the several national questions that were considered, Indian policy, the tariff, and nullification were the most important. King and his colleagues unanimously endorsed Andrew Jackson's attempts to induce the Cherokee Indians to move to a trans-Mississippi reservation.[3] On the tariff and nullification issue, King introduced a resolution that called for a federal constitutional convention to pronounce upon the doctrine of implied powers. The Senate approved the resolution unanimously, but the House refused to concur. A set of compromise resolutions embracing both the tariff and nullification questions was brought up in place of King's original proposal. King voted for a resolution declaring the tariff unconstitutional, and, when that failed, for another that disavowed the right of Georgia to condemn the actions being taken by the State of South Carolina. Subsequently, he voted against a statement of principles condemning the course of South Carolina as unwise and hypocritical. The compromise resolutions, combining censure for South Carolina and a protest against the tariff, were unacceptable to the gentleman from Glynn County, who aligned himself with

the minority bloc of adamant State Rights partisans refusing to
accept the compromise.[4]

The Troup party, which controlled the legislature, endorsed a
movement for a convention to revise the Constitution of 1798.
Like the citizens of other states during this era, Georgians sought
to alter their basic law to conform with the needs of an expanding
population and changing political ideals. Two specific features of
the government were under attack: the size of the legislature,
which promoted long and expensive sessions; and the inequality
of representation by counties. So vigorous was the agitation on
these points that an extra-legal convention was called to meet in
Milledgeville in February 1833. Under this pressure the legislature issued a call for a convention. King was a member of the majority that approved the movement, legalized it, and set the date
for the official convention in May 1833.[5]

An active delegate to the convention, King introduced the first
motion after the swearing in of members and participated frequently in the week-long debates. On the question of senatorial
representation he voted for revisions that would have set up a
Senate of thirty or of thirty-six members, and against a forty-five-
member group. To reduce the size of the House, the proposal was
put forward that free white population, rather than the federal
ratio which included three-fifths of the slaves, be used as the basis
of representation. By both vote and argument King opposed the
free white basis. His county, Glynn, was small in size, had the
lowest free white population in the state, and counted the highest
ratio of slaves to free. On the federal ratio basis, Glynn's representative population was five times greater than it would have
been under the new proposal.[6] To judge from his actions, then,
King favored a drastic reduction in the Senate, but defended the
advantages which slave ownership conferred on some of the population.

Only part of the story appears from individual votes. A closer
examination of King's record shows that he voted in the minority
on every motion, except one, for which a roll-call was taken. Clearly, he was an obstructionist, and the explanation is to be found in
the partisan aspects of the convention. Leaders of the Troup party
had spearheaded the agitation for a convention, and the Troup
majority in the legislature of 1832 had legitimized the movement.
However, in the election of delegates the Clark-Union party
gained control of the convention, and the proposal to use free
white population as the basis for representation struck at the politi-

cal strength of the Troupites in the plantation counties. From the outset, therefore, the Troup delegates obstructed the work of the convention, even going so far as to register a complaint in the journal against the partisan spirit of the deliberations. Unable to have their way, or even to secure an acceptable compromise, the Troup partisans led the campaign against the ratification of the amendments proposed by the convention. They succeeded in bringing about a decided rejection of the proposals, with the vote closely following the party lines of previous elections.[7]

The ratification vote on the amendments to the constitution was the last in which the followers of Troup maintained their unity. George Michael Troup retired from active political life in 1833, and John McPherson Berrien, former attorney general in Jackson's cabinet, made a strong bid to convert the party into an anti-Jacksonian group. John Forsyth headed the Troup Unionists who refused to follow the rest of the party into opposition to Old Hickory. Out of this split came the formation of the State Rights party of Georgia. Thomas Butler King was one of the few old Troup leaders who won election to the Senate in 1834 as a State Rights candidate. The legislature was Unionist by a large majority, a Unionist governor already held office, and the entire Union congressional ticket was elected.[8]

The most prolonged and bitter party battle of the legislative session concerned the issue of federal relations. In 1834 the case of James Graves, a Cherokee Indian, threatened again to raise the question of Georgia's jurisdiction over her Indian inhabitants.[9] The governor's message dealing with the Graves case was referred to the standing committee on the state of the Republic, which brought in general resolutions regretting the attempt of the United States Supreme Court to assume jurisdiction. William Crosby Dawson, a strong State Rights partisan, offered a substitute resolution declaring Section 25 of the Judiciary Act of 1789 "unconstitutional, inoperative, null, and void."[10]

King spoke at length in support of Dawson's report. He pointed out to his hearers that the Union was a compact of sovereign states, buttressing his argument with a long historical review. He hailed the Virginia and Kentucky resolutions as restatements confirming the sovereignty of the states and expressed surprise "to hear the old federal doctrine of 1789 advocated in the Senate of Georgia in 1834."[11] Avowing himself unafraid of the word *nullification,* he urged his colleagues "to declare in the face of Congress and the world, that those acts [under which the Supreme Court assumed jurisdiction] are unconstitutional, null and void."[12] South Carolina, King asserted, had found in nullification the only remedy against nationalizing tendencies. Warning his fellow senators that the economic and political life of the South was being threatened by the consolidationist interpretation of the Constitution, he made a forecast worthy of John C. Calhoun:

The time is rapidly approaching when the majority in Congress will be vastly increased from the non slave holding States; and unless the south shall soon rally round the Constitution, and confine the action of the General Government within its proper limits, it requires no spirit of prophecy to foresee that the time is not far distant when that majority, regardless of the interests of the slave holding States, will resort to a course of legislation for their own benefit, that may involve us in ruinous intestine wars, or in submission to a Government without limitation of powers.[13]

King's argument elicited high praise from State Rights papers in the capital and in Savannah.[14]

Although King's speech enhanced his reputation it failed to convince his colleagues. The State Rights minority stood firm for a while on the principles set forth in Dawson's resolutions, but in the final balloting they supported milder resolutions that merely protested against the interference of the Supreme Court in a state criminal prosecution. State Rights and Unionist members were almost unanimous in opposing federal intervention; they differed only in the terms of their protest.[15]

Besides gaining fame as a State Rights orator, King registered his opposition to the Bank of the United States and voted to censure President Andrew Jackson on four counts: for removing the deposits, for requiring the resignation of the Secretary of the Treasury, for retaining the Postmaster General in his cabinet, and for attempting to have a protest recorded in the journal of the Senate of the United States.[16] Several local bills that King proposed were defeated, but on the last day of the session he pushed through an act giving state aid to the opening of the port of Brunswick.[17]

When King returned to Milledgeville in November 1835, he devoted his major attention to the question of aid to internal improvements. He proposed three bills connected with the Brunswick schemes. Most important was the act incorporating the Brunswick and Florida Railroad Company, which passed early in the session. Closely related was the act permitting the sale of three hundred acres of the Brunswick town commons, thus making good waterfront acreage available to private owners. Finally, a move to repeal the act of the previous session granting state aid for the opening of the port of Brunswick was successfully blocked.[18]

During the preceding summer much excitement had arisen in Georgia over the use of the mails to distribute abolition literature. In King's home county of Glynn, three separate meetings in August and September had endorsed resolutions assailing William Lloyd Garrison, the Tappan brothers, and other abolitionists and calling on the governor and the legislature to take action to preserve the peace of the state.[19] In his annual message Governor Lumpkin took notice of the agitation of abolitionists and suggested that the legislature consider what steps should be taken to combat the danger. Lumpkin's Democratic floor leader introduced seven resolutions on the subject, firm, but far from bellicose. King and eighteen other State Rights doctrinaires offered amendments that strengthened the original wording and called on citizens of the northern states to pass positive laws against abolitionists. However, when their amendments were rejected, they joined in the unanimous approval of McAllister's resolutions.[20]

In 1836, when he was seeking outside capital to be invested in the Brunswick schemes, King did not seek reelection, but when he returned to the Senate in 1837 he enjoyed increased prominence. Of the first three proposals submitted to the Senate after its organization, King offered two, one of which was to occupy the legislators for the greater part of the session. Although there was a standing committee on internal improvements, King moved the appointment of a joint select committee of forty-two to consider the subject, and the motion carried. The following Saturday, King presented to the committee his views on the needs of the state; McAllister, the Democratic floor leader, then opened the hearing for the representatives of different Georgia towns to present their views; finally, Seaborn Jones placed before the group a detailed plan for the blanket extension of state credit to private companies. Out of this concerted and bipartisan effort the committee fashioned a bill that looked not only to the completion of the state-owned Western and Atlantic railroad, but also to state aid for privately owned companies in general. King was given credit for the form which the bill finally took, and he piloted it carefully through many parliamentary shoals. He preserved it intact, but never brought it to the floor for final action; apparently the response on amendment test votes led him to withhold the measure from immediate decision. On the last day of the session, he called up a somewhat similar substitute bill from the House, but it failed to pass.[21]

Before the end of the session King successfully sponsored amendments to the charters of the Bank of Brunswick, the Brunswick and Altamaha Canal and Railroad Company, and the Central Bank of Georgia. In addition, he secured charter authorization for the Brunswick Lumber Company and introduced an act to set up limited partnerships. His proposal that the court records of Glynn County be kept at the town of Brunswick was endorsed, as well as his resolution to rent a house for the governor until the new mansion should be completed. As a legislator he suffered no outright defeats, although his amendment of the charter of the Brunswick and Florida Railroad Company, like the general railroad bill, was never brought to a final vote.[22]

The legislature of 1837 faced many problems arising out of the financial crisis that had struck the country some eight months earlier. Although Georgia felt the effects of the panic less than many of her sister states, only three banks, including the state-owned Central Bank, were maintaining specie payment. Since most of the banks were subject to forfeiture of their charters if they suspended specie payment, only action by the legislature could save them. Governor William Schley, whose term of office expired while the legislature sat, recommended that the legislators fix on some method of relief. He also recommended that the Central Bank be given more latitude in the issuance of bank notes. The Senate considered a measure that set a date for the uniform resumption of specie payment by the banks of the state. King joined his State Rights colleagues in opposing and delaying the bill, which was frequently amended and finally killed. He cast similar dilatory votes against a bill penalizing the Insurance Bank of Columbus, which was controlled by Nicholas Biddle, and this administration measure also was defeated. The Senate finally adopted a motion to lay all banking resolutions on the table for the balance of the session.[23]

The legislature of 1838 followed the pattern of the previous year. A State Rights governor, George Gilmer, occupied the executive chair, but both houses of the legislature remained Democratic. However, the Democratic party was plagued with internal divisions, and the State Rights leaders took advantage of every opportunity to improve their position. One of them, Charles Dougherty, was named to the presidency of the Senate, while Thomas Butler King was virtually the floor leader of the session.

The senators took up the banking question where they had left it the year before. In the face of a continuing depression, various proposals were put forward in regard to banking, some providing relief for existing institutions, others suggesting new principles of control. The Committee on Banks, of which King was a member, reported a number of these measures for action. The State Rights party continued the obstructive tactics that it had pursued in 1837, exploiting the divisions within the ranks of both parties to preserve the status quo. King joined the majority who denied special privileges to the Central Bank, which was regarded as a Democratic institution; he also voted with the majority who opposed relief for banks that had suspended specie payment. On the other hand, he voted for an act to permit free banking and for an unsuccessful bill to speed the collection of bank notes.[24] Although these votes are not conclusive, they indicate that King opposed governmental interference in banking, particularly action that was aimed at relieving legal obligations.

King set forth his views on banking more clearly in a series of resolutions founded more on sectional and political bases than on economic theory. In the preamble, he condemned the Bank of the United States because its policies had injured the South, but he emphasized the need for a large banking capital to promote the commerce of the South. He suggested that the governor appoint a commission to draw up the charter for an exclusively southern bank, the total capital to be equal to the value of southern exports. Each southern state was to have a branch of this bank, the stock to be divided according to the value of exports. This stock, in turn, was to be held half by the state government, half by the citizens of that state. Each state was to have the right to withdraw from the scheme at any time, and other states might join. This contribution to banking policy found an early grave. The motion to print the resolutions failed, forty to thirty-seven, and the measure did not arise again.[25]

When the national banking system came up for consideration, King voted for resolutions that declared the Bank of the United States to have been "unconstitutional, inexpedient, and dangerous to the liberty of the people."[26] The pet bank system was declared a failure, and the issue of Treasury notes unconstitutional. Another resolution called for the appointment and removal of the Secretary of the Treasury by the United States Senate, rather than the President. Such an attack on the policies of the Van Buren administration was unpalatable to the Democrats, who countered with a set of resolutions asserting that the Bank of the United States had been unconstitutional and the pet banks inexpedient. The Independent Treasury was endorsed, as well as the issue of Treasury notes redeemable in specie. Although King missed the final rollcall on these resolves, his earlier votes leave no doubt that he disapproved of their adoption.[27]

Governor George R. Gilmer's message gave encouragement to the supporters of internal improvement, for he called for support of the state-owned Western and Atlantic to be supplemented by aid to private companies. King, as chairman of the Joint Select Committee on Internal Improvements, reported a bill embodying the executive recommendations. The prospects for passage were clouded by several factors: the continuing financial depression, the need for the state to concentrate its resources behind the Western and Atlantic, and other piecemeal legislation. This last, in fact, seems to have been decisive; Savannah, Macon, Brunswick, and other towns were unable to agree. The Chatham County (Savannah) delegation showed more interest in a bill favoring the powerful Central Railroad, and the old rivalry with Brunswick flared up again. King's bill combining the interests of the state works and private companies was broken up; the Western and Atlantic received support, but the general aid feature was defeated. He had to be content with amendments to the charter of the Brunswick canal and railroad companies and a new charter for the Brunswick Insurance and Trust Company.[28]

With the end of his Senate term in 1838, Thomas Butler King brought to a close one phase of his public career and embarked on another. In six years he had grown from an inexperienced candidate to a veteran politician, disciplined in the school of adversity as a member of the minority party. In the workshop of state politics the apprentice learned his trade, and year by year he gained the journeyman skill that was to serve him in his later work. He had emerged as the foremost leader of those who wished to see private enterprise, aided by the state, develop a transportation network. Although his general aid bill had not passed, he had secured privileges for the corporations that rested on the development of Brunswick. He gained some fame as a nullificationist orator and always stood with the most obdurate State Rights partisans. Insofar as national issues had entered into Georgia politics, he had voted against the policies of Andrew Jackson and Martin Van Buren. The distinguishing marks of his career had been party loyalty and persistent pursuit of his aims. With the close of the session of 1838, he left the legislative halls at Milledgeville for the wider arena of the Twenty-sixth Congress.

When he had been named to the platform committee in 1835, King joined the inner circle of State Rights leaders. The party caucus chose him as a candidate for Congress the following year, on a ticket that carried electors for Hugh Lawson White and Philip P. Barbour for President and Vice-President. From Boston, where he was seeking capital for the Brunswick development schemes, King issued a strong State Rights declaration, denying the power of Congress to legislate on slavery in the District of Columbia and the territories and denouncing the petitions of abolitionists. This statement was not even presented to the public until after the elections took place, and the candidate must have expected the defeat that he met. As the time for the State Rights convention of 1837 approached, King's name was put forward as a worthy choice for governor, and newspaper reports identified him as the favorite of the southern part of the state. In the convention, however, he ran an honorable fifth in the field of nine, with George R. Gilmer receiving the final approval.[29]

In 1838 the State Rights party once again presented Thomas Butler King to the voters as a candidate for Congress. This time King campaigned vigorously. During the summer and fall of 1838 he travelled about southern Georgia promoting local subscriptions for the Brunswick and Florida Railroad Company and keeping himself before the eyes of the voters. In a personal platform he stated his views on current political issues. He declared the establishment of a national bank unconstitutional and inexpedient and attacked the pet bank system. He opposed the Independent Treasury as it had been presented by the Van Buren administration, but qualified his opposition by saying that he objected most to the excessive concentration of power in the hands of the President. He surveyed the leading presidential candidates and concluded that all had been guilty of unpardonable sins against the South. Clay was unacceptable because of his high tariff views and his championship of a national bank. Webster he considered too much of a Federalist to deserve the support of Georgia. Harrison he dismissed as entertaining the same opinions as Clay and Webster. Van Buren he called unprincipled. He concluded that none of the candidates inspired his confidence, but that he would support any candidate who received Georgia's electoral vote.[30]

Under the general ticket system then in use, the entire congressional delegation of the State Rights party was elected. King re-

ceived 32,090 votes, standing fifth in the field of eighteen candidates.[31] His popularity in his home county was noteworthy. The
Brunswick Advocate expressed gratification that

the vote for Mr. King is nearly unanimous, and indeed the few Union
votes that were polled, could only be procured by placing Mr. King's
name on the same ticket, thus affording to the whole state a convincing
proof of the manner in which he is appreciated by his immediate
neighbors and constituents.[32]

With this encouraging evidence of local and state-wide support,
King entered a new sphere of political activity.

Another measure of his growing stature as a local and sectional
leader was to be found in his participation in the commercial conventions that took place between 1837 and 1839. In a broad sense
these conventions dealt with the changes wrought by the industrial
revolution, and the central theme about which they revolved was
the growing divergence in the economic interests of the North and
the South. Consulting together in non-political gatherings, leaders
of the agricultural South considered their problems of credit, marketing, and transportation, and debated the means by which the
South might escape its dependence on the North. As sectional
movements, the conventions marked a step in the development of
a distinct nationalism for the South.[33]

Although the conventions that met in Augusta, Charleston, and
Macon from 1837 to 1839 assumed a greater significance in the
light of later events, they were called primarily to deal with immediate problems arising out of the Panic of 1837. The suspension
of specie payment and the stringency of credit combined with a
prolonged decline in the price of cotton to render the lot of the
planter almost insupportable. On October 16, 1837, delegates from
Georgia and South Carolina met in Augusta, Georgia, to consult
about means of relief from current ills. King was one of the most
active members, serving on both the resolutions committee and
the publicity committee, participating in the debates, and speaking at the dinner given by the citizens of Augusta. On the opening
day of the convention, George McDuffie presented an analysis of
the economic condition of the South. For the section's dependence
on the North, he blamed the protectionist tariff, the discriminatory financial policy of the federal government, and—most of all
—the lack of enterprise of planters and merchants of the South.
The resolutions committee presented a verbose report that recited
anew the ills of the South. To avoid dependency on the North, the

South should establish direct trade with Europe. Profits from southern staples would then no longer flow out of the section, and credit and imported goods would be available through the local financial and commercial communities. It was realized that these ends could not be attained overnight, but Southerners were urged to support the objectives set forth. Committees were appointed to publicize the work of the convention and to memorialize the legislatures of South Carolina and Georgia for laws permitting limited co-partnerships.[34] The delegates adjourned to meet again in six months.

At the second direct trade convention in Augusta, some two hundred delegates from seven states met on April 2, 1838. Thomas Butler King was unanimously chosen as president of the body. He named Robert Young Hayne as chairman of the committee on resolutions, which brought in a report repeating and emphasizing the earlier resolutions. The convention specifically called for the establishment of agencies in southern ports by European manufacturers and urged the founding of banks to handle foreign exchanges, but the delegates confined themselves to exhortation rather than planning.[35]

King served as temporary chairman for a somewhat similar convention at Macon, Georgia, in October 1839. This Cotton Convention met in answer to a call issued by a group of cotton planters who had consulted together in New York the previous July. There they had worked out a scheme to support the price of cotton in the foreign market and had sent General James Hamilton, Jr., to Europe to make the necessary arrangements abroad. The Macon Cotton Convention heard a report from General Hamilton and a detailed presentation of the plan by Thomas Butler King, who served as chairman of the Resolutions Committee. The committee report called for the banks of the South voluntarily to join in a uniform plan to advance money to planters on cotton, which designated agents in Europe would hold off the market until the best price could be obtained. In a transaction of this kind, the committee argued, no one could lose. The borrowing would be kept at home and the marketing abroad; the planter would have his money from the bank; the bank would issue its notes secured by bills of lading and insurance; the consignee would make an adequate commission by holding his cotton for the best price; and the whole credit structure would be self-cancelling when specie was remitted in payment. Such a plan would revolutionize the system of cotton marketing by shifting the burden of credit from the planters to the banks.

The planters who met at Macon adopted the plan of action put forward by King. Standing committees of merchants and bankers were appointed in the major cotton ports of the South to make financial arrangements, and a central committee was appointed to handle inter-city cooperation.[36] Yet despite the ambitious planning of King, Hamilton, and their associates, this scheme to control the cotton market in the interest of the planters never materialized. Two weeks previously the Bank of the United States of Pennsylvania had suspended specie payment, and even as the convention was meeting banks in the South began to follow suit. Thus was precipitated the sharp secondary depression that was to bring years of hard times to the cotton producing areas. On the Liverpool market cotton dropped by one fourth to one third, to continue its downward trend to the 5-cent low of 1844-1845.[37] Even while they were planning so elaborately at Macon, King and his fellow-planters must have realized the probability of failure. In the words of one analyst: "Here, as later, cotton planters talked much but did little . . . ."[38]

Although long on talk and short on performance, the southern commercial conventions of 1837-1839 pointed up the growing divergence of the sectional economies and foreshadowed the later crisis of the Union. So far as Thomas Butler King was concerned, none of his previous activities had spread his name so widely before the public. For the ex-Senator from Glynn County and untried member of Congress it must have been gratifying to find himself ranked with George McDuffie, Robert Y. Hayne, and James Gadsden, his co-officials in the conventions. It was a resounding send-off as a sectional spokesman for the newly elected gentleman from Georgia.

· IV ·

A Gentleman from Georgia

WHEN ANNE ROYALL, the Washington gossip, made her usual survey of the new congressmen in 1839, she picked Thomas Butler King as "the flower of the Georgia delegation."[1] He was at this time thirty-nine years old, unremarkable in size, but finely made and arresting in looks. His deep-set, piercing gray eyes dominated a pale, cleanly modeled face. He wore his dark hair short in the fashion of the day, except for a fringe of beard along the line of the jaw. He had a firm chin and sternly-set lips. A certain gravity of countenance did not prevent him from creating a favorable first impression, for he was a ready conversationalist, affable in manner.[2] He had a persuasive tongue which he could employ to advantage in responding gracefully to a toast or in pronouncing a eulogy on the death of a friend, but he gained no great fame as an orator or debater. His formal speeches were notable for their marshalling of statistics and their enthusiastic optimism rather than for oratorical display. Through experience he gained a command of anecdote and invective that made him a formidable opponent in the give and take of a political campaign.[3]

It was a matter of great concern to King that his political activities so frequently kept him away from his wife and children. Anna Page King, slightly her husband's senior, devoted herself to the care of their eight children, the eldest of whom was just entering adolescence. Mrs. King never accompanied him on his political travels, and she opposed his activities in politics to some extent. At one time she reproached him for breaking his promise to her not to stand again for nomination.[4] She devoted herself to domestic affairs, which included not only the upbringing of her own children but also the supervision of more than three hundred laborers on the plantation.

Outside the immediate family circle King had many dependents. To his slaves he is reputed to have been a kind master, and the well-built hospital that he maintained for them only a stone's throw from his home evidences his concern for their health. Years later his son Floyd compared the different attitude that he encountered on a Louisiana plantation: "Here negros were a speculation, with us on the coast of Georgia they were an estate; we neither bought nor sold, that is [,] nothing of the kind was done on our plantations during my life."[5] In his early and most successful planting operations King managed his own slaves. He relied especially on the driver, Tony, who in the later years when an overseer was employed made separate oral reports on production figures.[6]

During the years when politics occupied so much of his time, King employed at least two overseers. The intermediary position of this employee made his relationship a difficult one; master and overseer usually parted company after a year or two. Yet one of King's overseers stayed at his post for more than eight years, and there are few indications of any friction between the two men. The fact that two tutors left King's roof with regret and expressions of high regard confirms the record of good relations between employer and subordinate.[7]

King's interests outside his business affairs were diverse, ranging from church activities to racing for high stakes. He was appointed to collect money for the enlargement of a Protestant Episcopal church and served as a trustee of the meeting ground of the Waynesville summer colony, a joint project of Methodists, Presbyterians, Baptists, and Episcopalians. He was an early subscriber to Audubon's *Birds of America* and promised to assist the naturalist with sales among his friends. He served as president of the Aquatic Club of Georgia, which issued a challenge to all comers to race their boat, the stakes on one race to be $10,000. Among other diversions, he enjoyed surf-bathing, poker games, and good liquors.[8]

When the Twenty-sixth Congress met in Washington in December 1839, King took his seat among the Whig opponents of President Martin Van Buren and quickly identified himself with them by opposing the Independent Treasury Bill. On a closely related bill giving the Secretary of the Treasury the power to re-issue treasury notes, King delivered his first speech in Congress.

He asserted that the proposed authority was unconstitutional,

since treasury notes were bills of credit. His argument merely
served as a prologue for a denunciation of Democratic policies.
This legislation was clear evidence of a plot by Andrew Jackson
and Martin Van Buren to monopolize for the government the
banking of the country. Jackson's "hard money" had been merely
a ruse in the general war on credit, preparing the way for Van
Buren's paper money, which was practically authorized by the
present measure. Lest he be thought a proponent of the Bank of
the United States, King hastened to state his view that both
Banks had been unconstitutional. Furthermore, they had oper-
ated against the interests of the South. He favored a separation of
government and banks, and he advocated a system in which northern banks could no longer profit from southern industry or control southern commerce. The administration measure he considered a thousand times more objectionable than the Bank of the
United States. It would concentrate all the banking of the country
in New York, drain the country of specie, and attract gold into
the coffers of the government. Southern cotton growers and cotton
exports would be expected to supply the enormous amounts of
specie that would be needed to sustain the system. He compared
the Independent Treasury with the fiscal measures of Alexander I
of Russia, and concluded: "This, sir, is the relief and reform which
may always be expected from the iron hand of despotism, when it
is necessary to sacrifice the interests of the people to acquire
power."[9]

For anyone who knew his previous career, King's maiden
speech had a familiar ring. As a member of the State Rights party
he had looked to a strict construction of the Constitution to protect the people from executive domination and a nationalized
financial institution; he had attacked Jackson and Van Buren for
using despotic methods and plotting against the public welfare;
he had condemned the Independent Treasury as an attempt to
consolidate power and debase the currency. As a spokesman for
planters he had assailed the domination of northern banks and
had advocated direct trade and a new system of cotton marketing.
As a promoter he had profited from the loose system of credit that
depended on state chartered banks. Yet never before had he combined so many elements in so virulent an attack.

King soon felt himself at home in his new duties. As his first
term in Congress drew to a close, he wrote his wife: "We have
nothing new here. The dull business of this *President making
Congress* goes on in the usual routine."[10] He, too, contributed to

the President-making, by serving as chairman of the Georgia delegation to the Young Men's Convention in Baltimore in early May
1840. There he joined in the acclamation for William Henry Harrison as the Whig candidate for President.[11] When he returned to
Washington he used his energies, and the franking privilege, to
bring the State Rights party in Georgia into the General's camp.[12]
His own campaign for renomination he left in the hands of his
brother, Andrew L. King.

For the State Rights party in Georgia the election of 1840 became a turning point. Some leaders considered an open alliance
with the tariff-minded Whigs a betrayal of party principles. Three
of the State Rights delegation in Congress bolted to the Union
party, but the "faithful six" rallied the organization under the
banner of Harrison.[13] From the state convention at Milledgeville,
Andrew L. King reported triumphantly that Thomas Butler King
had been renominated and that the chances of both the state and
national tickets in Georgia looked good. However, other political
supporters found a widespread distrust of Harrison's views on the
Bank of the United States and some dissatisfaction with the new
alignment even in King's home county.[14] Walter T. Colquitt, the
former State Rights Congressman who was now running on the
Union ticket, published a pamphlet to justify his about-face, and
King wrote an answer which appeared under the pseudonym, "A
State Rights Man of 1825."[15] After the adjournment of Congress
in July, King returned to Georgia to take part in the lively canvass, but a fever forced him to break off his speaking tour.[16]

The fever which sent King to Retreat to recuperate also struck
Anna King and the children. On top of illness came new financial
liabilities, for he had been a co-signer on a promissory note of
William S. Rockwell. When the note was not paid an indebtedness
for $12,200 suddenly threatened King, whose fellow endorser al-
ready had $25,000 in judgments against him.[17] This was almost the
last straw on King's financial burden. Since spring he had been
counting on strict economy and a good crop to help him meet the
demands of his own creditors. A friend who was advising him on
his tangled affairs had warned him then: "You must rely on provi-
dence for another crop which will come in before you are pressed
and then if the worst must come—with this crop and the sale of
100 Negroes you will be above all apprehension of distress."[18]
Fortunately, the crops at both Retreat and Waverley turned out to
be good; if prices held up, another year's crop would rescue his
over-extended credit.[19] King was not alone, of course, in his finan-

cial straits. The Brunswick development had failed openly after the canal company stopped digging at the end of 1839, and his fellow planters and the merchants of his area were in despair.[20]

These personal misfortunes were partially offset by good news from the political front. The "Log Cabin and Hard Cider" campaign had produced a resounding victory for the national Whig ticket, and in Georgia all but one of the State Rights-Whig candidates for Congress were elected. In the final tally King stood seventh among the nine party candidates, surpassing the average of his opponents by about 4,000 votes.[21] He was assured of two more years of service, this time as a member of the majority party in Congress.

Delayed by his illness and his troubled business affairs, King did not return to the lame-duck session of the outgoing Congress until January 1841, and even then his attendance was irregular. He remained in Washington to attend the inauguration of President William Henry Harrison, the funeral of the President which followed soon after, and the special session of Congress that began May 31, 1841. For the first time he belonged to a party which controlled both the executive and legislative branches of the government. He had learned his political lessons as a member of the opposition; with his party in power he now had an opportunity to play a different role.

Although the death of President Harrison deprived the Whigs of their nominal leader, they could still enact the program of legislation which Henry Clay had drawn up for the old hero's approval. On one point nearly all Whigs agreed: the repeal of Van Buren's Independent Treasury Act. Thomas Butler King took the lead in the House of Representatives to bring the repeal bill to the floor. Several attempts at delay were fought off, and King voted with the majority, 103 to 102, to bring the measure up for decision. Two days later he joined the safer majority of 134 to 87 which voted to end the Independent Treasury.[22]

On the question of substituting a national bank for the Independent Treasury, the Whigs began to display their factional differences. In the struggle for leadership of the party between Henry Clay and the former Vice-President, John Tyler, King enrolled in the ranks of the Senator. On the last day of debate over the bill to establish a national bank, he spoke for three quarters of an hour, arguing for the constitutionality and expediency of a bank.[23] In his diary John Quincy Adams noted King's "ingenuous account of the change of his opinion from an undoubting convic-

tion that a bank was not essential to the regulation of the currency, to a decision still more clear that it was."[24] Shortly thereafter the House proceeded to vote on the bill, and King was among
the 128 to 98 majority that voted for its passage.[25]

Party differences began to develop more clearly when President
Tyler vetoed the bill. A second bank measure, tailored to meet
some of the President's objections, was also vetoed. The intra-
party fight was now in the open, the break between Clay and Tyler
complete. King, who had helped push the second bank bill through
the House, now joined in an unsuccessful attempt to override
Tyler's veto.[26]

Despite the President's opposition to the bank, the Whig leaders in Congress moved forward in the enactment of their program.
One of the major acts of the special session was introduced by
King. On July 7, 1841, he presented a bill calling for the establishment of a Home Squadron by the Navy. The accompanying
report presented arguments for the adoption of new naval policies
by the Congress. Americans were said to think of naval warfare in
terms of the privateersmen and individual battles of the War of
1812, but steam vessels made such terms obsolete. Already, British
steamers, auxiliaries of the Royal Navy, had the power to blockade
a large portion of the American coast, and the use of steamers as
war vessels was only in its infancy. The committee not only approved the request for increased naval appropriations to provide
for a Home Squadron, but also added a resolution that the Secretary of the Navy report to the next session of Congress on the
possibilities of establishing a subsidized line of American merchant steamers, convertible to war uses.[27]

King guarded his legislative proposal carefully. He managed to
postpone debate until the committee report was printed, and
when the merits of the bill were argued he answered critics vigorously. On the final vote the bill met little opposition. As George
H. Proffitt, an Indiana Whig, commented, "Those who brought it
in had the power to pass it, and meant to pass it, whether or no."[28]
He went on to say that King's report would convince any doubter
of the necessity for a home squadron, and that even though his
state would not benefit from the expenditures he favored the bill.
Only eight votes, and those Democratic, were recorded against the
measure on final passage, and it was speedily approved by the
Senate and the President.[29]

The Home Squadron Act, the first piece of major legislation
with which Thomas Butler King's name was connected, reflects

some of his views and methods. Several complementary lines of thought can be distinguished in the report that accompanied the bill. It presented arguments in support of the measure that were primarily nationalistic in their appeal. It pointed out the weakness of the country's defenses and held up the advances of rival nations for emulation. The current bad relations with Great Britain, arising out of the excitement over the trial of Alexander McLeod, were exploited by the emphasis on British offensive capabilities. At the same time, the report appealed to sectional interests. Residents of the eastern seaboard could easily see the benefits to be derived from a mobile squadron of ships based in American waters. Manufacturers could envisage the profits to be garnered through contracts for government steamers. The commercial leaders of the country were encouraged to hope for the creation of a lucrative subsidy system based on French and British models. The black menace of West Indian troops played upon the fears of the inhabitants of the defenseless South. Here was a basically nationalistic bill which would rally sectional support and varied economic interests.

Naval authorities of the day were sharply divided over the relative merits of sail and steam as methods of propulsion. In debate Henry A. Wise, the chairman of the committee, spoke for the advocates of sailing ships, while King emphasized the revolutionary changes that steam was bringing about. The final bill represented a compromise, for the Home Squadron was to be made up of a majority of sailing vessels, but the advocates of steam power received an opportunity to demonstrate their theories.[30] Almost as revolutionary was the resolution that the Secretary of the Navy inquire into the expediency of using armed steamers to carry the mail. This proposal, combined with the emphasis on the French and British subsidy systems, clearly pointed the way to a new departure in governmental policy. A comparison of the committee report with that of the Secretary of the Navy shows that the major differences between the two lay in the emphasis on steam power and the efficacy of subsidies. The committee report closely paralleled the suggestions of Matthew Fontaine Maury, a naval officer who for three years had been campaigning for reforms in the navy. In addition to recommending the expansion of the navy, the operation of steam war vessels, and the subsidizing of mail steamers, Maury favored the reorganization of the Navy Department and the whole system of naval education.[31] Similar views were to be reflected in later legislation sponsored by King.

In addition to combining nationalistic and sectional appeal and uniting the interests of the advocates of sail and steam, the Home Squadron Act shows a clear awareness of partisan realities and a knowledge of legislative preparation. The act bore the endorsement of the administration and emerged from the committee with the backing of the whole group, not as the handiwork of a single dominant member. It was supported by a written report, replete with statistics, that was circulated by the party newspaper. The debate on the measure was postponed until the report should have time to create a favorable atmosphere, and when the time for argument came the facts of the report were not questioned.

The enactment of the Home Squadron Act and the publication of the accompanying report were feathers in King's cap. From the iron manufacturing state of Pennsylvania his brother Henry King reported general approval, and correspondents from other states joined in the commendation.[32] The *National Intelligencer* led the party press in endorsing a measure so "obviously expedient and universally approved."[33] Besides gaining applause for its sponsor at the time of passage, the act has since then been recognized as one of great significance in the rise of American naval power.

. . . it resulted in the establishment of an organization which was to evolve through successive stages into the North Atlantic Squadron of the 1890's, the Atlantic Fleet of the 1900's, and finally the United States Fleet of today—the supreme embodiment of the now universally recognized strategic principle of the concentration of power.[34]

It is doubtful, however, that King was looking so far into the future.

In another matter connected with national defense, King showed a frankly sectional attitude. When the fortifications bill came up for discussion, he protested against the allocation of $75,000 for deciding upon the site of a new armory. He thought $5,000 a more appropriate sum for the task and ventured to suggest a simpler solution. After pointing out that the South had only one armory, Harper's Ferry, and the West had none, he proposed that legislators from the two sections should join forces to promote armories in each area. As for the locations, he felt the representatives of the South would have no difficulty on agreeing. He himself favored the selection of the falls of the Chattahoochee River as the site and gave a number of reasons. Departing from this blatant logrolling, he insisted that the public interest demanded that one new armory be connected by water with the Gulf of Mexico, which he predicted would be the theater of the next war.[35] King's proposal was defeated.

Although King was usually to be found among the Whig majority, he faltered in his allegiance to Henry Clay on general revenue measures. He went along with the administration proposal of a loan as a temporary solution to some of the government's financial difficulties,[36] but not on the tariff. For a permanent solution of the problem of revenue, many Whigs looked to a general revision of the tariff upward. As a stopgap, they introduced a temporary tariff measure, and the debate ranged through the usual arguments. King expressed his decided opposition to the principle of protection. In answer to a protectionist speech by John Quincy Adams, he argued that Adams falsely represented the workings of the British Corn Laws. Should the corn laws be repealed, he maintained, the price of American grain would be lowered. Whatever the merits of this argument, King put his finger on the political meaning of Adams's appeal to the West to support a protective tariff. In a passage typical of his style of debate, he protested:

Now, sir, one word in regard to this unnatural alliance of the West with the East. Where do the people of the Western States find the best and most extensive market for their productions? In the South—in the cotton-growing States! not in the East, or manufacturing districts of the Union. Where do the farmers of Kentucky, Ohio, Indiana, Illinois, and all the great West and Northwest send their corn, bacon, horses, hogs, and mules? Do they send them to the Eastern manufacturers? No, sir; they send them to the South. Whose interests ought they, therefore, to consult—the manufacturers of the East, or the planters of the South, [sic] Let them decide when the question of a tariff for protection comes up. The honorable gentleman from Massachusetts has said that the question of a protective tariff is a question between free labor and slave labor—this being, when interpreted, a question of taxation on the South for the benefit of the North! How, [Now,?] sir, when this question shall be presented, I shall join the honorable gentleman from South Carolina [Francis W. Pickens], and demand to know where the great State of Kentucky stands in regard to the compromise act? Is it possible that the South, which affords a market for the products of the West, and manufactures of the East, is to be deserted by the former and plundered by the latter? We shall see, sir.[37]

King evidently did not consider the temporary measure protective. He even spoke in its favor, but Adams damned his erstwhile opponent's effort with faint praise.[38] After speaking, King moved to bring the bill to a vote, and his name is listed among the majority who voted for the temporary tariff.[39]

King also wavered in his support of Clay's program for distributing the proceeds from the sale of public lands. President Tyler had pronounced a qualified approval of distribution, and the existence of a Whig majority seemed to indicate an early passage of the measure, but sectional interests complicated the situation. By parliamentary maneuvers in the Senate, Thomas Hart Benton forced Clay to unite with his distribution scheme a pre-emption law which had strong Western support. At the same time, Thurlow Weed, the New York Whig leader, was lobbying actively for a bankruptcy bill that enjoyed Eastern favor. In the complex vote trading that attended these measures, King's position is not entirely clear. He joined the Whig majority in a move to cut off debate and in other attempts to bring the distribution bill to a decision, then reversed himself on a move to lay the bill on the table. On the final vote he was bracketed with the Democrats and a few dissident Whigs who were recorded against the measure.[40]

When the lawmakers ended their labors in September, King journeyed briefly to Philadelphia, where he underwent a surgical operation of an undisclosed nature.[41] Then he returned to Georgia to face the dismal financial prospects that awaited him there. As the year had passed reports from his home area had become more and more discouraging, and many of his friends were in despair.[42] His overseers wrote letters telling how the cotton was delayed by the rains, showed promise briefly, and then fell prey to the cotton lice and the late rains.[43] Some of the crop must have been salvaged, for toward the end of the year King informed his brother Henry in Pennsylvania that he would manage to "slide along for another year."[44]

King's optimism had led him astray. His financial affairs, precariously balanced for so long, came tumbling about his ears in January 1842. On the 17th of the month he drafted a letter to his creditors confessing his inability to pay his debts, even with a forced sale of his property. He had received no adequate offers for the one hundred slaves that he had put on the market. So gloomy was the prospect that he left Washington, where he had returned for the regular session of Congress, with the intention of resigning his seat and settling his affairs. From February until May he remained at home arranging for the disposal of all his property—Waverley Plantation, the summer cottage at Waynesville, and the slaves.[45] Fortunately, Retreat, which had been settled on his wife at the time of their marriage, remained untouched. He had the dreary consolation, too, of knowing that he was not alone in his misfortunes. His friend S. T. Chapman wrote from Columbus, Georgia, asking for the text of the new bankruptcy law, and added: "All is dark and gloomy here. Hundreds are sinking in the general wreck. . . ."[46] Mrs. King wrote her husband of the extraordinary course of two young gentlemen of the community; one enlisted as a sailor, and the other insisted on becoming a carpenter.[47]

As a result of their financial losses, the Kings' home life underwent some changes. Mrs. King began to carry the keys to her pantry and to indulge in petty economies. Even in what they referred to as straitened circumstances, however, the Kings lived in sumptuous fashion. At Retreat, Mrs. King was hostess to a household of twenty, including guests who had been detained by adverse winds. The family circle still numbered among its members a tutor for the boys and a governess for the girls. Young Butler began to help about the plantation, but this could hardly have resulted in many savings, for his Negro man, Sam, attended him every evening when he brought in the cows. Although he may have felt the pinch of poverty, King still played in card games where the debts averaged $200 for the losers.[48]

There was enough money and labor available to carry out improvements on the home plantation. The boys' tutor, Henry S. McKean, used his engineering training in the design for a new road. A new cotton warehouse was built, and new equipment was bought for the gins. From the plantation at Waverley, which was lost in the financial debacle, more gins were brought to Retreat. Several gins of a new type were erected. King also arranged to send cotton to New England manufacturers to provide supplies of lint for experimental purposes.[49]

After four months of preoccupation with private affairs, King returned to Washington to take an active part in the Twenty-seventh Congress. A long and involved battle over the tariff occupied much of the time of his colleagues, but he left the arguments to others, taking good care, however, to record his opposition to any of the tariffs currently being considered. His own energies were devoted to naval matters, in which he was beginning to be recognized as an expert. Young naval officers, impatient with conservative seniors "who have not seen the Color of ocean water for these twenty years,"[50] looked to him as their special advocate on the Committee on Naval Affairs. Some of their ideas were em-

bodied in the Naval Reorganization Bill which drew from King
his only long speech of the session. In the interests of efficiency
and economy, he called for an end to the old board of navy commissioners and its replacement by seven bureaus with assigned
functions and responsibilities, uniform accounting practices, and
increased clerical forces.

With remarkably little opposition, and with only minor alterations, the Naval Reorganization Act of 1842 became law. The
bureau system which it inaugurated was to remain for a century
the basic administrative plan of the naval service.[51] Many naval
officers welcomed the changes. Their gratitude to King for his
activities in their behalf can be measured in part by the tribute
they now accorded to him. Two warships of the home squadron
which he had sponsored were ordered south on a cruise, and King
was invited to be a guest on the steamer *Missouri* during her voyage to Savannah.[52]

The arrival of King and the warships touched off a round of
festivities and public demonstrations. The officers of the *Missouri*
entertained four hundred ladies and gentlemen on board the ship
anchored in Cockspur Roads, and the citizens of Savannah recipro-
cated with a public dinner. King came in for a large share of the
compliments that were exchanged. Even the Democratic *Savannah
Georgian,* a newspaper usually critical of his actions, congratulated
him on earning the esteem of the naval men and spoke in approving terms of his answer to a toast.[53] King apologized to his wife for
the delay in his homecoming:

You cannot be more surprised or annoyed at my prolonged stay
here than I am. But such has been the disposition of all parties here
to toast and feast the officers of the Missouri and my humble self. The
truth is it has been impossible for me to get away.[54]

Perhaps the enthusiasm of the reception helped to sweeten the
taste of political defeat. King had just been one of the victims of
the general Whig losses of the off-year elections.

The congressional elections of 1842 showed even more clearly
than the previous ones that the old State Rights Party of Georgia
had cast its fortunes with the national Whig party. The nominating convention proposed the names of King and two other in-
cumbents, Richard W. Habersham and Roger L. Gamble, as candidates for re-election. The congressional campaign was waged on
national issues rather than local ones. A national bank, a tariff
with incidental protection, and the distribution to the states of

the proceeds from the sale of the public lands were offered to the voters as the principles of the party. The nominating convention also endorsed at this early date the candidacy of Henry Clay for the presidency in 1844.[55]

Because of the prolonged session of Congress, King had remained in Washington until too late to make an active canvass in his home state. He delivered his only campaign speech in Savannah, shortly after the *Missouri* anchored. This last-minute effort, which was part of a drive by the Whigs to capture the vote of Savannah's laborers and foreign population, proved unavailing. The counting of the ballots showed that even while King and the officers of the *Missouri* were being feted, the Whig ticket had suffered a thorough defeat. King received only 32,823 votes, standing fifteenth in a field of sixteen candidates. The average number for the Democratic candidates was over 35,000.[56]

After a brief stay at Saint Simons Island, King returned to Washington for the final session of his term of office. He took little part in these last deliberations of the Twenty-seventh Congress, but he regarded his retirement from politics as merely temporary. Clay's prospects for occupying the presidential office seemed good, and King expected to profit from a Whig victory in 1844. "All now say," he wrote his wife, "that if Mr. Clay is elected in 1844 I must be placed in the cabinet."[57] Buoyed up by a general improvement in his health, he refused to be discouraged by recent reverses, whether financial or political. The future offered many possibilities.[58]

King could look with some satisfaction upon the record of the last four years. Elected as an anti-Jacksonian, he had fought the last financial measures of Martin Van Buren. With the triumph of the national Whig party he had participated in the repeal of the Independent Treasury and the enactment of laws more in keeping with his own economic ideas. In his speeches he had upheld the rights and interests of the cotton planters of the seaboard South. On the national bank issue he reversed his former stand and accepted the Whig program for a national institution. While he had worked harmoniously with his party majority in Congress, he had maintained an independent position on the tariff, willing to accept the principle of incidental protection, but refusing to vote for Clay's permanent tariff. In the realm of personal advancement he had risen from a subordinate position to recognized leadership of the Committee on Naval Affairs. Two major measures with which his name was identified had been introduced from that committee and enacted into law. He had already shown his ability to work capably and harmoniously with his party. A political victory at the next election held out hopes of greater prominence and recognition.

· V ·

The Whig Veteran

EVERY POLITICIAN must keep close to the bases of his power, and for King this meant continued activity in Georgia politics. In June 1843 he attended the Whig gubernatorial nominating convention in Milledgeville as a delegate from Glynn County. He was named to the Committee of Twenty-one that presented the agenda of the convention, and that functioned after the meeting as the Whig state committee. In consulting among themselves before the convention, the Whig leaders had discovered some dissension in the ranks over the choice of candidate for governor. The principal rivals were George W. Crawford and William C. Dawson. King favored Dawson, but in a compromise move nominated Duncan L. Clinch and then withdrew his nominee in favor of Crawford. Tensions existed among the Whigs, but they maintained an outward harmony in choosing Crawford as the candidate and naming King to the list of delegates to the Whig National Convention in Baltimore.[1]

As chairman of the state committee, King fulfilled several functions. He consulted with party leaders at the summer retreat of the planters of Burke County, and he was the confidant of local politicians with special problems.[2] It fell to King as chairman of the committee to name the candidates for two congressional seats vacated by the resignation of John B. Lamar and the death of John Millen. The party was evidently well satisfied with King's leadership, for he received proxies from one third of the committee members, accompanied by assurances that whomever he chose would be acceptable to them.[3]

The results of the summer's activities were gratifying to the

Whigs. They captured the governorship and both houses of the legislature, and elected two men to fill vacancies in Congress. One of the encouraging events of the campaign was the emergence of an effective stump speaker in the person of Alexander Hamilton Stephens.[4]

Enheartened by their success in 1843, the Whigs of Georgia turned quickly to the next year's race. The campaign began early in March with a visit by Henry Clay, the almost certain Whig nominee for the presidency. Thomas Butler King was among the leaders invited to greet the great man on his arrival in the state, and he and other Whigs accompanied Clay on his tour of Georgia. Later in the spring the Georgia delegates to the Whig National Convention in Baltimore gave Clay their vote as the party nominee. King took part in these proceedings and stayed on for the Young Men's Convention that ratified the nomination, serving as a vice-president of the assembly. From Baltimore he went on to Whig rallies in New York, New Jersey, and Pennsylvania, where the enthusiastic reception of his speeches delighted him.[5]

King returned to Georgia to make an intensive campaign to recapture his old seat in Congress. In a tour of the First District, which embraced the entire coastal area, he concentrated his fire on the Van Buren administration, blaming the Democrats for the financial distresses of recent years. He acknowledged that he had changed his mind on the question of a national bank, and he spoke in favor of the Whig plan to establish an institution which would serve as a check on irresponsible state banks. He pointed out that he had voted against the Tariff of 1842 and promised to vote for a modification of it as soon as the debt was paid. He made much of Clay's distribution scheme, saying that Georgia's share of the funds should be devoted to the education of the poor. He advocated the annexation of Texas only when it could be done peaceably and honorably. He eulogized Henry Clay as a statesman.[6]

The Democrats charged King with inconsistency and vacillation. In contrast to his current opinions they quoted his campaign speeches of 1840, in which he had denounced Clay and the bank violently. They brought up his record in the state legislature of hostility to the interests of Savannah. They even pointed to his financial misfortunes as evidence of incompetence, and at one Democratic meeting a toast was proposed to "Thomas Butler King—The voters of the first Congressional District are too intelligent to trust their business to a man who cannot manage his own affairs."[7]

The Democratic nominee was Charles H. Spalding, like King a resident of the coastal islands. The two candidates toured the district separately, each expressing a desire to meet the other on the same platform. When in August a series of joint debates took place, King continued his general discussion of national issues, but he also regaled his audiences with anecdotes that one Democratic editor alleged to be unprintable because of their vulgarity. King's ability to tell humorous stories evidently nettled his opponent, who rather fretfully declared that "if the qualification of candidates rested upon their ability to amuse, he thought the claims of a *circus clown* superior to Mr. King's and *Jim Crow* should be the undisputed President of the Country."[8] But the Whigs had learned from the campaign of 1840 the uses of humor and ballyhoo. At one all-day gathering in McIntosh County nearly five hundred voters assembled. An excursion steamer brought Whigs from Savannah, and the Clay Minstrels serenaded the group with campaign songs, including the chorus:

> Tom Butler King, he is the man
> With whom we'll beat the Loco clan
> The gallant King the boys do say
> Deserves to run with Henry Clay.[9]

Such tactics must have been sound, for on the day of the election the Democratic paper of Savannah conceded that King would have a sizable majority.[10]

All told, the Whigs captured four congressional seats. Alexander H. Stephens and Robert A. Toombs carried the Seventh and Eighth districts by large majorities, Thomas Butler King the First by a comfortable margin, and Washington Poe the Third by a close vote.[11] These four did well to win half the seats in Congress in 1844, when Henry Clay was leading the national ticket to defeat. Instead of gaining from Clay's name, the Georgia Whigs had to carry the burden of his candidacy in addition to their own. Clay's opposition to the annexation of Texas met little favor in Georgia, nor did his high tariff views catch the fancy of the cotton planting area. Most Whig leaders in the state found it expedient to qualify their approval of the Whig tariff program. King's correspondence indicates two other obstacles to victory in 1844. The anti-slavery stand of many Whigs in the North put Georgia partisans on the defensive. King's friend S. T. Chapman uncovered an election-eve plot by the Democrats to accuse the Georgia Whigs of an alliance with abolitionists, and an observer in Washington attributed the Democratic successes in Georgia to the use of this stratagem. It was also suggested that Senator John M. Berrien should "have remained at home & canvassed the state thoroughly and completely,"[12] instead of going on a national speaking tour.

The campaign of 1844 generated intense personal antagonisms, and even after the returns were in the shooting was not over. On January 6, 1845, King and his defeated opponent, Charles H. Spalding, fought a duel on Amelia Island, Florida Territory. After exchanging two shots, the gentlemen shook hands and left the grounds together, and King considered the episode to have had an honorable conclusion. According to one version, King had challenged Spalding for insulting him during the campaign and then wasted his shots in a grand gesture. A Savannah kinsman of Senator Berrien reported the affair more lightly: "The difficulty between Mr. T. B. King and C. Spalding resulted fortunately in bad shooting and amicable adjustment."[13]

King must have had great confidence in his shooting, supreme reliance on the justice of his cause, or an utter disregard for consequences, to flirt with death in an appeal to arms. A different outcome would have cast a heavy shadow over the wedding of his eldest daughter the following week. The marriage of Hannah Page King to William Audley Couper on January 15, 1845, allied King by marriage to one of the most prominent families of the area.

During the ten months that elapsed before the meeting of the next Congress, King devoted his attention to the development of his wife's plantation. He experimented with the use of guano, with different methods of manuring, and with other practices of land improvement. He kept in touch with a Baltimore firm on the subject of a specially designed plow and moldboard. His ginning operations were so successful that he was consulted about equipment and methods. A neighbor who attained some eminence as an agricultural experimenter admitted that King surpassed him in the growing of turnips, a crop that King was trying out as a cattle feed. He exchanged information with other planters on seeds and methods of making the best use of labor. King's agricultural practices, combined with a favorable growing season, brought a good crop yield for the year.[14]

While planting and harvesting went on, so did politics. All was not well in the ranks of the Georgia Whigs, for Senator Berrien had alienated many of them by his independent course in Congress. They also resented his failure to bolster the state campaign of 1844 with his presence; instead he had traveled conspicuously through the North, leading some observers to conclude that he was seeking a place in Clay's problematical cabinet. Hard cash was involved, too, for Berrien and his coterie had made only reluctant contributions to the party funds for the state election campaign of 1845. One of King's supporters wrote with some asperity: "If he and his friends expect uninterested persons to pay the expenses of a campaign from which they are to reap the benefit I think they will find themselves mistaken."[15] There was some discussion of abandoning Berrien as the senatorial candidate when his term should expire in 1847, and his appointment to the newly created supreme court of Georgia offered a method of easing him out of his position. Berrien awakened to the danger and resigned his seat to clear the way for a decision. After winning back his wavering followers and securing re-election for his own unexpired term, he made a brilliant speech defending himself against the charges that had been made against him. King, who had been eyeing Berrien's seat in the Senate, was advised by his friends to abandon his immediate hopes.[16]

Clay's defeat caused King to give up hope of appointment as Secretary of the Navy. Berrien staged a comeback, and with it recovered his grasp on the senatorship. Therefore, it was as Representative from the First Congressional District of Georgia that King journeyed to Washington in November 1845, to take his seat in the Twenty-ninth Congress. President James K. Polk's followers, with a good working majority and capable leadership, quickly organized the House, and King was assigned to the committees on naval affairs and patents. In the first of these, of course, he was in familiar harness.

By his votes and brief comments, King recorded his opposition to such Democratic measures as the establishment of the Independent Treasury and the Walker Tariff.[17] His only full dress speech of the session dealt with the Oregon question. Instead of advocating President Polk's proposal to end unilaterally the joint occupation of the territory, he called for arbitration of the dispute with Great Britain. In the course of his remarks, he criticized the reckless conduct of foreign affairs by the Democrats and at the same time deplored "throwing our foreign relations into party contests for political power."[18] Polk's Oregon policy merely furnished pretexts for the work of radical agitators, such as the movement for the abolition of slavery, "which seems ever ready to seize hold of the elements of discord."[19] Moderation in diplomacy and the emigration of hardy pioneers into contiguous territory would naturally and inevitably include Oregon in the nation's march to greatness. He looked forward to the day when the whole Pacific slope would be settled by Americans.

The possibility of war with Great Britain lent a justification for a number of measures that King brought out of the Committee on Naval Affairs, bills to double the appropriation for the Brooklyn Navy Yard, to construct drydocks at Pensacola and Savannah, to build a fort at the entrance of Cumberland Sound in Georgia, to transfer the revenue service to the Navy Department, and to amend the naval reorganization act.[20] All of these were concerned with the maintenance or expansion of the existing naval establishment. More significant were the policy changes that the committee proposed, part of a long campaign to modernize the Navy.

King's ideas on naval policy can be seen more fully in the committee reports, which gave an opportunity to present detailed arguments for change. In a recommendation to build twelve armed steamers, the committee reviewed general strategic concepts, compared the respective merits of iron and wood in naval construction, advocated competitive bidding for contracts, and especially endorsed a change from sailing ships to steam-driven propeller craft. King's favorable review of the claims of the naval architect and inventor, John Ericsson, showed that the legislator was committed to a policy of innovation and experiment.[21]

Under King's leadership the committee also recommended that the government should undertake to subsidize three commercial shipping lines to Liverpool, Le Havre, and Panama. To justify such a course, the report pointed to the success of the well-established British system, which gave Great Britain a large auxiliary fleet, subject to immediate use if war broke out. The subsidy which the committee proposed was to be paid to the private companies only if their steamships met naval specifications for conversion to war purposes and were subject to immediate use by the government in time of war. As an additional argument in favor of a subsidy, it was pointed out that the Chagres line would facilitate the movement of settlers into Oregon. Thus, the westward expansion of the nation supplied King with ammunition in his fight to improve the merchant marine and the Navy.[22]

The outbreak of the war with Mexico gave additional emphasis to King's nationalistic arguments. It was therefore logical that he should support Polk's request for power to prosecute the war, even though he had opposed the President's foreign policy. By approving war measures, he also catered to public sentiment in Georgia, where the war was popular.[23]

The prolonged session of Congress made it difficult for King to conduct his campaign for re-election in 1846, and he struggled with the added burden of recurrent asthma.[24] Fortunately, the outlook in the First District was good. Among the Whigs no opposition to his renomination was discernible, while his measures for the advancement of Savannah had won him the approval of many Democrats in that city. King's friends who managed his renomination in the Whig convention predicted that the Democrats would not oppose him in the First District. Some dissatisfaction arose among the Whigs because of a rumor that King had promised the succession to a Savannah follower, and the incumbent sent a denial to quiet the fears of the back-country party leaders.

In mid-July a small group of Democrats placed a candidate in the field without holding the usual nominating convention. Their choice, Solomon Cohen, issued a dignified address which promised that the campaign would be less personal than the preceding one. The Democratic newspaper, the *Savannah Georgian,* was less restrained, attacking King particularly for opposing the Walker Tariff. It accused King of logrolling in connection with the Rivers and Harbors bill, when the Savannah River project might have stood on its own merits as a separate measure. On the personal level, King was accused of being a visionary and a bungler, incompetent in business, and of being born in Pennsylvania. The *Georgian* hinted that King's "opportune" illness was only serious enough to keep him in Washington working as a member of the Whig committee set up to circulate franked documents.[25]

From his sickbed in the capital King dictated an address to his constituents, attacking the Polk administration, the Independent Treasury, the Walker Tariff, and the Mexican War. He favored a tariff of at least thirty per cent specific duties, declaring that no lower rates would supply the needs of the government. He also defended a limited protection of American industry. As in the previous campaign, he advocated the distribution of the proceeds from the sale of public lands, coupling this with a denunciation of Democratic measures reducing the price of the lands. He also made much of his efforts in behalf of Savannah.

As the *Georgian* charged, King's illness did not keep him entirely idle in Washington. Throughout the summer he worked with other Whig leaders, particularly Truman Smith of Connecticut, to capture the next Congress for the Whigs. To finance a special campaign in Iowa and Wisconsin territories, the two men appealed to businessmen in Boston, New York, and Philadelphia. In return for financial aid, the Whigs were to try to replace the Tariff of 1846 with one more to the liking of their friends in the East. Bostonians were cool to the proposal, and one correspondent wrote frankly: ". . . it would be impossible for me, to procure the cooperation of my friends, unless we have a *pledge* from the Whigs. . . ."²⁶ The response from New York was equally discouraging, but Philadelphians were more generous. Truman Smith reported to King that he had received from the Pennsylvanians enough funds to send an agent west with $3,000, and his way would be prepared by intensive distribution of Whig propaganda at public expense through the use of the franking privilege. The campaign was designed primarily to build up Whig voting power for a revision of the tariff, but it incidentally served as a check on the popularity of Whig presidential hopefuls. The results of this plan to bring Iowa into the Union as a Whig state failed, but the first elections in the new commonwealth showed surprising Whig strength.²⁷

Returning to Georgia in September, King showed himself to good advantage in a short tour through the district. The results of the election confirmed his strength in his own bailiwick. In an off-year election he had increased his margin of victory by more than three hundred votes, defeating Cohen by a count of 3,324 to 2,227. Democratic editors complained of agricultural duties that prevented Democrats (but not Whigs) from voting, but it seems more likely that King increased his majority mainly because of his efforts in behalf of Savannah.²⁸

After the election he enjoyed a brief period of relaxation at his island home in Georgia. There he had the pleasure of seeing his first grandchild, Anna Couper, now nearing the end of her first year. The plantation was flourishing, confirming the reports of the overseer throughout the year. However, finances were not yet easy. Several of his creditors reminded him of old obligations, and he had found it necessary before he left the North to borrow money from his brother Henry and to float a loan with a Boston bank. His brother Stephen wrote to him about a single debt of $23,000, adding that he supposed he was Thomas Butler King's largest creditor. Somehow, King found the money—or the credit—to import some blooded stock to improve the quality of the cattle at Retreat. He looked for good returns on the current crop and hoped to retrieve something from the wreck of the old railroad scheme at Brunswick, which began to show signs of revival.[29]

When King returned to Washington, Congress was absorbed in the prosecution of the war with Mexico and in measures that made heavy demands on the Treasury. It is therefore remarkable that King, a member of the opposition, was able to secure the passage of bills requiring considerable appropriations. In behalf of his Savannah constituents he introduced petitions and bills for dredging the Savannah River and building a custom house. Both measures were lost in the legislative shuffle, but King managed to have the custom house project included in the civil and diplomatic appropriation. The House and the Senate disagreed over a long list of amendments, and in the complicated jockeying by members to add or remove projects King's $30,000 provision for the building of a custom house in Savannah was retained. After conferences and trading on the very night of adjournment, the two houses finally concurred in the law.[30]

In the same hurried evening session, King pushed through his scheme for further subsidization of the transatlantic mail, along with a naval procurement bill. The first section of the act appropriated $1,000,000 for the building of four steamships for the naval service. Then, in words following almost exactly the recommendations of King, the Secretary of the Navy was directed to conclude contracts with two designated agents to handle the Atlantic and Caribbean mails. Edward K. Collins was to carry the mail from New York to Liverpool in ships approved by naval authorities. Similarly, A. G. Sloo was to be the contractor for a line of ships from New York to New Orleans, with calls at Savannah, among other ports. The Sloo contract called for an extension to Chagres, Panama, and a separate contract was authorized for the Pacific mail to Oregon. The specific money required for this projected network was not mentioned in the act; subsequently, nearly $900,000 was required.[31]

King supported the administration in its war appropriations and even proposed to double a specific allocation of money for the Pensacola naval base. King's support of this measure undoubtedly sprang from several sources. As usual he was willing to spend money liberally on the Navy, and the Pensacola base had proved its value during the Mexican War. There was the obvious advantage accruing from large federal expenditures in his section, even if the primary benefit was to Floridians. Finally, a number of his personal friends were interested in a proposed railroad which

would terminate at Pensacola. He also introduced a measure of
more interest to his general constituency when he proposed that
the Secretary of War make a survey of the inland waterway from
Savannah to the St. John's River. At the same time that he voted
for war appropriations, however, the gentleman from Georgia recorded his disapproval of a war of conquest.[32]

Nationalistic as he showed himself in some regards, King stood
firmly with his section in the voting on the Wilmot Proviso. When
David Wilmot first tried to attach his ban on the extension of
slavery to an appropriation bill, King recorded his opposition.
When the proviso was added, he voted against the bill. Later the
Senate returned the bill without the proviso, and again King
showed his hostility, helping to prevent the addition of the re-
strictive clause.[33] The Twenty-ninth Congress concluded its session
soon after this vote, and the members began their exodus from
Washington.

King delayed his return to Georgia about a month, spending
part of the time in New York. The merchants of that city, in appreciation of his leadership in the passage of the steamship subsidy, joined forces to give a dinner in his honor. Already his role
had been praised by the Whig *National Intelligencer;* now Horace
Greeley's *Tribune* acclaimed the man whose "ardent, unremitting
and successful exertions" had procured the establishment of a line
of steamships from New York. The dinner was "intended as the
expression by all parties of grateful feeling for the benefits obtained through his agency."[34] In reply to compliments to his leadership and breadth of view, King spoke for the better part of an
hour. He outlined the policy of the British government in steam
navigation and presented statistics on the economic results. It was
on the success of English policy and the preeminence of the British
in the development of ocean steamers that "he predicated his
opinion of the necessity of Governmental interference for the
establishment of a national line of steamers."[35]

From the plaudits of the New York merchants, King returned
to Georgia, only to find that there, too, public business monopolized his attention. There was little time to enjoy the society of his
family, and perhaps to investigate the growth of the many exotic
plants that he had ordered sent to his plantation from the North.
In April he was elected a director of the Central Railroad and
Banking Company of Georgia and was delegated by his fellow directors to represent them at a railroad convention in Chicago.
The appointment was reinforced by an invitation, extended to

him as a legislator, which he received from the sponsors of the convention.[36]

Before departing for Chicago, where the convention was to meet in July, King joined with other dignitaries to welcome Daniel Webster to Savannah. There was a connecting link between these honors to Webster and the plans of the Central Railroad, for the "god-like Daniel" in his speech found occasion to direct his hearers' attention to the glorious prospect of joining Savannah to Pensacola by rail. This project was already dear to the hearts of some of his hosts, including the Representative from the First Congressional District.[37]

In these dinners for Webster in Savannah and for King in New York can be seen the outline of the alliance of planters, merchants, and manufacturers that made the Whig party a formidable political organization. Few figures in the party exemplified better than King the mutual and reciprocal economic interests that tied the elements together. Equally significant was the Chicago convention that King was scheduled to attend, for it was a barely veiled attempt to capture the allegiance of the West and add another economic bloc to the alliance.

The Chicago Rivers and Harbors Convention had many political implications, but it was advertised as a non-partisan gathering. It originated at Rathbun's Hotel in New York among a group of Westerners who had been antagonized by Polk's veto of the Rivers and Harbors bill in 1846. Determined to focus the resentment of their section against the administration's policy, they called the public meeting in Chicago. The leading Polk newspaper in Washington attacked the principles that the sponsors proclaimed, but some Democratic organs forsook their party allegiance to give publicity and support to the meeting. Democrats and Whigs alike were numbered among the delegates.[38]

Thomas Butler King was a member of the temporary steering committee and one of the vice-presidents of the convention which opened July 5, 1847. The first day was spent in celebration of the national holiday—the Fourth had fallen on Sunday—and in organizing the nearly 4,000 delegates. The next morning was devoted to the reading of letters from distinguished guests who had found it impossible or impolitic to attend. Martin Van Buren, Henry Clay, Thomas Hart Benton, Daniel Webster, and Silas Wright all expressed sympathy for the development of the transportation facilities of the West. True to Democratic doctrine, Van Buren and Benton were cautious about the principle of federal aid, but the latter went to great pains to show that he had long been a champion of western development. Webster publicly endorsed the general purposes of the meeting and pointed out that Whig leaders had always been in favor of internal improvements with federal aid. Webster's fears that Democrats would gain from the meeting had led him to reject an invitation to attend. Privately, he wrote King:

Pray defend it [his rejection] as far as you think it may deserve defense. I have no idea that the Whigs ought to give up now all the vantage ground they possess, in having so long maintained the doctrine of Internal Improvements.[39]

At the afternoon session the committee brought in a series of fifteen resolutions, generally declaring that the improvement of rivers and harbors was properly the concern of the national government, that the needs were urgent, and that candidates with soundness on these points should be elected to office regardless of their party affiliation. After brief debate and minor alterations the resolutions were passed unanimously, and the president of the convention appointed King as one of the two Georgia delegates on the publicity committee. Besides serving on every one of the committees, King delivered one of the principal addresses of the meeting.[40]

When King returned to Saint Simons Island he was urged to attend the state railroad convention in Atlanta, but several domestic matters demanded his attention at home. Decisions had to be made on where to send the children to school, and the money for tuition had to be raised. Fortunately, Andrew King, who had made a success of his sugar planting operations in Cuba, offered to assume the burden of college expenses for his two eldest nephews.[41] This was especially good news, for although the Retreat cotton crop had proved to be a good one, King received only gloomy forecasts on the price outlook from his factor.[42] Besides these personal concerns, political fences needed mending, for the trip to Chicago had prevented his attendance at the state Whig Convention during the summer. These varied affairs kept him busy until the reassembling of Congress.

Since the Whigs had captured the House of Representatives in the off-year elections, the political arena in Washington offered King more opportunities than usual. He could look forward to increased responsibility as Chairman of the Committee on Naval Affairs. In addition, his years of service made him one of the most experienced members of the House, for less than half the members

had served in the preceding Congress. President Polk could hope
for little more than necessary bills to emerge from a Whig House
and a Democratic Senate. Above all, this was a presidential election year, and partisanship would tend to dominate the proceedings of Congress.

King frequently took part in the debates of the session, but seldom delivered a set speech of any length. He usually ventured on-
to the floor of the House as chairman of his committee, and almost
invariably he appeared as an advocate of larger or additional appropriations. Some of the sums involved were petty, as in the case
of a proposed bonus payment to naval professors; others were for
considerable sums, such as the $150,000 to build a drydock at the
New York navy yard. King was kept busy sponsoring new bills
and defending those already reported.[43]

King also debated bills concerned with private claims against
the Navy, administrative details, and humanitarian reforms. The
claims were so numerous that the chairman of the naval affairs
committee pleaded with his colleagues to establish a system to
eliminate routine private relief bills. For the humanitarian attempts to eliminate corporal punishment and abolish the liquor
ration in the Navy, he showed only a perfunctory sympathy. He
chided the advocates of these reforms for loading an appropriation
bill with irrelevant amendments.[44]

In the running feud with President Polk on the conduct of the
war with Mexico, King acted as a spokesman for his party. The
Whigs took advantage of their majority in the House to demand
from the President an account of his diplomatic dealings in regard
to the Mexican general, Santa Anna. When Polk refused to comply
with their request, King moved that his action be referred to a
select committee, but the House declined to go along. To Democratic charges that the Whigs had not supported the war, he
pointed out that his party had faithfully voted for the necessary
appropriations, even though they disapproved of the Democrats'
policies and Polk's conduct of the war. Although this partisan
bickering tended to become bitter, King avoided personalities in
his defense and twice protested against intemperate wrangling in
debate. At the same time he provided a focus for the Whig attack
on Polk by including in the general civil and diplomatic appropriations a provision to remove the sunken hulks of ships that
impeded navigation in the Savannah River. In debate he denied
that his measure had been proposed in order to embarrass the
President, but Polk was convinced that this item had been in-

cluded from partisan motives and determined to veto the bill if
it carried the Savannah appropriation.[45]

King continued to lead the fight for mail subsidies to expand
the American merchant marine. He sponsored and defended laws
aimed at carrying out the measures which he had introduced during earlier sessions, and gave his support to new subsidies. When
Robert Barnwell Rhett, of South Carolina, introduced an amendment calling for direct voyages of mail steamers from Charleston
to Havana, King succeeded in adding Savannah as a required port
of call. In the exchange between the two congressmen can be seen
the strong commercial rivalry of Charleston and Savannah for the
trade of the southeastern coast. In further debate on the same bill,
King urged that the Secretary of the Navy, as well as the Postmaster General, be given a hand in the award of mail contracts.
Such dual authority he based on the same principle that he had
embodied in his own subsidy bills. Mail steamers, he argued,
should meet the standards of a board of naval inspectors, in order
to be convertible to war uses. The House did not approve of his
argument, and the members may have been influenced by the
workings of the subsidy measure of the previous session. Under
that generous grant of authority the Secretary of the Navy was
receiving bills for setting up a Pacific mail system over which the
Postmaster General had little authority. Contractors were competing for profits with small regard for the needs of the postal service.
Yet, despite the flaws in the operation of King's subsidy law, the
House approved without objection the $874,600 for mail steamer
contracts in the general Navy appropriation. The Senate and
President Polk concurred.[46]

King's only long speech of the session was in support of mail
subsidies. In it he summoned up from earlier debates and reports
familiar arguments. The United States depended on foreign-owned
lines to carry the transatlantic mail. The British therefore received
the profits from high American postal rates, while they enjoyed
low rates on their own subsidized ocean steamers. At the same
time, by their governmental policy they encouraged the growth of
their merchant marine. After a long statistical review of the results,
King drew the conclusion that only through a similar program of
subsidies could the United States lines compete with their British
rivals. He drew special attention to the defensive value of the vessels which would be added by this measure to the national maritime service. He concluded by presenting joint resolutions author-

izing the opening of bids for American flag lines to Le Havre and Antwerp.

This speech was little more than a recapitulation of parts of King's committee report on trade routes to China, which he presented on May 4, 1848. He began with a ten-page review of Anglo-American trade with China, its nature, value, and potentialities. From the survey the author concluded that China constituted an enormous potential market for American manufactured goods, particularly cotton. The next eight pages of the report were devoted to an examination of the trade routes to the Orient. The shortest route from Europe to China ran through Panama, and from that port the shortest course to Shanghai passed close to San Francisco. Mail for the Orient, and other cargo which required speedy delivery, would naturally fall into the hands of whoever developed the route first. The United States should exploit its geographic advantage. With a confident glance into the future, the writer saw the development of transcontinental rail connections, such as Whitney's planned railroad to Oregon or a line from the Mississippi to San Francisco. With the completion of such a network the United States would absorb the carrying trade and commerce of the East, and New York would replace London as the financial center of the world. For accomplishing the first step to these desired ends, resolutions looking toward the opening of the Asiatic trade routes were proposed. The Secretary of the Navy was to be empowered to maintain a regular mail service to Hawaii by Navy steamers and to inaugurate the same type of service to Shanghai. Further resolutions called for the same official to contract with a private firm for a continuation of these mails within two years.[47]

Even though King's proposal was tabled it attracted attention both in Congress and in the press. The Senate embarked on a general discussion of the policy, with Democrats leading a sucessful attack on extending the commitments of the government further. The *New York Herald* approved the establishment of a two-ocean network, as did the Whig organ in Washington, the *National Intelligencer*. The China trade report attracted special notice. The *Philadelphia Ledger* endorsed its glowing predictions, while the *National Intelligencer* devoted one whole page to its publication and carried an additional column of editorial analysis and favorable comment. In September and October the same newspaper ran a series of seven articles on the subject of the China trade, which made frequent references to the report. In this manner King contributed to one of the most persistent American myths, the unlimited market in China for manufactured goods.[48]

In the closely related field of land transportation, too, King supported the principle of government aid to expand the nation's commerce. He presented resolutions from the Georgia legislature approving Asa Whitney's project of a railroad from Lake Michigan to Oregon, and alluded to future transcontinental connections between the Mississippi and San Francisco. From the naval affairs committee he reported a bill to grant to the Alabama, Florida and Georgia Railroad Company alternate sections of the public land along the route of their contemplated roads, under certain conditions. Despite persistent parliamentary maneuvering in which he worked closely with his junior colleague, Alexander H. Stephens, he failed to bring the bill to a final vote.[49]

In the midst of his congressional duties King faced again in 1848 the recurrent problem of the politician, re-election. He had given his friends and family some reason to believe that he might not seek office again. However, as the incumbent and as the sponsor of legislation which had benefited his district, it might be reasonably assumed that the nomination was his for the asking. His political friends encouraged him to run again, and he began making plans with his closest supporters on the choice of delegates to the nominating convention and on publicity for the race.[50]

As King's advisers had predicted, the convention named him the Whig candidate for the First District, but the meeting was not wholly harmonious. When it became apparent that King would be renominated, the supporters of James Lindsay Seward bolted the convention. King's private report on the meeting assured him that his prospects remained bright and that Seward had little backing. Later, Seward announced for Congress as an Independent, throwing the Whigs into an argument over the political morality of his action that lasted all summer. The Democrats of the First District contributed to the confusion by not nominating a candidate.[51]

While King worked in Congress during the summer, his friends sent him encouraging reports on the political scene in Georgia. Probably the most helpful occurrence took place in Philadelphia, where Thomas Butler King helped to nominate Zachary Taylor as the Whig candidate for the presidency. The First District leaders were much relieved; in fact, they had urged their candidate earlier to come out openly for Old Zach. King's friend W. W. Paine expressed the general consensus: "If Gen. Taylor is our candidate and the Democrats run Seward you will in my opinion beat him 400 or 500 votes. Should Mr. Clay be our candidate and Gen. Taylor run on his own hook—Seward may beat you."[52] The results of the National Whig convention were therefore more than satisfactory to King's backers.

Since Seward was leading a Whig splinter movement, King profited greatly from the failure of the Democrats to nominate a candidate. His efforts in behalf of Savannah had gained him such widespread support in that city that the Democrats were willing to see him return to Congress. In fact, even while the Democratic newspaper of the city sang the praises of Cass and the Democratic party, it gave favorable notice to King for his part in securing an appropriation for the new custom house, for his efforts to remove obstructions in the Savannah River, and for his proposal to build additional mail steamers. This happy state of affairs did not continue through the summer. On August 25 the *Georgian,* which had carried no Democratic candidate for the First District at the masthead with the regular party ticket, proposed the name of Joseph W. Jackson. Their nominee accepted the call to duty, but pleaded age and infirmity as excuses for not canvassing the district. Seward, whose chance for a Democratic endorsement had now gone glimmering, announced his withdrawal from the race, and King was left with only a feeble rival for his seat. Yet opposition still existed in another quarter, within his own family. His wife reproached him in almost bitter terms:

I dare say I would have been mortified had your *name been rejected*—but you promised me you would not consent to be again put up for a *target to be shot at.* And I believed you! . . . If you would but stay with us, how much better it would be—how much happier I would be. I have said all this before.[53]

Others in the family were more enthusiastic about his political activities. Lord and Thomas Butler, Jr., both referred to the probable victory of Zachary Taylor, and the former added the hope that "the old scamp will have the *manners* to make you Secretary of the Navy, or some foreign ambassador. . . ."[54] Butler made a more practical contribution by supervising the preparation of the buggy that King would use in the last days of the campaign.

While all these domestic and political reports were coming in, King remained in the North, first at his duties in Washington and then on a brief vacation advised by his doctor. It was probably more than good fortune that his health had recovered enough for him to attend a political rally in Albany, New York, where he made a soothing speech to the Whigs in Thurlow Weed's territory.[55] About three weeks before the October election date he returned to Saint Simons Island for a one-day visit before departing on the political canvass. The Democratic *Georgian,* which had praised him earlier in the summer, now discovered that King's efforts in behalf of Savannah were no more than any representative would have made. How, asked the editor, could voters support such a man, who was openly against the Tariff of 1846? But the favorite charge against him was guilt of association. Had he not joined John Quincy Adams, William Slade, and Joshua Giddings in endorsing the proposal to limit the veto power of the President, a protection for minorities? Had the Philadelphia paper which praised King not pleaded the abolitionist cause in the same issue?[56]

These partisan criticisms proved to be mere rearguard sniping, for King defeated Jackson by nearly nine hundred votes. In the November presidential election Zachary Taylor carried the state. Once more King could hope for a prominent place in the majority party—and a share in the spoils of office.[57]

The last session of the Thirtieth Congress was almost wholly taken up with one absorbing topic, the extension of slavery into the territories acquired by the Mexican War. In spite of their preoccupation, however, the lawmakers despatched their regular business, and Thomas Butler King followed the same course he had taken in previous sessions. As Chairman of the Committee on Naval Affairs he presented a number of bills aimed at restoring the Navy to a peacetime footing. Of such a nature were measures to substitute marines for landsmen on shipboard, to transfer the Pacific naval agency from Lima, Peru, to San Francisco, and to shift the control of vessels from the Secretary of War to the Navy. Again King opposed the complete abolition of the spirit ration to sailors. In defense of the general naval appropriation bill he answered the charges of extravagance leveled by Horace Greeley. In the money bill once more was an appropriation for $874,600 to fulfill the contracts for mail subsidies under the jurisdiction of the Secretary of the Navy, and the total appropriation for the Pensacola navy yard amounted to more than $450,000.[58]

On January 16, 1849, King presented an elaborate report which recommended the building of a railroad across the Isthmus of Panama.[59] This was closely related to the system of subsidized mail steamers which King had sponsored, and the method of lending government aid was similar. William H. Aspinwall and his associates in the Pacific mail contract petitioned Congress for financial aid in building a rail line linking the Atlantic and the Pacific oceans. They had acquired from the government of New Granada the lapsed charter of a French company, but Aspinwall saw no hope of obtaining enough private capital to complete so huge a project. In pleading for government aid, the contractors pointed out the advantage to the United States of having a means of transporting troops and supplies to forces on the Pacific coast, particularly in case of war. They asked for no direct grants of money, but rather for Congress to give the Secretary of the Navy the authority to contract for twenty years for the transporting of mail, troops, and supplies across the Isthmus. The payment was not to exceed that given by the government to the Edward K. Collins line of steamers that carried the Atlantic mails. With assurance of such indirect government aid, the promoters were confident of success.

King's committee endorsed the proposition with additional emphasis on the future advantages for American trade generally. Mileage tables that included the comparative distances between Asiatic ports and ports in America and Europe were presented in tabular form to point out the savings in time and distance which such a railroad would effect. The needs of American emigrants to California would also justify the lending of government aid—not the hundred thousand who were expected to flock to the newly found gold region this year, but the future population of the new area of the United States. Because of the nature of their work, Californians were expected for a long time to constitute a market for products from the older states. It was also pointed out that the treaty of 1846 between the United States and New Granada virtually committed the United States to a defensive alliance with that country. The ownership by citizens of the United States of a railroad across Panama would give reality to the right of transit for which the United States had bargained. Summarizing all the arguments, the report contained the speculation that over the course of twenty years the actual savings to the American government would amount to more than $85,000,000. The committee therefore recommended that the petitioners' request be granted, with the amount of compensation to be limited to $250,000 annually.

The House never discussed King's ambitious proposal. In the Senate a similar bill received little better treatment. Thomas Hart Benton introduced the measure; he was supported by Jefferson Davis in his efforts to schedule debate. When Benton's bill was taken up, Stephen A. Douglas offered a substitute more nearly in accordance with King's measure in the House, but the Senate soon turned to the discussion of other matters.[60] The issue of slavery in the territories was coming to outweigh all other problems of the day and to draw a line between North and South that Thomas Butler King would find it difficult to erase.

The members of the Thirtieth Congress from the Southern states had already had to face the divisive effects of the extension of slavery. Alarmed at the tendencies he saw developing in the government, John C. Calhoun headed a group of Southerners from both parties who met in caucus to consult on defending the rights of their section. This meeting placed some of the members of Congress in a difficult position, for many of them disagreed with Calhoun on the gravity of the dangers he professed to see. The Whigs, in particular, could hardly be expected to become enthusiastic about a movement that would obliterate party lines. After a long famine their party was about to enjoy the fruits of victory, and if they followed Calhoun's lead they would lose the confidence of the rest of their party. Abstention from the caucus, on the other hand, might be regarded at home as disloyalty to their section. In this dilemma the Southern Whigs, following the leadership of the Georgians, decided to attend the meeting and either turn it to their own ends or frustrate the designs of their fire-eating colleagues.[61]

In the deliberations of the caucus King showed his opposition to any radical disunionist moves and his solidarity with the other Georgia Whigs. At the first tumultuous meeting on January 15, 1849, he voted with other moderates to exclude reporters from the proceedings. When Calhoun's Address to the Southern States was put forward as a presentation of the views of the assembly, the Georgia Whigs who tried to lay it on the table were in the minority. Unsuccessful in the first vote, they resorted to delaying actions, and the majority agreed to recommit Calhoun's address to a committee for revision. In other meetings of the group King supported successive delaying motions by his fellow Georgian Alexander H. Stephens to adjourn *sine die,* to issue a declaration that it was inexpedient at the time to publish an address, and to adjourn for a month. None of the motions carried. John M. Berrien, Whig Senator from Georgia, brought in from the committee of revision an address very different in content and tone from Calhoun's. King supported this mild address to the nation, and when it was rejected as the choice of the caucus he joined the large body of Whigs and moderate Democrats who refused to sign the published Calhoun address.[62]

· VI ·

Appointments and Compensations

WHEN THOMAS BUTLER KING returned to Washington in December 1848, it was no secret that he hoped to receive from President-elect Zachary Taylor the appointment as Secretary of the Navy. For several years King had made a specialty of naval legislation and had been the acknowledged spokesman of the Navy in Congress. In addition, he had served the "Commerce Whigs" of the eastern seaboard by sponsoring the two-ocean network of mail steamers which brought profits to the ship-builders and subsidies to the steamship companies. However much the knowledge gained from these activities might qualify him for the position that he sought, the route to a cabinet post led through the maze of partisan politics. The Whigs had won the presidency, but had King rendered such notable service to the party, and to the winning candidate, that his claims for preferment would be considered? He could point confidently to his record over the past few years.

After the defeat of Clay in the election of 1844, the Whig leaders in Congress began their search for a candidate who could win in 1848. For a brief while in 1846 some of them seized the idea of creating a boom for General Winfield Scott, and King's acquiescence, at least, is implied in a note from a Scott supporter who was leaving for the West "to put in motion the *Scott* ball—to keep it rolling until the Hero of Chippewa is elevated to the Chair of State."[1] Along with Truman Smith of Connecticut, too, King sounded out the far western areas of Iowa and Wisconsin on the names of Scott, John McLean of Ohio, and Thomas Corwin of Ohio. However, the McLean and Corwin balloons never got off the ground, and Scott's was punctured by the publication of some of his letters, unfortunately phrased. Henry King informed his brother Thomas that Scott was no longer acceptable in Pennsylvania, but in the same letter he inquired about the possibility of running General Zachary Taylor.[2]

As the news of Taylor's victories arrived from Mexico, the General's name became familiar throughout the country. Even after his theater of operations became quiet the continued popularity of the Hero of Buena Vista convinced Whigs that here was a potential winner. For enthusiasm to be converted into voting power, however, required skilled direction of the political machinery. Favorable delegations had to be named to nominating conventions, and close coordination had to be maintained among different factions. Assuming that Taylor would be the principal nominee, the prize of the Vice-Presidency still remained open, and various interests had to be consulted, various possibilities assayed. It was in the role of behind-the-scenes management and liaison that King played a part in the pre-convention maneuvers of 1848. John O. Sargent, the Whig journalist who had been so influential in the election of William Henry Harrison, reported to King the situation in New England. Sargent was convinced that only Taylor could lead the Whigs to victory in the northeastern and central states. As for the Vice-Presidency, Abbott Lawrence, merchant, manufacturer, and railroad builder of Boston, was willing to be put forward but was not running hard; he would let his friends know his decision by May 1, 1848.[3] In New York, the Taylor supporters kept in touch with King and were particularly concerned with the problem of a minority who still clung to the idea of nominating Henry Clay. One Taylor man reported a letter from a "wise man" in Albany: "Our people mean to have success, and they do not think success can be had with Mr. Clay for a candidate."[4] Sargent tended to discount the strength of Clay's following in New York. "The Weed & Seward cliques have been going for Clay to accumulate a little capital to trade upon. They are now about ready to sell out."[5] Their aim was to secure the Vice-Presidential nomination for Millard Fillmore, thought Sargent, but Governor John Young of New York might have himself in mind for the post. From New Orleans, another survey of Whig chances informed King that Taylor was a winner, Clay a sure loser.[6]

In Georgia, too, the Taylor fever had caught hold. The *Republican,* the Whig organ in Savannah, had put Taylor's name up on the masthead for the presidency as early as July 1847, but the nominating conventions, county and state, were not scheduled until nearly a year later. In March 1848 the consensus was well expressed by R. R. Cuyler, one of King's particular friends in Savannah: "I remain of opinion that Mr. Clay—as much & justly as he is admired, cannot carry Georgia. General Taylor can carry the State."[7] County and district Whig conventions confirmed the Taylor trend by either endorsing Taylor or instructing their representatives to vote for a Taylor delegation at Philadelphia. At Whig meetings in May, King was renominated for Congress and also chosen as a delegate to the Whig National Convention. Publicly, the Georgia delegation was committed only to the choice of the national convention; but privately, W. B. Hodgson, a prominent Savannahian, confided to King: "In the Philadelphia convention you will be placed between two fires, and endanger your place as Secretary of the Navy. But it is neck or nothing, with 'Old Whitey.' "[8] In fact, he added, if the national Whigs did not choose Taylor, he favored an independent Taylor ticket that would at least keep the Whigs of Georgia in power.

At the Philadelphia convention King was conspicuous in promoting the Taylor cause. He acted as the floor leader of the gathering, making the initial organizing motions. In turn, he was named one of the vice-presidents of the convention and was appointed chairman of the credentials committee. Although the Taylor forces had the same number on the committee as their opponents, the resolutions they brought in favored Taylor. Specifically, the pro-Taylor delegate from Texas was recommended for a permanent convention committee. On the fourth convention ballot Zachary Taylor was chosen as the standard bearer of the party in the forthcoming election. The vice-presidential nomination, however, did not go as King had hoped. He himself received a complimentary vote on the first ballot, but the second place on the ticket went to Millard Fillmore, rather than Abbott Lawrence.[9]

During the summer King kept up his activities in behalf of Taylor. He maintained close touch with Whig leaders in the North and helped to spread campaign documents to all sections. He also spoke in New York and New Jersey for the Whig ticket. His most important service in the cause was performed at Albany, New York. A group of Albany Whigs were threatening to bolt the regular ticket because of Taylor's non-partisan attitude, and Thurlow Weed wrote to King that if General Taylor did not write a letter emphasizing his party affiliation, "God only knows what is to happen."[10] Furthermore, his candidate Fillmore was being at-

tacked in the South as an abolitionist, and it was feared that the
southern Whigs were less than enthusiastic about the vice-presidential candidate. A mass meeting was arranged in Albany, and
King interrupted a brief vacation to address the dissidents and
assure them that the southern Whigs were loyal supporters of the
entire Whig ticket.[11]

Upon his return to Georgia, King embarked on a two-week campaign tour in his own behalf, beginning in Savannah with a speech
on the activities of Congress and the progress of the Taylor campaign in the North. He had time for only a few meetings in the
up-country before the October 2 election, but the results were
gratifying. He even carried the home county of his opponent, Jackson. With his own election assured, he devoted the month that
ensued before the presidential voting in November to a thorough
canvass of the First District to insure Taylor's victory. Taylor carried the First District by an even greater majority than King had
won in the October election.[12]

Having served the President-elect so faithfully, King looked forward to the reward that his political activity merited. The post of
Secretary of the Navy had long been the object of his ambition,
and his congressional career as well as his political services recommended him for the position. His hopes for the cabinet post
amounted almost to expectation, and the probability of his appointment was acknowledged both publicly and privately. Nathan
K. Hall, law partner of the incoming Vice-President, alluded to
the likelihood of the appointment in a speech in Congress, and it
was common currency among the editors who practiced the pas-
time of cabinet building, in Georgia and elsewhere.[13]

His past activities might give him claims to preferment, and
other men might think King deserved the Navy Department, but
King was too knowledgeable a politician to think that the post
would fall into his lap. The exact method of presenting his claims
posed a problem. R. R. Cuyler, a close friend in Savannah, inquired of King shortly after the election "if pains had been taken
to acquaint General Taylor with your services in his behalf . . .
for if it has not been done, you should not be asleep."[14] Yet the
only suggestion that Cuyler could offer was that King should send
a letter of congratulation to the General. What King needed was
a friend at court who would urge his appointment without de-
grading his claims to the level of the petitions that had begun to
overwhelm the President-elect at his Louisiana home.[15] It was
through another hero of the Republic, Commander Charles Stew-

art, who had captained the *Constitution* in the War of 1812, that
King hoped to influence General Taylor. What more patriotic and
disinterested source could there be? Commander Stewart's son was
an intimate friend of Taylor's and was charged by his father "to
use every possible exertion in King's behalf."[16] While he remained
in Louisiana, Taylor certainly included King among those he was
considering for his official family, but he decided to wait until he
reached Washington to make most of the appointments.[17]

The real key to a place in the cabinet lay in the hands of John
Jordan Crittenden, Governor of Kentucky. Taylor had already
offered him the State Department, which had been refused, but
he planned to visit Kentucky on his way to Washington and persuade the Governor to reconsider his decision. Although these
facts and intentions remained a secret, Taylor's confidence in
Crittenden was well known, and letters began to pour in upon the
Whig governor from applicants for office and their friends. Among
them was a powerful plea for King's appointment to head the
Navy Department. Just ten days before Taylor was due to arrive
in Frankfort, John O. Sargent, who became the editor of the administration newspaper of the new regime, wrote to Crittenden in
King's behalf. After pointing out the strong press support for his
friend, the political services that he had rendered, and his "national" view, Sargent continued:

Here we have experience, ability, popularity, services and the will of
the party as expressed through its journals, uniting to recommend one
individual. . . . If he is passed by, it must be in favor of some individual of fewer qualifications, less acquaintance with the duties of the
office, less popularity, no more eminent services, and one who must
come into the place which the Navy, the Press, and the Party—or *in
other words the Country*—have universally and uniformly assigned to
another.[18]

After reviewing the sentiment of the South, Sargent stated that
"it would be a subject of sore disappointment to the Whigs of New
England & New York who united with Mr. King in the movement
for General Taylor if he should fail to receive the appointment."[19]
When Taylor visited Crittenden at Frankfort, the two men conferred on the cabinet possibilities; such a plea as Sargent's could
hardly have failed to figure in their conversations. Taylor's Kentucky host advised him to consult Stephens and Toombs, two
Georgia Whig Congressmen, on political matters in Washington.[20]

Without knowing precisely what passed between Taylor and

Crittenden, it is clear from this last advice that King had been discarded as a cabinet choice, for Toombs and Stephens had no intention of promoting the ambitions of Thomas Butler King. The Savannah Whig editor, J. L. Locke, had warned King soon after the election against their "malign influence," advising him to rely on his Whig friends in the North rather than "on our particular friends in the up country."[21] Both Toombs and Stephens had expressed themselves as opposed to King in letters to Crittenden before he saw Taylor; instead of King, they wished to see George W. Crawford of Georgia named as one of the President's principal advisers. Stephens, in particular, urged the appointment of Crawford rather than King, and expressed alarm at the thought of placing King in the cabinet.

I did not at first have any serious thought about Mr. King of our State being put at the head of the Navy. But recent rumours awaken my apprehension. Now my dear Sir this will not do. You know Mr. King, but I know the people of Georgia. And if you will allow me I will suggest to you that Mr. Crawford at the head of the War Department or Mr. Toombs Atty General will suit us much better.[22]

When Crittenden advised the President-elect to consult Toombs and Stephens in Washington, the decision against King's appointment had most probably already been taken. Publicly, however, his name continued to be mentioned by newspapers as a likely head for the Navy Department throughout the month of February. Only on March 5 did the news become official: George W. Crawford was to be Secretary of War and William Ballard Preston of Virginia, Secretary of the Navy. Georgia had her cabinet appointment, but it was Crawford, not King.[23]

The choice of Crawford must have been made largely on the recommendations of the Whig leaders of the state, particularly Toombs and Stephens. It would be easy to explain Stephens' preference merely on personal grounds, for he and Crawford had been intimately associated for years, yet Stephens specifically disclaimed any personal reasons for his advice to Crittenden, alluding instead to the needs of the party in Georgia.[24] Some secret may lie hidden in the labyrinth of state politics, perhaps in the 1843 election for Governor when King was the party chairman and Crawford the candidate, or in the episode of 1846 when Senator Berrien resigned his seat and was overwhelmingly reelected.[25] To Anna Page King the answer was simple enough to encompass in a few words: that her husband had "ever been & ever will be an object of jealousy—to Judge Berrien & the up country members."[26] Certainly the fear of promoting the influence of a rival in state politics would work equally on both the Representatives and the Senator. There was also an underlying economic factor, best summed up in an article in the *Savannah Republican*. The editor expressed disappointment that King had not received the Navy appointment, but rejoiced that he remained the representative of Savannah, "whose commercial importance is already advancing a little too fast to suit the notions of a certain clique in Georgia, who arrogate to themselves the management of every thing great— both political and commercial. This is the reason Mr. King did not receive the appointment of Secretary of the Navy."[27]

Although King failed to receive from Taylor the appointment which he coveted, the President called on him to help solve the most important and delicate problem which faced the new administration, the political future of California. Even before the election of 1848, the question of California had engaged the attention of the Whigs in Congress. John Middleton Clayton, who later became Taylor's Secretary of State, took the lead in the Senate to unite the Whigs and the moderate Democrats of Congress behind a measure that would erect territorial governments in areas that had just been acquired from Mexico, leaving the question of slavery to future decision by the Supreme Court. This "Clayton Compromise" seemed to offer great hope as a means of avoiding the antagonisms that were developing between strong anti-slavery partisans and the more extreme slavery advocates. To Clayton's measure King gave his support in the House of Representatives, but the Whig leaders in Congress were unable to hold their own party united behind the measure and failed to attract the Democratic votes needed to pass Clayton's bill.[28]

In the interval between the election and the inauguration of the new administration, the Whig leaders redoubled their efforts to devise a solution to the problem of slavery in the territories. If they could surmount this difficulty before Taylor assumed power, the greatest threat to their party unity would be removed.[29] When Congress convened again in December, Clayton once more proposed a method: admit California and New Mexico as states, thereby removing the controversy from the halls of Congress. Robert Toombs of Georgia held high hopes for the plan:

We have been in a good deal of trouble here for the last month about this slavery question, but I now believe we begin to see the light. I came here very anxious to settle the slavery question before the 4th. of March. The longer it remains on hand the worse it gets; and I am confident it will be harder to settle after than before the 4th. of March. We have therefore concluded to make a decided effort at it now. [William Ballard] Preston will this morning move to make the territorial bills the special order for an early day, which will bring the subject before us. We shall then attempt to erect all of California and that portion of New Mexico lying west of the Sierra Membres into a state as soon as she forms a constitution and asks it, which we think the present state of anarchy there will soon drive her to do. . . . I think we can carry this or something very like it. The principle I act upon is this: It cannot be a slave country; we have only the point of honor to save; this will save it and rescue the country from all danger of agitation. The Southern Whigs are now nearly unanimous in favor of it. . . .[30]

But Toombs proved to be a poor prophet. Preston's bill embodying the statehood plan was defeated just before the sands of the Thirtieth Congress ran out. King, with other Southerners, voted against the bill after anti-slavery provisions were attached to it.[31]

The Whig leaders having failed to remove the question from the floor of Congress, it remained to be seen whether their soldier in the White House could find a solution. No one knew his ideas on the subject, and he gave evidence that on inauguration day he remained undecided.[32] Once in office, however, he adopted wholeheartedly the plan that Clayton had advanced the previous December. Officially the government refrained from action, but a course had been charted. Clayton, now Secretary of State, wrote hopefully of the prospect to Governor Crittenden in Kentucky:

As to California and New Mexico, I have been *wide awake*. Everything is done as you wanted with it. The plan I proposed to you last winter will be carried out fully. The states will be admitted free and Whig.[33]

Anarchic conditions might drive the Californians to form a constitution and ask for admittance as a state, but they would be more likely to act if they knew that the Taylor administration was sympathetic to such moves. Taylor and Clayton needed a sound Whig to carry the news to California, and their choice to serve as messenger to the new American territory fell on Thomas Butler King.

No fanfare attended King's mission to California. The newspapers reported only that he was occupying the time before the reconvening of Congress by a trip to California. Ostensibly, he undertook the journey to inspect the mail steamship lines and to examine the route for the trans-Isthmian railroad that he had recommended in his latest committee report. Privately, King carried the commission of the President as a special agent.[34]

King's letter of instructions from Secretary of State John M. Clayton enjoined him to carry out several duties. In addition to carrying dispatches to the naval and military commanders in California, he was to assure the people of California of the President's concern for their welfare and his efforts in their behalf. King was also to advise the people of California on the adoption of measures best calculated to promote the President's wishes. Another duty was to acquire information about the country. Finally, King was to report immediately any attempt to establish an independent government or to alienate any territory gained by the treaty of Guadalupe Hidalgo.

Most of the authority of the executive branch of the government was enlisted to aid King in his mission. A blanket authorization was sent by the Secretaries of State, Treasury, War, Navy, and Interior to their employees and subordinates in California to assist him in carrying out the objects of his mission. So important was speed considered that Secretary of the Navy Preston wrote personally to W. H. Aspinwall in New York to hurry the passage of King's party to Panama and thence to San Francisco.[35]

Two other agents accompanied King to California. One of his companions was Lieutenant Cadwalader Ringgold of the United States Navy, who had gained distinction as commander of a ship of the Wilkes Antarctic Expedition. It is probable that Lieutenant Ringgold was known to General Taylor, since he belonged to a service family. His two brothers served as regular army officers, and one commanded a battery at the battle of Palo Alto. Ringgold acted as an assistant to King and submitted confidential political reports to the Secretary of the Navy. King's other companion of the journey was Colonel Robert S. Garnett, a former aide to Taylor. From Havana, where Garnett joined King and Ringgold, the civilian of the trio wrote of the political temper of his fellow Fortyniners.

There are a number of democrats aboard—more than one half, Hunkers, who declare they will act with the Whigs. There is but *one* opinion among *all on board* respecting the formation of a *State Govt.*, and that is *favourable.*[36]

The omens for his mission seemed good.

On June 4, 1849, King and his party arrived at San Francisco
to find that the people of California had anticipated the desires
of President Taylor. General Bennet Riley, the military Governor
of California, had on the previous day issued a proclamation calling for a constitutional convention to organize a state government. Taking advantage of the movement already under way,
King addressed a mass meeting in Portsmouth Square, San Francisco, June 12, 1849. He informed the people of the failure of
Congress to provide a government for California and urged his
hearers to organize a state government and apply for admission to
the Union. He was pleased at the enthusiasm with which he was
received; at a dinner in his honor two days later, he found the
response equally gratifying. Also he was careful to spread the administration views by word of mouth among influential Californians.[37]

By June 20 King had arranged with General Persifor F. Smith,
the commander of the Pacific Division, to make a tour through the
mining districts to survey the resources, products, and possibilities
of the country, as his instructions directed. The tour took place as
scheduled, beginning July 5, and occupied approximately forty
days. The route followed roughly the line of foothills east of San
Francisco from the Tuolumne to the American rivers. In his official report to the Secretary of State, King passed lightly over this
part of his travels, implying that he concerned himself primarily
with exploration.[38] Privately, he reported his activities in detail.
Both he and the two generals, Riley and Smith, made frequent
speeches at points along their route, urging the people to take
immediate steps to form a state government. In this manner, most
of the concentrated population of the northern part of California
learned of the desires of the administration.

Proper explanations [King wrote to Secretary of State Clayton] have
produced the same result at all the places we have visited. No doubt
is now entertained by any one that the convention will be well attended, a constitution speedily framed and adopted. The demagouges
[sic] who opposed us at first in the hope of profiting by delay and confusion now find the current of public opinion so strong in favour of
the immediate formation of a State government that they have turned
suddenly round to swim with the tide. . . .[39]

He had few doubts about the success of the administration plan
in California.

Just after his return from the mines in the back country, King made use of the generous authority granted to him by the administration. To advance the statehood movement, he called upon Commodore Thomas ap Catesby Jones to send the steamship *Edith* to the ports of southern California to pick up the delegates from that section and bring them to the constitutional convention in Monterey. Although the vessel was wrecked en route, all the delegates save one arrived in time for the working sessions, which began September 3, 1849.

On August 20, 1849, King fell sick with dysentery, an almost universal experience for California immigrants. In King's case, the illness became extremely serious. The newspapers reported that his recovery was doubtful and his friends and attendants feared for his life. Fortunately, a navy surgeon was at hand to render competent medical care. When the worst of his illness was over, the patient was moved to the naval station at Sonoma to recuperate. He recovered slowly, and it was some time in November before he was able to take an active part in public affairs.[40]

Because of his illness King missed the meeting of the state constitutional convention in Monterey. Even in his enforced retirement, however, he was not idle. He had come to a decision to throw his lot in with the new state that was taking form. Accordingly, he wrote a letter to the Governor of Georgia resigning his seat in Congress.[41] As he recuperated from his illness he made plans to seize the opportunities offered by California to an aspiring politician.

The political situation in the embryonic state was confused. The immigrant population had brought with them the habits and forms of previous political affiliation, but no party organizations existed. As a result, the first elections in California lacked the partisanship of elections in the old states. Because of his tour King was well known in the mining areas, and he had received frequent notices in the San Francisco newspapers during his sojourn among the Californians. As a public figure he enjoyed an advantage in his quest for office, and he aimed high. A whirlwind election campaign took place between October 13, when the convention ended, and the election day one month later. During this time the newly-resigned ex-Representative from Georgia appeared in the lists as a candidate for a senatorship from California in the United States Congress. According to Lieutenant William Tecumseh Sherman, King "was generally regarded as the Government candidate for United States Senator."[42]

In his bid for the senatorship King had the endorsement of a leading San Francisco newspaper, the *Pacific News*. Even before his resignation the *Pacific News* had given him publicity by printing his report from the Committee on Naval Affairs on the advisability of building a railroad across the Isthmus of Panama. It praised King's foresight in establishing the Pacific mail steamer service before the discovery of gold. When King announced his resignation from Congress and placed his name before the people as a candidate for the Senate, the *Pacific News* redoubled its efforts. King's name went up at the masthead as the first of a list of nonpartisan candidates. His running mates were John Augustus Sutter for governor, John B. Frisbie for lieutenant governor, and P. A. Morse for representative in Congress.[43]

At the election of senators by the newly-organized legislature, a warm fight developed. John Charles Fremont was selected on the first ballot, but a runoff was necessary to choose the occupant of the second Senate seat. The principal contenders were William McKendree Gwin, Henry Wager Halleck, and King. The Georgian's supporters broke ranks after the first vote, and Gwin picked up the two votes necessary to elect him on the third ballot. King's gamble for a Senate seat from California failed, but he did not abandon his earlier announced decision to throw in his lot with the new state. After his defeat he joined with three other men to open a law office in San Francisco. He also took a prominent part in the ceremonies honoring the retiring military governor, General Bennet Riley.[44]

The steamer *Oregon*, which left San Francisco on January 1, 1850, carried a number of distinguished passengers, including Thomas Butler King and the prospective members of Congress. King and the two representatives-elect, George W. Wright and Edward Gilbert, hastened on to New York via the mail steamer, the *Empire City*. When they arrived at New York on February 7, the politicians faced an uncertain welcome. The issue which had sent King westward the previous spring was still the center of discussion in Congress. King had encouraged the Californians in their moves toward state government in unmistakable terms:

> You will have no difficulty in being admitted as a State. I pledge myself to it, and I PLEDGE THE ADMINISTRATION, and I think I may speak equally confidently for the next Congress. Form a State government, send your senators and representatives, and then admission is certain.[45]

Now would come the proof for his assertions.

King had left Washington to carry out the agreed policy of the President and the Whig high command, and party members from both North and South were united in favor of the admission of California as a state. In the ten months since his departure, the harmony had disappeared. The Southern Whigs, following the leadership of Robert Toombs and Alexander H. Stephens, refused to join the Northern wing of the party in organizing the House. King's role as the administration spokesman in California was reported to be the cause of the Whig dissension, ". . . a break between the Ewing-Clayton Cabinet and the Southern Whigs, which will not be healed in the course of this session."[46] The Senate also resisted administration directions. Henry Clay had returned to the upper house and set himself up in opposition to President Taylor. The President and a majority of the Whigs continued to support the admission of California as a state, but the Democrats lost no time in turning the Whig division to good account.[47]

In his first annual message to Congress President Taylor stated his position on the question of slavery in the recently acquired territories. He urged Congress to accept the decision of the people of California as embodied in the constitution that they would soon present to Congress. But Democrats and dissident Whigs questioned the propriety of the President's actions in helping to form the "decision of the people." On the last day of 1849 the House of Representatives called on Taylor to send them all the information in his hands concerning the actions of the executive branch of the government in California. He complied by sending them the reports of his cabinet officers.

President Taylor's views on California are set forth in two official statements, his annual message of 1849 and the special message that accompanied the departmental reports. In the first, Taylor dismissed with one paragraph the explosive question of statehood:

No civil government having been provided by Congress for California, the people of that Territory, impelled by the necessities of their political condition, recently met in convention for the purpose of forming a constitution and State government, which the latest advices give me reason to suppose has been accomplished; and it is believed they will shortly apply for the admission of California into the Union as a sovereign State. Should such be the case, and should their constitution be conformable to the requisitions of the Constitution of the United States, I recommend their application to the favorable consideration of Congress.[48]

Clearly, he still held to the old Whig plan of Clayton's, anticipating official action by the Californians.

The second message answered his congressional critics. Taylor pointed out that he had made no changes in the administration of California, even leaving Polk's appointee, General Riley, as commander and governor of the territory. King, he insisted, was essentially an observer. True, he had through King expressed his desire that the people of the territory should form a state government and apply for admission. However, the instructions given to executive officers in the area by his order emphasized that all measures of domestic policy adopted by the people of California must originate solely with themselves. He neither sought certain ends nor desired to dictate the course of events; rather, he hoped to avoid "occasions of bitter and angry dissensions among the people of the United States," and had "put it in the power of Congress, by the admission of California and New Mexico as States, to remove all occasion for the unnecessary agitation of the public mind" which prevailed during the territorial stage of government. He concluded his defense with an appeal to the patriotism of Congress:

Seeing, then, that the question which now excites such painful sensations in the country will in the end certainly be settled by the silent effect of causes independent of the action of Congress, I again submit to your wisdom the policy recommended in my annual message of awaiting the salutary operation of those causes, believing that we shall thus avoid the creation of geographical parties and secure the harmony of feeling so necessary to the beneficial action of our political system.[49]

His plea fell on deaf ears.

The opposition took advantage of the split within Whig ranks. The Democratic *Daily Union* led a chorus of criticism of President Taylor's "usurpation" of the powers of Congress. King came in for his share of the blame.

We remember that, while the Mexican war was pending, the Whig party wrongfully charged Mr. Polk with having done, in time of war, through the agency of General Kearny, what General Taylor has done in time of peace, through the agency of General Riley and T. Butler King.[50]

Four days later the same organ devoted its lead editorial to an attack on King's interference with the domestic affairs of California, contrary to his instructions. The *Union* called Riley's actions as civil governor the reestablishment of the Mexican government, and in the same vein King became Taylor's ambassador to the Californians. By implication the editor saddled King with responsibility for the holding of the constitutional convention and for the provisions of the constitution. King and Riley appeared in the columns of the Democratic newspaper as villains misleading a docile and obedient populace.

In the House, King was denounced by Samuel W. Inge, a Democrat from Alabama, who assailed him as the emissary of the administration to overthrow the government of California, and as a political schemer, responsible for the anti-slavery clause in the California constitution. Inge also charged King with being the agent by whom President Taylor instructed Governor Riley to issue his proclamation of June 3, 1849. Finally, Inge argued that the whole government of California was a creation of the cabinet, illegal and fabricated.[51]

The attack on the floor of the House came only four days after King's ship docked in New York. King replied by inserting in the administration newspaper in Washington a refutation of the charges that had been made. He denied categorically that he had received any instructions, either from the President or from members of the cabinet, regarding the subject of slavery. He insisted that he did not attempt to influence the people of California to decide the question of slavery one way or the other. He pointed out that he did not arrive at San Francisco until after General Riley had issued his proclamation calling for a constitutional convention, and that it was impossible for him to have given instructions to the governor.[52]

King defended both his own actions and the President's plan of immediate statehood in his formal report to the Secretary of State. He opened with a graphic description of the chaotic governmental situation of California when he arrived there. He outlined the efforts of the people to set up their own territorial government, and the conflict they had with Governor Riley. He presented the urgent need for full statehood for the gold country. He affirmed the right of the people of a state to decide for themselves the question of slavery or no slavery and quoted the words of John C. Calhoun in support of this contention. King's defense of his own actions was brief but convincing. When he reached California, the call for a constitutional convention had already been issued; therefore he could not have given orders to General Riley to issue it. When the elections were being held for the convention, he was exploring the back country and had at his command none of the machinery by which he might have affected the choice of delegates in so huge an area; therefore, he could not have packed the convention with delegates to whom he could dictate. While the convention was in session, he was ill or convalescing at a point 130 miles distant from the gathering; therefore, he could not have dictated the provisions of the constitution. He pointed out the fact that, though many of the convention delegates were from the South, the vote on the anti-slavery clause of the constitution was unanimous. He reiterated in categorical terms that he had received from the President and the cabinet no secret instructions, oral or written, regarding the question of slavery.

... nor was it ever hinted or intimated to me that I was expected to attempt to influence their action in the slightest degree on that subject. That I never did, the people of California will bear me witness.[53]

Residents of the state substantiated the truth of his statement. His sturdiest defender in Congress was a Democrat, Delegate Samuel Royal Thurston of Oregon. On March 25, 1850, Thurston delivered a speech calling for the admission of California as a state, in which he effectively answered all the accusations against King. He was the only man then in Congress who had been present when the constitutional convention of California was in session, and could speak authoritatively.

Whatever General Taylor or his Cabinet may have intended I cannot say, but what some of the facts are, I do know, and dare say them. And I do say—first, that if General Taylor and his cabinet had tried to dictate terms to the people there, they could not have succeeded; secondly, that they did not try; and thirdly, that the project of forming a State government was the project of the people; and it would have been done had General Riley never issued a proclamation for the purpose.[54]

In later years other actors on the California scene confirmed King's assertions. As a national issue the admission of California had been settled, but in Georgia King later found it expedient to publish in pamphlet form a vindication of his conduct in 1849. The pamphlet contained letters that King had gathered from men who were prominent in California at the time of his mission.[55] Brigadier General Bennet Riley, governor of California when King arrived, asserted that he acted on his own authority in calling the constitutional convention; he had received no instructions, orders, or intimations to issue his proclamation. He added, further, that he knew of no attempt by the administration in any way to control the people in the formation of their government.

Commodore Thomas ap Catesby Jones confirmed the prior action of both the people and General Riley and claimed for himself the credit for beginning the statehood movement. Judge Kimball H. Dimmick of California added his denial of King's influence; he had discussed the issuance of General Riley's proclamation with the Governor a month before King arrived, and was assured at the time that the proclamation would be issued. William McKendree Gwin, the Democrat who had beaten King in the contest for the senatorship from California in 1849, confirmed King's statements in every regard. He touched particularly on the adoption of the anti-slavery clause in the California constitution, adding:

That you had any agency in its adoption is utterly impossible, and I do not think you could have influenced the vote of a single member of the Convention on this question, if you had been there and exerted yourself.

As I have made this statement on numerous occasions, public, and private, I see no objection in thus addressing you on the subject.[56]

Other testimony, unsolicited by King, bears out his contentions. Thomas Jefferson Green, a member of the Senate of California, writing of King's illness which had prevented his having any part in the constitutional convention, said: "I never met in California a more pro-slavery man than yourself."[57] Years later, William Tecumseh Sherman, who was present during King's illness in 1849 and who attended the constitutional convention as an observer for General Smith, recalled the disinterest of two of his companions on the slavery question. "I never heard General Smith, who was a Louisianian, express any opinion about it. Nor did Butler King, of Georgia, ever manifest any particular interest in the matter."[58]

The unsupported, partisan charges against King died away amid the thunder of bigger guns—Calhoun speaking on the rights of the South, Webster on the Union, Seward on the Higher Law, and Clay pleading for compromise. Although King was in Washington during the great debate, it is doubtful that he heard it, for he suffered from a recurrence of his illness. Despite sickness, by the end of March he had put the finishing touches to his report on California.

Although some of the congressmen professed to believe that King exerted undue influence on the formation of the California government, they showed their appreciation for the information he brought back by having ten thousand copies of his report printed. Like King's other reports, it was full of information, statistics, and sanguine predictions. The author surveyed the mineral and agricultural resources of the new territory. He examined the estimates of the mineral wealth then being mined by placer methods and prophesied a continuing outflow of the golden stream. He predicted that the mining of gold-bearing quartz ore would produce still greater returns. He laid particular emphasis on the agricultural resources of the country. He had found the climate equable and temperate, except in the desert valleys. The soil produced cereals and grasses in abundance, along with grapes that were converted into delicious wines. The country, in his opinion, offered almost unlimited opportunities for development. The commercial potentialities of the new area were great. The population for a long time would afford an immense market for the products of the eastern part of the Union, and with the development of an Isthmian railway San Francisco was destined to become the great warehouse of the trade with the Orient.[59]

King remained in Washington while the impasse continued between President Taylor and his opponents over the California question. Taylor maintained his insistence that California should be admitted at once as a state, without reference to the other problems of the day. As a faithful soldier in the Taylor camp and one of the few Southerners who remained loyal, King might expect a reward from his chieftain. The possibility was increased by the rumors of dissension in the cabinet. George W. Crawford, the Georgian who had been preferred over King for a cabinet post, was under attack because some of his legal clients had received a large award in settlement of a long-standing claim against the government. The recalcitrant Congress lost no time in embarrassing the administration by attacking the conduct of the Secretary of War. With a cabinet overturn in the making, King might yet hope to occupy the chair of the Secretary of the Navy.[60]

The contest between the executive and the legislative branches of the government ended unexpectedly with the death of President Taylor, July 9, 1850. Once more King's name figured in the speculations about the cabinet of the new President. But King wrote his son that he did not wish to be a member of President Fillmore's cabinet and had "so informed his friends."[61] Undoubtedly, the administration owed King a debt for risking and losing his political life on the California mission, but Fillmore, the compromiser, would hardly be expected to reward the Georgian so signally for his unwavering support of Taylor.

Despite his stand on the California question, King had lost surprisingly little strength at home. While he was on the West Coast the legislature of Georgia had passed a resolution censuring him for his conduct. A further indication of lost power came when a Democrat was chosen at the special election to fill King's seat in Congress. However, both these might be considered normal political defeats, for the Georgia legislature was Democratic, and King's successor won his place partly because of a gerrymander by the same Democratic body.[62] Peterson Thweatt, one of the most influential of the Georgia Whig editors, wrote King encouragingly:

Men in Georgia and warm personal friends of George Crawford, who could not tolerate my protest, in the appointment of Gov. C to the exclusion of yourself, now *give in* and admit that *I was right*. And even at this day though you are not now any thing like as *strong* in Georgia as you were then (the cause of which I presume you are aware) yet I firmly believe that if you were now made Secretary of the Navy, you would not only strengthen the administration in *Georgia,* and more particularly in the *United States,* but you would be able to regain what you have lost at home—and even without that appointment, it appears to me you might regain, if you have lost any thing in your district, by going out among the people and *explaining your position.*[63]

Encouraging as this report was, it failed to deflect King from his intention to return to California. He had investments and professional ties in the new country. Another California senatorial election would occur within a year, and a friend in the West assured him that his chances for election were good.[64] Most important of all, he finally received the reward that his services to the administration had merited. In October 1850, Millard Fillmore appointed Thomas Butler King Collector of the Port of San Francisco, at a salary of $10,000 a year.

· VII ·

California: Land of Opportunity

THE MONTH and a half following his appointment as Collector of the Port of San Francisco was a busy time for Thomas Butler King. In October 1850 he returned to Saint Simons Island, where the prospect of an indeterminate but certainly long absence must have filled every moment with decisions and preparations. Young Thomas Butler, Junior, was attending college in Athens, Georgia, when he read the news of his father's appointment. He immediately wrote his mother, asking that she use her influence with the new collector to secure him an appointment in some subordinate office at the San Francisco Custom House. His request was granted, and a month later he accompanied his father north to catch the steamer for Chagres, Panama. The last few days before the ship sailed the Kings spent in Philadelphia and New York, where the new collector conferred with political and personal friends. On November 26, 1850, father and son took leave of Henry Lord Page King, who had come down from Yale to see them off on the steamer *Ohio*.[1]

The journey from New York to San Francisco was still a strenuous undertaking, even after the Forty-niners had tried and proved so many paths. The Kings travelled by steamer to New Orleans and Chagres, across the Isthmus by canoe and muleback, and again by steamer to San Francisco. For the younger King, at least, the voyage to New Orleans was lightened by the opportunity to become acquainted with Miss Lillie Devereux, to whom his brother Henry had already lost his heart. The crossing of the Isthmus was less pleasant. It took the better part of three days to cover twenty miles, and no food was to be had for twenty-four hours of that time. Worse still, the brandy ran low, so that some members of the party had to depend on the resources of the ranches along the way to relieve their thirst. The cities of Panama and Acapulco on the Pacific side offered a welcome contrast to the rigors of the crossing. The Kings dined with the American consul and paid a visit to the theater on Sunday night—the most fashionable night, Butler assured his mother. He also reported to her on the wonders of the cathedral, with its solid silver altar weighing "about 5 tun, [*sic*]" and remarked on the similarity of a native fiesta with the Christmas antics of the slaves on Saint Simons—"the only difference was they were a much more miserable looking set—and measured their beef by the yard."[2]

San Francisco, which the travelers reached on January 8, 1851, was more to the young man's liking, although he found the city as noisy as New York, with "every other door a gambling house—in which they have a band playing all the time."[3] They had been ashore no more than twenty minutes, he reported, before his father was deep in consultations with friends, and in the ensuing days the elder King was occupied from 6:30 A.M. to 11:30 P.M. "F[ather] has not had one moment to himself," Butler wrote. "I do believe he likes it."[4] Father and son settled in two comfortable rooms at the Union Hotel, where their domestic wants were relieved by Davy, a Negro whom they had brought from Saint Simons.[5] Within a week both senior and junior King took up their duties at the Custom House, where the retiring collector, James Collier, had been in charge for more than a year.

Collier had received his appointment because he and his brother had served the Taylor cause in the campaign of 1848, but the appointment proved to be an unfortunate one for the Whig administration. When Collier assumed his duties, conditions in California were chaotic because of the influx of goldseekers and the confusion of governmental authority. Faced with novel conditions, he approved of some measures that were contrary to the letter of the revenue laws. He permitted the use of ships in the harbor of San Francisco as warehouses. The bonds which he took from importers later proved to be unenforceable. More important were the charges that he used his office to enrich himself and his family. Upon his return to Washington, his accounts were found to be more than $750,000 short.[6] Collier's successor took on an extraordinary burden with the transfer of authority.

When Thomas Butler King assumed his office at the Custom House on January 14, 1851, he inaugurated new policies. In general, the new collector required importers to comply strictly with the letter of the law. He was prompt and energetic in carrying out specific instructions, but he refused to assume authority on doubtful questions, referring such problems to his superiors in Washington. Inevitably, this reversal in policy aroused opposition among the merchants who had been accustomed to Collector Collier's liberal interpretations of the law and lax administration. As a result, King found himself constantly in hot water with the San Francisco merchants. The newspapers of the city took up some of these differences of opinion and discussed them endlessly; other matters required extensive correspondence with the Treasury Department. The slowness of communication between San Francisco and Washington kept decisions pending for months and added to the difficulties of the collector's tasks.

King's characteristics as the administrator of the nation's fifth largest port can best be seen in his handling of the outstanding problems that arose during his term of office. His first major reform in collection practices was to require the storage of all imported goods in warehouses, according to the law. Secretary of the Treasury Corwin had instructed him to stop the use of ships in the harbor as warehouses, and he had made arrangements for renting premises in San Francisco for a government warehouse before he left Washington in 1850. Even so, warehouse space was at a premium, and importers had to pay extra for lighterage because of the lack of docking facilities. The Chamber of Commerce appointed a committee to try to persuade King to return to the former practices, but he refused to recede from his position. The Collector convinced his fellow San Franciscans that his instructions permitted no deviation from standard practices. This strict enforcement of the warehousing requirements had an unfortunate sequel when the government warehouse was destroyed by the great fire of May 3-4, 1851. Strangely enough, it was the national administration, rather than King, that received the blame for the losses which the merchants sustained in the fire. The fire may actually have helped King by making the merchants realize that claims against the government could be filed if losses occurred in a federal warehouse.[7]

King's policy of enforcing bonds also raised differences of opinion between the new collector and the merchants of San Francisco. When King succeeded Collier, he turned all unfulfilled bonds over to the United States District Attorney for prosecution, and the trials began in the federal district court in September 1851.

The Democratic *Alta California* and the *Herald* attacked King for his part in the proceedings, while the Whig *Daily Evening Picayune* defended the collector vigorously and published a long statement by him. The climax of the controversy came when a mass meeting of merchants appointed a committee to wait upon King and enlist his aid in obtaining relief from authorities in Washington. King was quite willing to support their petition, and Corwin eventually granted him the authority to delay action on penal bonds. Yet the new instructions did not arrive until he had made himself thoroughly unpopular by following the usual practice in regard to bonds. It was somewhat galling to him to learn that Corwin had finally reversed the policy after the merchants had brought pressure to bear through Senator William M. Gwin, rather than listening to the reports of the collector. In the matter of forfeited bonds, King was again the victim of slow communications with Washington and of disregard for local conditions on the part of his superiors.[8]

King did not always appear before the public as a virtuous civil servant dutifully enforcing unpopular decrees. An incident of March 1851 brought a storm of protest down on his head, particularly from the Democratic press. King received information that the mails were being used to smuggle goods, and sent the surveyor of the port to the post office to witness the opening of the mail bags from the steamship *Columbia*. Surveyor Hart Fellows met a rude reception from the postal authorities, went aboard the *Columbia,* impounded the remaining mail sacks, and proceeded to open them himself. Postmaster Charles C. Moore and the Democratic newspapers were incensed at King's interference with the mails, and King was affronted by their refusal to permit an inspection. Both officials issued public letters explaining their side of the controversy. Legally, both sides were at fault, for the postal clerks should not have refused permission to inspect and King's subordinate exceeded his powers when he opened the mail sacks. The whole tempest in a teapot is noteworthy only because it illustrates King's vigorous performance of what he considered his duty.[9]

Another incident connected with King's office gave his enemies an opportunity to ridicule him. To promote efficiency, the San Francisco collector was named a special depositary of Treasury funds with authority to pay out customs receipts in the Pacific area for duly authorized federal expenditures. King was therefore responsible not only for the collection of customs but also for the safekeeping and disbursement of federal funds. At his direction, a vault with three-foot masonry walls reinforced by iron grating was built in the Custom House to protect the government specie. Soon afterwards, the supposedly fireproof Custom House was destroyed in the great fire of May 1851. Young Butler King sent home a vivid account of the disaster:

The flames broke out about half past ten—or eleven o'clock on the night of the third of this month—and by daylight of the next morning —as much property was destroyed as was in the great fire of four or five days in New York all most the whol City it was. Father very unfortunately had just left that afternoon to go up into the country for a day or two—the first time he has been away for an hour in months. I saved all the important papers of the Custom House . . . and I had the money down in the vault—but whilst I was attending to the papers at the Custom H—the fire spred all over town . . . there were hundreds burned to death. The fire came on them so quickly—that though they knew it was coming they had not time to escape. I came very nere being in the same fix—for the steps that is stare case were all on fire when I came out of the Custom House. I got a little burned but had put some buckets of water by me and after doing all I could I threw the water over myself put my hat over my face and made a rush.[10]

After the fire the specie was found intact in the vault, and guards were posted about the ruins until a new vault could be built. King's foresight was praised, and his strong room was pointed to as a model for businessmen who were rebuilding their premises.[11]

So far, the Collector's precautions were commendable; it was when the time came for removing the specie to a new vault that he evoked ridicule. After a morning of preparation he assembled a company of armed sailors and Custom House employees, marshalled them in military fashion, and personally supervised the transfer of the funds amid a display of armed force. Opposition newspapers had a field day in their mock-heroic reports:

General King gallantly took his stand in a most exposed position upon the top of a pile of bricks, and with a six-barrelled revolver in one hand, and a formidable looking cane in the other, issued his orders for the removal of the treasure, with admirable coolness. . . . The whole conduct of the exploit exhibited military skill of the highest order, and heroic devotion worthy of all praise.[12]

King maintained, with some reason, that his show of force was necessary. San Francisco was notorious for its lack of law and order, and the city was currently submitting to the extra-legal rule of the Vigilance Committee of 1851. Sam Whittaker, later hanged by the Committee, confessed that his gang had actually discussed robbing the new Custom House after the fire. Paradoxically, the same papers that ridiculed King were supporting the stern measures of the Vigilantes.[13]

King's uncompromising policy of strict compliance with the laws eventually began to pay dividends in the form of an easing of the demands of his position. After October 1851 the Custom House seldom figured in the headlines of the newspapers, and references to the Collector touched mainly on his political activities. He settled into a quiet daily routine in his personal life and enjoyed improved health. Young Butler, who shared his father's quarters as well as his duties at the Custom House, noted the change:

We are getting on here now very well. All the infernal scoundrals who used to bother us have found it of no use to benefit themselves by all their deepness and smartness—And the business is not nearly so severe upon Father—this change for the better has done him much good I assure you—not only in allowing his health to improve but actually sometimes they allow him to keep in a good humor *all day*— which I assure you was not the case six months ago.[14]

It must not have been entirely comfortable to live with the Collector.

In contrast to the stormy early period, King's last twelve months of administering the Custom House passed by so quietly as to require no special notice. Father and son lived in the temporary customs building while new federal offices were being erected. In their leisure Butler tasted the pleasures of society, while his father devoted himself to a number of investments. Both Kings purchased city lots in San Francisco, San Diego, Sacramento, and Benicia, and in Port Oxford, Oregon, although none of these ventures is known to have brought large returns. The elder King also retained his interest in the law office which he had opened when he first arrived in California, and through this connection participated in the settlement of one of the most famous of the early California estate cases.[15] The greatest possibilities for wealth lay in acquiring and exploiting gold-bearing lands, a speculation that engaged King's attention as his term in office drew to a close. The duties of the collectorship began to pall on him, and the drawbacks of his position to outweigh its advantages, as he confided to his wife:

I have been so abused and misrepresented for the faithful performance
of my duties that I have become disgusted with the place and the
people. Collier, my predecessor is a defaulter and I perceive that
some of the papers in the Atlantic States speak of the defalcation as
having occurred at the San F—— Custom House and mix my name
with it.[16]

Writing to Corwin in a similar mood, King hinted that he would
like to resign August 1; later, he reconsidered his decision and
expressed his willingness to serve until the new administration
should be inaugurated in March 1853. He was chagrined to find
that his hint had been accepted as a resignation by Corwin and
President Fillmore, and that his successor had been appointed
immediately.[17]

   When King's successor took over his duties in November 1852,
there was a flurry of dinners, presentations, and testimonials for
the retiring official. Even King's erstwhile enemies joined in his
praise, and his conduct was held up to the incoming collector as
a model. Gone from the columns of the *Alta* were the strictures
of earlier days, and in their place appeared a eulogistic farewell.
After describing the trying conditions under which King assumed
office, the Democratic paper continued:

In all the transactions which our commercial citizens have had with
Mr. King, they have found him liberal, courteous, and accommodat-
ing. . . . Mr. King retires tomorrow from a position that has been
more prolific of labor and anxiety than of popular praise or pecuniary
profit.—Wherever he goes, or whatever he does, he carries with him
our sincerest regard and esteem for personal worth and official stability.[18]

These valedictory compliments pleased King, but they did not
wipe out the bitterness of earlier attacks. "I shall ever feel grateful to you and the President for bestowing the place upon me,"
King wrote to Corwin, "but were the duty to be gone over again,
no available consideration I assure you, would induce me to
accept it."[19]

   The office of collector of a port was far more than an administrative appointment. It could be a reward for party services that
carried a high salary, as King's post in San Francisco did. It could
be a stepping stone to higher office, as the collectorship of Boston
proved to be for George Bancroft. In any circumstances, the collector was a partisan politician, powerful because of his ability to
appoint subordinate officers. Each Custom House tended to be-

come the focus of local party activity, for there were centered the loyalties of the minor office-holders who had supported the party in the past and who might supply a corps of reliable workers in the next election. The San Francisco Custom House in 1850 was no exception. The collection district ranked fifth in the United States in the amount of revenue collected. The salary of the collector was $10,000, and other salaries were treble those for comparable offices in other collection districts in order to offset the inflated gold rush prices. Only a few of the staff of two hundred were appointed in Washington, and the payroll and other expenses of the San Francisco district in 1852 amounted to more than a million dollars. Thomas Butler King had a small army of assistants who were indebted to him for their appointments and salary. In addition, he helped to choose the site and superintend the building of a $400,000 Custom House and of a marine hospital, he arranged leases for temporary quarters for federal offices, and he was a subtreasurer with special powers. All these circumstances combined to make King the most powerful federal official on the Pacific Coast.[20] He was in a position to render his party notable service by organizing an effective Whig machine in California.

In the first election in 1849, before any party organizations were formed, Californians had chosen two Democrats, John Charles Fremont and William McKendree Gwin, as their senators. Nearly a year passed before Congress, by admitting the new state, accepted the two men as members. As was customary, Fremont and Gwin then drew lots to see which would have a six-year and which a two-year term. Fremont was the loser in this game of chance, and when Congress adjourned in 1850, he hastened back to California to seek reelection. As a candidate he enjoyed the advantages conferred by his flamboyant personality, the fame of his earlier exploits, and the relative length of his connection with California. On the other hand, he had acquired large landholdings based on Spanish grants, which put his personal interests in conflict with those of the newer arrivals to California, the squatters and the goldseekers. He had failed to achieve any great legislative triumphs, and his enemies pointed out that a land bill on California which he had proposed in the Senate specifically exempted his own holdings from review by the courts. A serious illness contracted during his return journey from Washington prevented him from conducting a vigorous campaign. In view of all these circumstances, the Democrats of California were not united in support of their incumbent senator.[21] If the Whigs could capitalize on the division in the Democratic ranks, they might elect one of their number to the United States Senate.

Such was the political situation when King stepped ashore from the *Tennessee* on January 8, 1851. He was immediately recognized by Democratic papers as the leading Whig candidate for senator. Indeed, hardly had he assumed the reins of office at the Custom House before he departed for San Jose, where the legislature met, in order "to take care of his chances for the U.S. Senate."[22] King's avowed candidacy and his active self-promotion injected new life into the senate campaign. The Democratic *Pacific News* noted that his arrival in San Jose had enheartened the Whigs of the legislature and that he would prove a formidable opponent. To the editor it appeared as if the administration "had expressed a man *to* California, for a specific object, with the demand that he must be expressed back, in compliance."[23] The *Herald,* also Democratic, stated flatly: "It is now a matter of certainty that he has come to this country, labelled and endorsed by the powers that be to their liege subjects here for election to the Senate."[24] Both President Fillmore and Secretary of the Treasury Corwin would doubtless have objected to the statement, but they certainly knew of King's bid for office and counted on him to build a Whig political machine in California. The election of a Whig Senator there would go far to extend the operation of the two-party system into the new domain of the West.[25]

In San Jose, King and the other candidates maintained open house, where champagne and roast duck were dispensed to the legislators who were to choose the new senator. The seats in the legislature were divided among twenty-seven Democrats, eighteen Whigs, and five Independents, but the Whigs were united on one man, while the Democrats could not agree on a single candidate. As the day of election approached, rumors of arranged resignations and political deals indicated the likelihood of a victory for King, which the *Pacific Daily News* seemed prepared to accept: "If elected, aside from his efforts in the political field, to make California a Whig state, he would no doubt exert himself faithfully and energetically to accomplish the most good for California."[26] The Democratic *Alta* also predicted that King would win the Senate seat.

A prolonged contest began on February 18, 1851, when the legislature sat as a convention to elect a senator. On the first ballot King received fifteen votes; on the second, sixteen; and on the third, seventeen. The Democrats split their votes among three candidates: Solomon Heydenfeldt, John B. Weller, and John C. Fremont. Nine ballots in all were taken on the first day, but the results did not vary appreciably. King's seventeen votes led the field, but the other forces showed no signs of weakening. The political correspondent of the *Pacific News* sourly reminded his readers of an earlier warning that he had voiced, "that only through a legislative caucus could the requisite *union* be effected" for a Democratic victory.[27] He pointed to the Spanish-American Californians as the keys to the situation, asserting that they would vote for no Democrat but Fremont and that if they were released from him their vote would go to King. The lesson, as he saw it, was that the other Democratic candidates should throw their support to Fremont.

Through six more days the balloting continued, broken only by unsuccessful attempts at a caucus by the Democrats. By the 131st ballot the contest had become a three-way race, with King and Heydenfeldt leading and the twelve Fremont supporters holding the balance. The earlier proceedings had engendered a good bit of acrimony, but now they took on the aspect of a good-natured farce. John Smith was nominated and withdrawn, the clerk was ordered to read instructive or cryptic Bible verses, and members began to circulate pen-and-ink sketches of the candidates and their backers. On Wednesday, February 26, the legislature seemed no nearer to a choice than it had been ten days previously. On the 141st ballot, Heydenfeldt's name was withdrawn and John B. Weller's was substituted. Although Heydenfeldt and one of his followers broke Democratic ranks to vote for King, the Whigs still lacked a majority. The convention thereupon adjourned until January 1, 1852, leaving the choice of a United States Senator to the next legislature.[28]

King's bid had failed, but not his aim. Since the senatorial seat now depended on the legislature that would meet in 1852, one issue was set for the state elections in September: How would the candidates for the legislature vote when the choice for senator confronted them? The Whigs must close ranks and enforce party discipline for the forthcoming battle. A Whig caucus of the legislature proceeded to read James M. Crane and his *Courier* out of the party for opposition to King during the convention. Shortly thereafter, the *Pacific News*, which had formerly supported Fremont, announced that it had become a Whig newspaper. The weight of patronage was used to encourage the faithful, and

Democrats complained that the Custom House payroll was used to subsidize a correspondent for three of the newspapers in the interior, thus to a certain extent giving tone to public opinion in the mining region.[29]

Party organization continued to develop, when in May 1851 both Democrats and Whigs held conventions, the first of their kind in the brief history of the state. The Whigs adopted a twelve-point platform which called on the federal government for extensive legislation in favor of California. High on the list were federal aid to a transcontinental railroad, aid to steam communication with China, and appropriations for river and harbor improvement. The platform rejected national Whig policy in regard to mining lands and other public domain. Where President Fillmore had called for either the leasing of the goldbearing lands under government supervision or outright sale of the lands, the California Whigs endorsed government ownership for the benefit of miners with no tax or restriction. Similarly, the California Whigs approved the extension of preemption rights to the bona fide settlers and improvers of private lands in California.[30] At the Whig convention, the dominance of King adherents was noted by an opposition newspaper, which foresaw in the Whig organization "the one purpose of sending Mr. Thomas Butler King to the Senate of the United States." The same paper commented that in "most of the recent nominations for State offices he [King] has triumphed," but predicted a division in Whig ranks because of King's success.

Inevitably, because of King's dominant position in the party and his well-publicized candidacy for the Senate, the administration of the Custom House became a political issue in California. The attacks on King—over the opening of the mails, the new and stringent warehousing and bonding regulations, and the removal of the deposits from the ruins of the federal building—were merely part of the development of party politics in the state. Similarly, the defense of King by Whig papers was also aimed at attracting voters. When the *Pacific News* switched politics for the second time in three months, a rival welcomed the return to Democratic ranks with a jocular paragraph:

Hung be the Custom House with black. Its worshipper has departed, and now pays his devotions at another shrine. . . . "King and the Custom House" will give place to the patent and euphonious combination of "Bigler and Democracy."[31]

The newspapers were aligning themselves for the approaching state elections.

To lead their forces as a candidate for the governorship, the Whigs chose Pearson B. Reading, an "old" Californian of polished manners. In contrast, the Democrats picked as their nominee a raucous ex-dockhand, journeyman printer, and lawyer, known as "Honest John" Bigler. Despite internal divisions, the Democrats claimed the allegiance of the agricultural and mining populations, but conceded San Francisco and Sacramento to the Whigs on the basis of their commercial interests. The platforms of the two parties differed very little. On the most important point, both favored the continued exploitation of government mineral lands for private gain without tax. Beyond that, the Democrats were less emphatic in supporting the claims of squatters on privately owned lands, nor did they subscribe to such sweeping demands for federal financing of internal improvements as did the Whigs.[32]

A new element was introduced into the campaign by the entry of a third ticket in the San Francisco city elections. In August 1851 members of the famous Vigilance Committee endorsed an Independent ticket of reformers for city offices. Although both Whigs and Democrats were represented on the Independent ticket, the entire list was denounced by the Whigs as a political maneuver to elect four Democrats to key positions, while the other names were declared to be mere window-dressing.[33]

The last week of August brought a climax of electioneering tactics. At night, "Reading Rangers" paraded about the streets of San Francisco by torchlight, cheering Whig candidates and chanting political doggerel. Both parties brought their campaigns to a close in San Francisco with mass rallies. Senator Gwin and David Colbert Broderick led a procession to the Democratic meeting, while their followers carried banners and transparencies lampooning King. Scenes purporting to illustrate the Collector's life were shown—King on a throne, with the legend, "Whigs tremble and obey your King"; a tavern with an advertisement, "T. Butler King's free Grocery at San Jose. Licensed to get drunk on the premises"; and the Collector and his armed cohorts removing the Custom House treasure. The Whigs replied in kind, taunting the Democrats with allusions to "water lots," San Francisco real estate that figured in a number of charges of political grafting.

On election day, Butler Junior reported the sad news to his mother: "We have not yet received the full returns of the election from the state. But from the appearance of things in general—I don't think the chances for Fathers election to the *U. S. S.* are very good."³⁴

In the state at large the Democrats won the election decisively; in San Francisco, the Independent ticket triumphed. Since the Whigs of the new legislature would constitute only a small minority, King's election to the Senate was now reckoned impossible. Even so, the Whigs kept up their efforts. The issue did not remain long in doubt, for when the legislature met in January 1852, the Democrats united on the eighth ballot to elect John B. Weller Senator from California. For the second time in twelve months King had failed in his quest for a Senate seat. He brought to the contest acknowledged ability, twenty years of legislative experience, wide knowledge of California, and the full power of organized Whig efforts in the state. They were not enough. Because of division in Democratic ranks, King came close to the senatorship, but once the Democrats had united on a candidate his only hope of election was gone.

These senatorial contests of 1851 and 1852 furnish evidence of the breakup of the two-party system. The national Whig party was drifting toward dissolution. While it lived, it helped to bind the nation together; with its passing disappeared one of the bonds of union. In California, the state which finally upset the North-South balance in the Senate, the Whigs never gained a firm foothold. Under the leadership of Thomas Butler King the Whigs of California made a strong bid to capture the state and send a Whig to the United States Senate. When they failed, California politics became a matter of factional quarrels within the Democratic party, a pattern later repeated in the country at large.

Few California Whigs were surprised by their defeat, and in analyzing its causes they tended to blame the bungling of the national party leaders. Two basic faults were frequently mentioned: the delay of the Fillmore administration in organizing the commission which would confirm land titles, and the failure of the authorities to begin construction of any of the public works authorized by Congress. Secondary reasons were found in disregard by national leaders of patronage recommendations from the state, the defection of the *San Francisco Courier,* and King's persistence in maintaining his candidacy. John Wilson, a staunch California Whig, informed Secretary of the Treasury Corwin of his solemn conviction that the administration was to blame for the defeat in the state elections and that "before their time is out, the state will irretrievably be locofoco, for many years to come, and that she will carry Oregon with her."[35] The resentment against the administration, particularly in regard to the appointment of Democrats to office in California, culminated in a protest from the Whig Central Committee and in the nomination of anti-administration delegates to the national convention the following year. A Whig nominee for Congress expressed the widespread bitterness when he asserted that he would campaign for any Whig nominee for the presidency except Fillmore, and added: "Mr. Fillmore has evidently adopted the *policy* of *buying his enemies,* without being aware that at the same time *he is selling his friends.*"[36]

Upon King's return to Washington in January 1853, he discovered that the lot of an ex-collector was not a happy one. Although Secretary of the Treasury Corwin had promised quick action on the San Francisco accounts, he delayed their final approval until the last days of the Fillmore administration. His Democratic successor, James Guthrie, introduced reforms in accounting as well as new personnel, and King's agent for settlement wrote pessimistically of the prospect. It took an act of Congress to relieve King of the responsibility for some of the losses from fire and the intervention of former Secretary of the Treasury Robert J. Walker to sustain some of King's rulings. The accounting, which King had hoped to conclude quickly, dragged on for years and ended in a series of lawsuits.[37] The resulting financial uncertainty was to hamper him in his subsequent business and political career.

· VIII ·

The Gilded Age: A Preview

IN THE SPRING of 1853 Thomas Butler King had reached an obvious turning point in his life. His quest for elective office in California had proved unsuccessful, and his long absence from Georgia seemed to preclude a resumption of his political career there. Now that the Whigs had lost power, he had no prospect of receiving further administrative appointments in the national government. His wife was anxious for him to return to Retreat and relieve her of the cares of the plantation, but such a course would have to await, at least for the present, the settlement of some of his business interests, acquired during his last year as Collector of San Francisco.

King's most ambitious speculative project was connected with gold mining—not the individualistic placer mining of the Forty-niners, but large-scale, corporate exploitation of quartz-bearing ore. Together with eight associates in the Old Dominion Gold Mining Company, he took an option on the adjacent lands of the South Carolina Gold Mining Company. His colleagues then appointed him their attorney to dispose of the property in London. The pursuit of this commission took King to England in the spring and summer of 1853. The basic scheme called for the formation of a joint Anglo-American stock company. The American entrepreneurs were to supply the gold-bearing lands, while the English backers would ship mining machinery from England to California and furnish working capital. Additional capital would be raised through stock subscriptions on both sides of the Atlantic. By August 1853 King had succeeded in carrying out his basic objectives. A group of English investors agreed to buy and ship the machinery to be used in working the mine and to supply £140,000 for working capital. Another joint stock company, the Carson's Creek Mining Company, was planned to manage these assets, and the stock was divided equally between the British and American backers.[1]

Some of the English capitalists whom King met in the course of his gold mine promotion approached him about another possible American investment, a railroad from Savannah to Mobile. They were attracted by the possibilities of the project, but distrusted the company representative who was seeking funds in London. Drawn into the scheme by his English friends, King wrote a glowing prospectus for the Atlantic and Gulf of Mexico Railway which he thought would materially assist in promoting the idea in London financial circles. He immediately wrote, also, to some of the Savannah backers of the railroad, men whom he had known in his earlier career, explaining how he had become involved, warning them against relying on their London promoter, and emphasizing the demands that English investors would make before committing themselves to such a scheme. As his own enthusiasm for the Savannah-Mobile railroad mounted, he delayed his return to the United States even after he had completed his gold mine deal. His sanguine imagination looked beyond the Savannah-Mobile line, seeing in it merely the eastern end of an "Iron Mississippi" connecting Savannah with San Diego, a possibility that he pointed out to his English friends. When he returned to the United States, he made contact with the holder of the Savannah-Mobile charter, Nelson Tift, and wrote his London acquaintances to smooth the way for Tift's attempt to attract foreign capital. He even contemplated a trip back to London to assist in making the financial arrangements, but his energies soon were directed at another, larger project, the building of a transcontinental railroad.[2]

In 1853 the idea of a transcontinental railroad held no novelty for either King or the general public. The dream of a rail line to the West Coast existed even before the United States had an undisputed claim to a Pacific outlet. Foremost among the publicists who built the dream into a possibility was Asa Whitney, and it was Thomas Butler King who as a congressman reported the endorsement by the Georgia legislature of such a scheme. The acquisition of Texas and the northern portion of Mexico opened new routes overland to the Pacific. After 1849 the question was no longer whether a Pacific railroad could or ought to be built;

political leaders were exploring the question of which route it should follow. Different sectional champions presented the claims of cities in their area to become the eastern terminus of the road: Stephen Arnold Douglas favored Chicago, Thomas Hart Benton, St. Louis, and Southerners proposed Memphis, Vicksburg, or New Orleans.[3]

Besides the problem of the selection of a route, there was the major question of how to finance a work of such magnitude. It was clearly beyond the means of any single man or small group of men. Benton, in his proposal for a national road from St. Louis, came out squarely for governmental construction of the line. Most plans suggested outright or virtual gifts of the public lands along the right of way to the companies or individuals, such as Whitney, who might accomplish the work. Some plans carried the suggestion that the United States should issue bonds in instalments as sections of the road were completed by some private company.[4]

Although many leaders advocated the building of a road with federal aid of some kind, the majority of congressmen always found some grounds for disagreement on specific proposals, either because they favored some section or group of individuals, or because of the philosophy of state rights. Increasingly, the twin problems of the preference of routes and the amount and kind of federal aid engaged the attention of the nation's lawmakers.[5]

The building of a transcontinental rail line held the promise of rich profits for those men who might be chosen to receive the benefits of governmental grants. Among those who hoped to create the favored company were a group of men who in July 1853 received from the State of New York a charter for the Atlantic and Pacific Railroad Company. The incorporators included a long list of public figures from nearly every state in the Union, but the moving spirits were Robert J. Walker, former Secretary of the Treasury, and Levi S. Chatfield, a New York politician. Their corporation was capitalized at $100,000,000 and was granted the privilege of operating in other states besides New York. On paper, the Atlantic and Pacific company had broad powers, large capitalization, and influential men associated with it. Concurrently, a move favorable to the company was being made in Congress. Senator Walker Brooke of Mississippi introduced a Pacific railroad bill providing for the grant of public lands and the lending of government bonds up to $30,000,000 for the building of the road. The provisions of Brooke's bill showed that it was clearly designed for the benefit of the Atlantic and Pacific Company, or one remarkably like it. Unfortunately for the promoters of the Atlantic and Pacific, Brooke's proposal failed to pass in Congress.[6]

Thomas Butler King, although not one of the original incorporators of the Atlantic and Pacific Railroad Company, was soon associated with it and became one of its guiding spirits. He had hardly returned from London before he plunged into the schemes of Walker, Chatfield, and their companions. This activity, together with other business affairs, prevented his returning to Saint Simons, from which he had now been absent for nearly three years. Instead of going there, he brought his family to Philadelphia, where they enjoyed a long-delayed reunion. His wife and children had little more than a visit with him, for in November 1853 he left for Texas, making the first of a long series of journeys on company business.[7]

The situation in Texas was unique. One of the best known and most highly favored transcontinental routes lay along the Thirty-second Parallel through Texas, and negotiations were currently being concluded with Mexico for the Gadsden Purchase, which would open up the best railroad route west of Texas. Secondly, Texas, which had kept its public lands at the time of annexation, could provide state land grants for a large portion of a transcontinental line. A third favoring element, surplus capital, had been added by the passage of the Compromise of 1850. As an indemnity for renouncing her claims to New Mexican territory, Texas received from Congress $10,000,000 in United States bonds. Of this amount, $2,000,000 was set aside as a permanent education fund.[8]

It was at this juncture, when Texas legislators had it in their power to grant charters, lands, and state credit, that Thomas Butler King, together with Levi Chatfield and ex-President Anson Jones of Texas, arrived in Austin during the session of the legislature in December 1853. In a public address shortly after his arrival, King urged the Texans to adopt a policy of liberal aid to railroads. He argued that aid to a transcontinental line would bring to Texas the current of migration and trade between the oceans, increasing the state's wealth and population. By adopting a generous policy, Texans had it in their power to gain the advantages that would accrue to the first transcontinental route. Descending to the practical in his peroration, he advised his hearers to pass a general land grant law, applicable alike to local roads and to a transcontinental trunk. He also spoke for the passage of loan legislation based on the investment of the school fund as an additional inducement to railroad builders. If both measures passed, the financing of Texas railroads could be managed without resort to the uncertainties of the foreign bond market, or even the New York market.[9]

After debating several alternative methods of aid to railroads, the legislature of 1853 adopted the general grant system recommended by King, to which it added a special law to provide for the grand design of reaching the Pacific. Under the general law any railroad company which completed twenty-five miles of road should receive title to sixteen sections of land per mile along the right of way. The transcontinental trunk measure was called the Mississippi and Pacific Reserve Act. It reserved from settlement a strip of the public lands two degrees wide along the Thirty-second Parallel. The governor was empowered to advertise for bids from individuals and companies to build a railroad within these bounds. After the successful bidder had surveyed a route, the original two-degree reserve was to be reduced to a width of sixty miles, and the builders of the road were to receive twenty sections of land for every mile of finished road. The contractors were required to post a guaranty of $300,000 to complete fifty miles of the line within eighteen months. At the expiration of ninety-nine years the ownership of the road was to revert to the state.[10]

On January 18, 1854, Governor Elisha Maxwell Pease issued a proclamation calling for bids on the construction of the Mississippi and Pacific Railroad. Within a month President Chatfield of the Atlantic and Pacific Railroad Company submitted a bid. However, this bid was replaced in July by another, submitted by Robert J. Walker and Thomas Butler King. Governor Pease accepted the second bid, and the prospects of the company looked bright. The contract was signed August 11, and put in escrow until August 31, 1854, pending the submission of the $300,000 bond. As security for their bond, King and Walker offered stock in private corporations. These securities were rejected by Governor Pease, who demanded United States bonds or state bonds. The promoters countered with an offer to increase the amount of stock in private companies, but this too was rejected by the governor. However, State Treasurer James H. Raymond accepted the stock as a valid fulfillment of the guaranty. In a letter of explanation to the stockholders of the Atlantic and Pacific company, Walker and King presented their side of the controversy. Their argument was cold

comfort to their associates; an appeal to the courts could not remove Governor Pease's opposition in time for them to complete
the first fifty miles within eighteen months, as contracted. The
bright prospects of the company vanished, and King and Walker
were left with a contract of doubtful value and legality.[11]

Neither Walker nor King was the type to abandon such a promising enterprise. In December 1854, at Montgomery, Alabama,
they reorganized the corporation as the Texas Western Railroad
Company, under a charter that had been purchased by the Atlantic and Pacific company during the preceding winter. They
framed a report to the stockholders of the old company explaining
their disagreement with Governor Pease. Under the circumstances,
they declared, the Atlantic and Pacific organization would have to
be abandoned. On the other hand, the Texas Western charter had
advantages which might outweigh the opportunities that were lost
with the Mississippi and Pacific contract. The new company
would become eligible for only sixteen sections of land per mile
instead of the twenty to be awarded under the other contract, but
the time for the completion of the first section of the road was
greater. The capital of the new company was set at the same
$100,000,000 figure, and former Atlantic and Pacific stockholders
were given the opportunity to exchange their stock for shares in
the new company on a one-for-one basis. The liabilities of the old
company were assumed, and future plans projected.[12]

Although the Atlantic and Pacific Railroad Company had been
essentially a paper corporation, it had taken some of the prelimi-
nary steps toward building a railroad. During 1854 Andrew B.
Gray, the former commissioner on the Mexican boundary, had
surveyed the route of the railroad from central Texas to San
Diego, California. He estimated the total cost of the 1,621 miles
of road from the eastern border of Texas to San Diego at
$44,470,657. The 783 miles from Marshall to El Paso, Texas, he
estimated would cost approximately $20,000,000. The location
survey for the first fifty miles of road was begun by Chief Engineer
E. A. Blanch in May 1854, and by January of the following year
he had surveyed the 125 miles from the Louisiana border to Dallas. Several contracts for grading were let in the spring of 1854,
and the first ground was broken at Marshall, Texas, July 4, 1854.
At one time as many as 230 men were engaged in grading, but the
organizational difficulties through which the company was going
forced a reduction in the number of laborers.[13]

The promoters of the new Texas Western Company proposed

to raise the $20,000,000 for the eastern (Texas) division of the
road by the sale of both stocks and bonds. One million shares of
$100 were to be offered to the public, with individual holdings
limited to $500,000. For each share the subscriber was to pay only
$5, and this payment was spread over a period of four years. Such
sales would provide $5,000,000 over the four-year span. The re-
maining $15,000,000 was to be obtained through the sale of bonds
secured by four-fifths of the land grants which the company would
receive as it completed twenty-five-mile sections of the road. The
lands of the company were to be pledged four-fifths to the redemp-
tion of the bonds and one-fifth to the payment of interest to stockholders. Once the initial funds were secured and the first sections
of road completed, the land grants would supply all subsequent
capital requirements. Upon the completion of the road, the stockholders would have a debt-free road, and a surplus of 1,638,400
acres of unencumbered land. This scheme was favorably compared
with the financing of the Illinois Central, whose bonds had been
sold abroad by Robert J. Walker.[14]

In 1855, as in the preceding year, King spent much of his time
travelling between Georgia, New York, and Texas on company
business. From the organizational meeting at Montgomery he went
home to Retreat for a brief stay before continuing on to New
York, where the railroad scheme was at a standstill awaiting his
arrival. With the abandonment of the New York charter, many
tasks faced the promoters. They had to arrange for the exchange
of Texas Western for Atlantic and Pacific stock, sound the market
for sales of the new shares, create favorable publicity for the reorganized corporation, and continue construction work in Texas.
Robert J. Walker was given full authority to settle the affairs of
the two companies, including the transfer of stock. In September
1855 he resigned the presidency, under fire for his settling of the
debts of the old company and the transferring of stock. Francis M.
Dimond, former vice-president of the Atlantic and Pacific Railroad Company, succeeded to the presidency of the Texas Western.
The payments of assessments on old stock and the sales of new
stock were so slow that the proceeds did not meet the rent and
current expenses of the New York office. However, stock sales in
Ohio and Kentucky and the reports from friends and agents in
that area encouraged the promoters to open an agency in Cincinnati to sell shares.[15]

The field work in Texas went forward uncertainly. The Boston
firm which originally had contracted with the Atlantic and Pacific

Railroad Company ceased operations. Jeptha Fowlkes, a director from Memphis, proposed to take a large force of Negro slaves to Texas to grade part of the road, but abandoned his plans after waiting nearly three months for his associates to approve his plans. Just before his resignation as president Robert J. Walker concluded a contract with James E. and Jonathan S. Brown to build one hundred miles of railroad, the first twenty-five miles to be completed by August 1856. After Dimond became president, these contractors sent an agent to Marshall, Texas, who hired local labor to begin the grading, pending the arrival of the initial contractor's party of twenty men, with carts and horses. Chief Engineer Blanch returned to Marshall from his surveying expedition to superintend the work of the new contractors.[16]

Despite their failure to attract much new capital, and the slowness and uncertainty of the field work, the promoters achieved some success in their attempts to publicize the route and the company. In the course of 1855 they issued three prospectuses, the longest and most important of which contained the report of the route survey by Andrew B. Gray. The engineer's enthusiastic endorsement of the route and his estimate of costs and receipts were excellent propaganda for the company. The Texas Western also benefited from the report of Secretary of War Jefferson Davis, who submitted to President Franklin Pierce the comparative surveys undertaken by his Department at the direction of Congress. In their publicity the promoters of the Texas Western made much of Davis' endorsement of the recommendation of Captain A. H. Humphreys that the Thirty-second Parallel route was to be preferred over all others. King contributed to the program of publicity by publishing in the *New York Herald* a letter on the route and its advantages.[17]

In November 1855 King once more journeyed to Texas to devote his talents to the accomplishment of two objectives. At Austin he worked to persuade the assembled legislators to pass further bills to aid railroads. He was also empowered by his associates to conclude a working agreement with the Vicksburg, Shreveport and Texas Railroad Company, whose completed track would supply the link between Texas and the Mississippi River. Late in the session of the legislature an act amending the charter of the Texas Western Railroad Company was approved, only to meet a veto by Governor Pease, who assailed the company as a creation of the Atlantic and Pacific speculators and denied their plea for an extension of the time for completing the first section of their road.

King was not dismayed by this rebuff. He considered the general
loan act to aid railroad construction far more important. By the
terms of this act, loans of $6,000 per mile of finished railroad were
to be granted to railroad companies from the $2,000,000 school
fund. This measure passed the Senate, but in the House action
was deferred until the supplementary session of the legislature
scheduled for the summer of 1856.[18] King was confident that the
measure would be enacted into law at that time, and he wrote
triumphantly to his son: "I have placed the Rail Road Company
on so firm a foundation that success is certain."[19]

King hastened back to New York to report his accomplishments
to the board of directors. During March and April 1856 the eastern
directors took a long step forward toward actual construction. By
June one thousand tons of sixty-pound rails were en route from
the Montour Works of Pittsburgh, Pennsylvania, to New Orleans.
King returned almost immediately from New York to Marshall,
Texas, to attend a session of the board of directors on Texas soil.
At this meeting, called at the instance of Louis Trezevant Wigfall,
the Texas stockholders aired their resentment of foreign control
of the railroad, but King expressed himself as pleased with the
outcome of the week-long meetings: ". . . our Company is assuming the form and substance of a real live bona fide Railroad Company with power and means of progress."[20]

The directors' meeting at Marshall illustrated some of the difficulties of the company in charting a course politically. Texas was
undergoing rapid expansion, and most legislators looked kindly
upon railroads as an aid to the growth of the state. At the same
time they resented outsiders, and the Texas Western had been
organized in Alabama and maintained its principal offices in New
York. Numerous projected lines were seeking charters and special
concessions, and each company had its advocates in the legislature.
The Memphis, El Paso and Pacific, for instance, had powerful
political connections, and its charter made it a formidable rival
of the Texas Western for the transcontinental route. In addition,
although Governor Pease had recommended and approved measures to aid railroads, he was an avowed enemy of the Texas
Western; fortunately, his second term as governor was drawing to
a close. It was obviously desirable for King and his associates to
encourage the growth of a favorable climate for private companies,
to placate or combine with rivals, and to work for a favorable
legislature which might offset the governor's animosity. July 1856
would be a crucial time, for the state capital would then be the

site of both a railroad convention to declare public opinion on state participation in railroad building and also of an adjourned session of the legislature.[21]

Looking toward these important meetings, King early in 1856 dispatched an agent to the interior of Texas to cultivate public opinion for the Texas Western and to exchange stock in the company for lands along the proposed right of way. His agent, C. A. Harper, reported great success in stimulating support for the corporation and in securing instructions to both convention delegates and legislators to vote for the loan provision passed by the Senate during the preceding session. Since it was important for the Texas Western to exert every ounce of influence upon the forthcoming convention and legislature, King prepared to join Harper at Austin in July. In the meantime, he visited Mississippi to propose a working agreement to the directors of the Vicksburg, Shreveport and Texas Railroad, which would give his company connections to the Mississippi River. After holding talks with the directors of the connecting line, he returned to New York, where he received instructions to conclude a merger agreement with the Memphis, El Paso and Pacific Railroad, but only after the session of the legislature had ended.[22]

The management of all this lobbying and jockeying with rival companies was left in King's hands, and the Texas Western Railroad Company achieved its main objectives at Austin in July. The railroad convention approved the general policies of aid to private companies, while the legislature passed a law calling for the grant of loans from the school fund of $6,000 for every mile of track completed. Several important changes in the charter of the Texas Western were passed over Governor Pease's veto. The name of the corporation was changed to the Southern Pacific Railroad Company, and it was given until February 1858 to complete its first twenty-mile section. These changes were not won without concessions, however, for the company was forced to fix its domicile in the state, have a majority of Texans on its board of directors, construct ten miles of track annually, and comply strictly with certain general regulations regarding land surveys.[23] While he was in Austin, King also worked out an agreement with the rival Memphis, El Paso and Pacific Railroad Company, whereby each corporation would build a separate line to a junction point and then build a common trunk line to El Paso.[24]

Until the fall of 1856 King had acted merely as a director of a speculative company; he travelled and worked in the hope that

his exertions would increase the value of the stock which he held.
In October his services were rewarded by an appointment as
"General Superintendent and Land Commissioner" of the Southern Pacific Railroad Company. Subject to the approval of the
board of directors, he had broad powers over the survey, location,
and sale of company lands and over the actual construction of the
road. His salary was set at $15,000 a year plus expenses, and he
was to have the services of a clerk of his own appointment. Heretofore, matters of organization and politics had occupied his attention. To these aspects were now added the problems of actual
construction and, above all, the need to secure working capital.
Contracts for laying the rails which were on their way to Texas
would require actual cash in the till of the company, to the
acquisition of which King now directed his efforts.[25]

Even by the most liberal estimates, the financial status of the
Southern Pacific Railroad Company was precarious. The corporation was saddled with the stock issues of two previous companies,
and large blocks of stock had been retained by the original speculators, other stock had been sold to the public at a discount, while
some had been used to pay for publicity or to buy lands along the
right of way. Except for some negligible assets the resources of the
company consisted of its charter rights and the enthusiasm of
some of its promoters. The charter rights depended on the successful completion of sections of the road; for each twenty miles
of road, the State of Texas would grant some 200,000 acres of
public lands and a loan from the school fund of $120,000. Com-
pletion of successive sections of the road would bring similar loans
and grants, but the first section would have to be completed by
February 16, 1858. It was imperative to move quickly, in order
that the company might acquire the assets that would support
further operations.

To secure working capital King launched a promotional campaign in New Orleans. He enlisted the aid of the *Daily Picayune,*
which during March and April 1857 extolled the virtues of the
route of the Southern Pacific and kept its readers informed of the
progress that the company was making. A strong bid was made for
regional support, with the naming of George Shall Yerger, a
prominent Mississippi lawyer and planter, as president, with an
understanding that Southerners were to have a larger voice in the
direction of the affairs of the corporation. King, Jeptha Fowlkes,
and Edwin Post were named as agents to transfer the books and
offices of the company from New York to New Orleans.[26] King

was overjoyed at the response when the subscription books for
stock were opened in New Orleans.

Thanks be to God!! [King wrote his wife] . . . I have laboured night
and day. Have written and talked a whole city into such a state of
enthusiasm as never animated it before—More than three hundred
thousand dollars of hard cash have been paid down on subscriptions
to stock within the last ten days.[27]

He failed to mention that the $300,000 represented subscriptions
to only half of the $12,000,000 in shares that had been thrown on
the market. The books were declared closed on April 11, 1857,
but were reopened again some ten days later.[28]

Both before and after the promotional campaign in New Orleans, King's duties as general superintendent took him to Texas.
Accompanied by his son Mallery, he travelled over the line of the
survey to Dallas, entered into negotiations with agents of rival
lines, and contracted for the laying of twenty-eight miles of track,
before returning to New York.[29] While he was in Texas young
Butler King, who had visited New York on business, warned his
father against some unnamed associates there, adding: "I think
you will find the 'rats' have been at play in New York, & that
you have not gone there too soon."[30] The New Yorkers, King
found on his return, did not take kindly to the idea of removing
the offices to New Orleans. Even his fellow agents appointed to
superintend the removal, Fowlkes and Post, showed little desire to
act. Not until September 26, 1857, was the New York office declared closed, and then it was accomplished by order of the board
of directors in New Orleans.

While King and some of his colleagues remained in the East,
the work of construction went forward in Texas. Aside from
minor complaints about labor, supplies, and sub-contractors, the
chief engineer expressed satisfaction with the grading and laying
of ties. If rail deliveries were accomplished as planned, he anticipated no trouble in completing the first twenty miles of road by
January 1, 1858. Jeptha Fowlkes contracted to build the next two
hundred miles of road at an average price of $30,500 a mile, and
he took an option on the building of the entire mileage to El
Paso. The real estate operations of the company proceeded under
the direction of C. A. Harper, who continued to secure deeds to
lands along the right of way and reported that the demand for
stock in exchange for land was strong in central Texas.[31]

The most serious threats to the progress of the plans of the company were to be found in the rivalry of the Memphis, El Paso and Pacific and in the resentment of some of the Texas stockholders toward outsiders. Politics entered into both matters. The rival road had long been considered a threat by the directors of the Southern Pacific, and King's merger agreement, which might have quieted the conflict, was rejected by the directors of the Memphis, El Paso and Pacific. Although the latter corporation was on the point of forfeiting its charter rights for failure to complete a specified mileage of road, the governor-elect endorsed an extension of the charter. King, who was still trying to push through a merger agreement, received encouragement from colleagues in Texas, but found his negotiations undermined by George S. Yerger, the new president of the Southern Pacific.[32]

Some of the Texas stockholders were restive because outsiders controlled the company. The answer to this problem, as well as the rivalry of the Memphis, El Paso and Pacific Company, appeared to several observers to be essentially a political one. Most of them agreed that State Senator Louis T. Wigfall held the key to the control of opinion in Texas. Chief Engineer Blanch, writing from Wigfall's home county, urged President Yerger and King to consult with the Texas senator and "let him know what the Company wants at the next legislature. . . . In fact Wigfall will be 'de facto' Governor."[33] Blanch felt sure that Wigfall could quiet the fears of Texans regarding outside control. As for the extension of time for the completion of the first section of the Memphis, El Paso and Pacific, Blanch assured Yerger that "Wigfall can kill this if he tries."[34] On the other hand, R. W. Loughery, a Texas director of the Southern Pacific, inclined to the opinion that some sort of merger with the other road was preferable to the existing rivalry, and here again Wigfall "could bring it about."[35] Wigfall's strong political influence was needed also to counteract the enmity of Thomas Jefferson Rusk, senior Senator from Texas in the United States Congress, who "will do any thing he can to cripple the Co[.] if thereby he can get his friends (who were backed out by Walkers action in the first move) into the M.E. & P. Co. . . ."[36] Robert J. Walker's name, invaluable in securing support in Texas in earlier days, now was accounted a liability to the venture because of his actions as Governor of Kansas.[37]

Despite rival roads and dissension within the company, the affairs of the Southern Pacific Railroad never looked brighter than in September 1857. Almost overnight the Panic of 1857 changed the prospects of the company, and of King. The contraction of credit put an end to land transactions and interfered with the construction. Even the forces of nature seemed to conspire to defeat the completion of the first twenty miles of track when heavy rains washed out embankments and, by delaying the cotton-picking season, brought about a shortage of Negro labor at a crucial time. The construction engineer urged King to send cash and a force of Irish laborers in order to repair the washouts and complete the laying of the track. Urging that the money be in the form of specie, not drafts, the engineer pointed to the approaching deadline for the completion of the section with the words: "Let me repeat, *send at once money & send hands,* or we are *gone.*"[38]

In order to save the charter, President George S. Yerger took a step that was to involve the company in complex litigation for three years. On October 17, 1857, he executed a deed of trust providing for the sale of the railroad, primarily for the benefit of the contractors. According to King's correspondents, the condemnation of Yerger's action was almost universal:

Did any one ever hear of a President taking care of himself in preference to the stockholders whose interests he ought to guard? . . . This deed of trust has killed Yerger in Texas, or at least this portion of it. His unheralded and unexpected appearance here, the privacy of his counsels, the limited number of his councillors, his sudden exit, and the extraordinary document he left behind, are matters of notoriety and common conversation.[39]

The state of public opinion was particularly important because of the imminent meeting of the Texas legislature in December 1857. Advocates of the company kept anxious watch over the prospects for action by authorities in Austin.

King was urged to take the lead in opposing Yerger's actions and to carry the fight to the meeting of the legislature. Jeptha Fowlkes, a director who opposed Yerger, harped on a familiar theme:

My opinion, is, you should enlist Col. Wigfall heartily in our interest —he has talents & boldness with powerful Texas associations. Let Col. Wigfall make 50 000$—what of it? There is enough for all! Without Col. Wigfall I fear yr. defeat.[40]

In January 1858 King took up residence in Austin to lobby for the interests of the company. To reinforce his arguments, he depended heavily on an appeal to Southern sectionalism, an aspect of the project that he had never emphasized so strongly before. In a memorandum supplied to Representative R. M. Powell, it was argued that the people of the North regarded the location of the transcontinental route as a sectional issue. The hope of the South lay with Texas, which by aiding the Southern Pacific to cross the continent "will become a vast counterpoise to the free states of the north west and fulfill the destiny which was claimed for her by the friends of annexation."[41] A vote for the bill uniting the interests of the Southern Pacific and the Memphis, El Paso and Pacific *"appears to me like voting against* the admission of Kansas as a free state. . . ."[42] The merger agreement was approved by the legislature. On other matters, success was not so certain. Wigfall, on whom so much depended, had gone over to Yerger's side, and he secured the passage of a law under which any railroad sold under a deed of trust should retain its franchise.[43] Good news for all friends of the Southern Pacific was the completion of the first twenty miles of road, making the company eligible for both land grants and loans from the school fund. The years of work had finally begun to show some fruit, but much depended on the legality of the deed of trust, which called for the sale of the company in June. If the creditors' claims against the company could be satisfied before that date, it might be possible to stave off defeat.

During the spring of 1858 King travelled from Marshall to New Orleans, Washington, and New York in a desperate attempt to keep the Southern Pacific from foundering in the depths of the financial crisis. Not enough cash was forthcoming to settle the outstanding debts, and the stockholders were divided into groups vying for the control of the newly-won assets. Jeptha Fowlkes led the forces of the stockholders and directors outside of Texas, while Yerger and Wigfall acted respectively for the contractors and Texans. King was caught in the middle. Common sense and political reality called for him to throw in his lot with Yerger and Wigfall; but all his hopes of a fortune depended on the stock which had been issued by the earlier companies, and a deed of trust sale would void most of these claims. On June 1, 1858, the Southern Pacific Railroad Company was sold at public auction to Jefferson M. Saunders for $40,000. He immediately sold the road to the creditors of the company for the same price. The following day a new directorate was elected; all the directors were Texans except L. P. Grant, one of the principal contractors. When the sale of the road was confirmed, King abandoned his efforts in behalf of the company. He returned to Retreat, broken in health and spirits.[44]

The state of King's health gave his family grave concern. In the interest of the railroad he had neglected to submit to medical treatment that had been recommended the previous spring. Throughout the early summer he was under the care of a physician in New York, but by the middle of August he was able to go to Saratoga Springs to convalesce. As his health improved, his interest in the Southern Pacific Railroad Company revived. During his illness and convalescence he was kept informed of the affairs of the corporation, and its signs of vitality in the face of overwhelming difficulties gave hope that all was not yet lost. After the sale of June 1, Jeptha Fowlkes, who had formerly occupied a subordinate place in the directorate, took up the fight for the stockholders outside of Texas. Regarding the whole deed of trust sale as fraudulent, he set about rallying the stockholders in a fight to regain control of the company. He issued a broadside calling on all supporters of the project to avoid personal issues and unite in the fight against the "new company" formed after the sale of the road. In the hope of raising $200,000 to meet the debts of the old company, he pledged $50,000 himself and called a meeting of stockholders in Louisville for August 24, 1858. Here he appealed for a subscription of fifty cents a share to make up a trust fund to pay off the creditors and regain control. After the meeting Fowlkes wrote King that he felt confident of defeating the new company; he also promised that although the feeling against King and all other former leaders in the company was strong he would recognize King's services of the past. Other reports on Fowlkes' activities ranged from the deepest pessimism to limited hope.[45]

With small expectations, King attended another stockholders' meeting in Louisville in November 1858. Seeing the enthusiasm aroused by Fowlkes' campaign to recover control, he regained some of his optimism. Since he lacked the cash to subscribe on his block of stock, he surrendered one half his holdings. Confidence in the company was restored to the point that the stockholders reportedly refused to entertain bids for $2 on stock that had been surrendered. King expressed the hope that the stock might sell at par value in another month. So entirely was his faith renewed that he reentered the employ of the company on the understanding that the stock he had surrendered should be returned to him in payment for his future services as a lobbyist. Immediately, he went to Washington, where he "made such arrangements as I think will prevent, for some weeks, the passage of any RailRoad project."[46] Thenceforward, it was in the role of national lobbyist that King was to play his part in the affairs of the Southern Pacific Railroad Company.[47]

For King the Pacific railroad adventure had been another characteristic hazard of fortunes. Like his political gambles in California, the stakes were high and the potential rewards great. Both the successes and the failures of the railroad reflected King's own nature and his services to the company. A member of the executive committee of three successive corporations, for five years he acted as the principal link between the financial headquarters in New York and New Orleans and the field of operations in Texas. He attended the sessions of every Texas legislature from 1853 to 1858, and, to judge by the concessions granted to his companies, he achieved success as a lobbyist. He successfully met the threat of competition from the Memphis, El Paso and Pacific Railroad by a merger agreement approved by the legislature of Texas. As a promoter he engendered the enthusiasm in New Orleans that supplied the Southern Pacific with funds to continue construction in 1857. While he was general superintendent, the major portion of the twenty-five miles of actual construction was accomplished and traffic operations were begun. He could claim a large share in whatever success the railroad achieved.

At the same time, King shared equally in the failures of the companies. He was a full partner of Robert J. Walker in the Mississippi and Pacific fiasco of 1853-1854. He presided over the formation of the Texas Western Railroad and helped guide its paper destinies. The successor Southern Pacific, with its large promises and small accomplishments, rested as much on his shoulders as on those of any single man. He condoned, if he did not originate, the dubious finance that from the beginning characterized the three corporations. The debts of each failure passed to the successor company and added to the difficulties to be surmounted. King therefore contributed to the weaknesses that made the Southern Pacific an early casualty in the financial panic of 1857. The wonder is not that the Southern Pacific Railroad achieved little, but that in spite of its precarious financing it came so near to success.

Even if failure seems to the modern observer to have been almost inevitable, King's contributions to the development of a transcontinental railroad were undeniable. He envisioned the idea of a railroad to the Pacific along the Thirty-second Parallel, he communicated his enthusiasms to others, and he managed to convert enthusiasm into action. He was a genuine pioneer of the transcontinental railroad movement, and when the continent was spanned the promoters used the same elements and techniques that King had employed. His promotion, finance, and lobbying for the Southern Pacific Railroad gave a preview of the gilded age that was to follow.

· IX ·

Retreat in the Fifties

AMID THE CHANGE and movement of his life in the 1850's, Thomas Butler King could count on one constant element, his home. To his dependents on Saint Simons Island he remained the head of the family, rather than the promoter of a railroad. On his trips between New York and the Southwest he frequently managed to spend interludes, long or short, with his wife and children, and it was at Retreat that he found the most appreciative audience for a recital of his triumphs or a place to rebuild his strength for the battles of the business world. What these visits meant in terms of the love and affection of his family can only be guessed at, but some of the relationships that existed can be traced in broad outline. In addition to being his home, Retreat was the basic resource on which the family relied for their existence. Although King's salaries or his speculations might hold promise of great wealth, the plantation furnished a relatively stable income, sufficient to maintain from year to year the family and the slaves who worked the land. With this economic base, King was able to devote his energies to the various business schemes that engrossed his attention. At the same time he could not neglect entirely the business of cotton growing, and his visits and long-range advice by letter kept him a planter. Absentee though he was, his judgments were regarded as decisive in plantation affairs.

In the early Fifties, while her husband was in California, Anna King managed the plantation with the assistance of their long-time overseer, George Dunham, and their son-in-law, William A. Couper.[1] Before King could once more take over direction of

planting operations, he had to make his journey to England to
complete his gold land speculation, and during his absence young
Butler took the reins. Subject to his father's instructions he exercised control from 1853 to 1858, with occasional assistance from
his brother Mallery. Within a year after he took control, Butler
came into conflict with George Dunham. The overseer first requested a salary increase and then gave notice of his intention to
leave the Kings' service by January 1, 1855. An argument between
Butler and Dunham in the summer of 1854 culminated in Dunham's leaving before the crop was fully harvested. King's role as
final arbiter in plantation affairs was illustrated by his managing,
on a brief visit home, to smooth over Dunham's departure and
restore peace between the two men. Thereafter, Butler devoted
himself to the care of the plantation, "out except at meals from
morning until dark."[2] After the crop of 1856 was laid by, he
hired a young overseer to take charge of the harvest while he
joined his father in New York to attend to some business affairs.
When his mother found Butler fully capable of running the plantation, she left the decisions of management to him, confining
her talents to the many other duties that confronted the mistress
of a plantation.

Only by careful management were the Kings able to extract
sufficient income from Retreat to sustain their generous scale of
living. Parts of the land had been under intensive cultivation for
more than fifty years, and this "old" plantation had to compete
with the new lands of the Southwest. The special Sea Island type
of cotton which was the staple on Saint Simons still commanded
a premium in the market, but improvements in manufacturing
technique had now relegated the long-staple cotton to the position
of a specialty product, rather than the preferred kind for quan-
tity production. The struggles of the Kings during the years from
1853 to 1858 therefore mirror the larger problems of all old
plantations in the East with their western competitors.

Customarily, between one hundred and one hundred fifty acres
at Retreat were planted to Sea Island cotton, and the resulting
crop brought in the cash income of the plantation. The rest of
the arable land was devoted to making provisions in the form of
corn, peas, and turnips. The total labor force remained more or
less constant at about 125 slaves of all ages and both sexes.[3] The
financial returns depended on the vagaries of the weather and the
market and on the productivity of the soil. The 1850's were a
prosperous period for many cotton farmers in Georgia, but not

for the Kings. They knew only one profitable year between 1853 and 1858. The poor crops were attributed to various causes, the chief of which was a succession of unpropitious growing seasons. In 1854 the promising crop was injured by rainstorms and further reduced by the overseer's defection. The poor returns from this year forced Mrs. King to borrow $4,000 from her factor. The crop of 1855 was slow in maturing and brought such a low price that the debt was carried over into the next year. In 1856 unfavorable weather again reduced the yield from an expected bag of cotton per acre to about half that amount. If the entire crop sold at the price of early shipments, it brought in something over $9,000. The year 1857 was almost disastrous. Both the cotton and corn crops were killed by a late cold spell and had to be replanted. Consequently, the crop was both late and small, and the Kings could only congratulate themselves that even so they were more fortunate than most of their neighbors. The $3,700 that this crop sold for was not sufficient to defray the expenses for the year.

Faced with a mounting debt, the Kings redoubled their efforts to secure good yields from the land. By Thomas Butler King's direction, and under the supervision of young Butler, the cotton was planted in flat beds, instead of the former high beds. Neighboring planters, who had looked upon the innovation with suspicion, soon adopted this successful method. The selection of good seed, especially for the turnip crop, became a matter of great concern. The most efficient aid to better crops seemed to be heavier fertilizing of the land. Different types of manure were tried, and the amount of manure increased by one-third. Young Butler also set up experimental plots where he tested phosphate and guano as fertilizers. Other improvements were made on the plantation equipment. Young Cuyler King undertook to renovate the old gins, and new gins were purchased in an attempt to improve the quality of the product for marketing. To handle transportation problems, a large flatboat, "fully worth $500,"[4] was built by local labor. In spite of all these efforts to improve production, Retreat remained economically unprofitable in the years from 1853 to 1858. Although the unseasonable weather received most of the blame, it was apparent to the Kings that their lands were becoming worn out.

The obvious solution was to bring new lands into cultivation. When a nearby plantation was put up for sale, King and his eldest son tried to purchase it, for the control of the entire area would permit the reclamation of an intervening marsh for culti-

vation, but their negotiations were not successful. After two years
of dickering, Butler secured a neighboring tract of over one
hundred acres to add to the Retreat holdings, although only a
third of it could be used for cotton. Before the year was out he
had also begun to prepare nearly a hundred acres for cotton at
Oatlands, another adjacent holding. Nevertheless, he considered
these moves merely temporary expedients; the only real solution
lay in a removal to richer lands.

But for the love of the Lord [Butler urged his father], get a place in
Texas—this year—so that I or some of us can take some of the hands
out there this Autumn, even 1000—acres to begin on—will be better
than starving here, for almost all the resources for manuring these
two places have been exhausted— . . . I am disgusted with these poor
lands—it keepes [*sic*] them killed in order to pasture the cattle necessary to be used in order to make any thing off them—[5]

The events of 1857 reemphasized the need to find a better location. A long drought in June was succeeded by heavy rains in
July. In August sickness among the slaves kept as many as twelve
or fifteen absent from the fields every day. A storm in the middle
of September ruined a fourth of the crop; the returns paid most
of the year's expenses, but did nothing to reduce the old debt
which the factor had been carrying for three years. The Kings
were caught in a dilemma: they needed to move to new lands in
order to make a success of planting, but they could not acquire
by planting the capital to make the move.

This bald summary of plantation affairs at Retreat helps to
explain King's exertions in the business world, particularly the
railroad speculations that occupied him during the same period.
Although the Pacific railroad gave scope to his talents as a lobbyist and promoter and appealed to his broad view of economic
development, it also offered a quick road to wealth which would
free him from reliance on a declining plantation and enable him
to provide for the future of his children. Such, at least, were the
grounds on which his wife justified his long absences from home
on railroad business. She knew that King expected to retrieve his
fortunes by a sudden financial coup. "I would not discourage
you," she wrote, "believing you to be more happy in trying to
better your fortune by this kind of excitement than you would be
at home looking back on the past [.]"[6] She hoped that he might
realize enough money to purchase a neighboring plantation, "a
much surer investment than any other you can make."[7] She also

appreciated the earnings that enabled King to carry some of the
losses incurred by "three short crops in succession."[8] The Panic
of 1857 and the failure of his immediate hopes she accepted as
the decrees of an unkind fate. Her greatest regret was that with
success "we could have gone some where—where we could have
had all of our dear children settled around us—."[9] But Anna's
feeling of regret was tempered by the knowledge that even though
her husband had failed financially he would no longer be sub-
jected to the dangers of constant travel, and could now enjoy the
comforts of a prolonged stay at home. They would make the best
of what remained to them.

So long as her husband or son resided at Retreat, Mrs. King
had little to do with the main business of the plantation. When
young Butler took over in 1853 and proved his reliability, she
greatly appreciated being relieved of the responsibility. "I am so
glad," she wrote her husband, "to shift the burden off my shoulders on to his young ones. . . ."[10] Nevertheless, she constantly surveyed the state of the crops and livestock, watched the weather
and prospects closely, and kept an anxious eye on the cotton
market. The kitchen garden and the orchards were under her
immediate care, and the products of the latter were "prized by
all—family and neighbors."[11] The flock of fowls also belonged to
her jurisdiction.[12] Her flower garden, to which her husband contributed new plants from time to time, was a source of special
pleasure and relaxation to the busy mistress of the plantation.
Relieved of the cares of planning farm operations, she still carried
many responsibilities. She frequently complained of the burdens
imposed by the duty of extending hospitality to guests, but her
husband took her protests with a grain of salt. "The fact is," he
pointed out, "you all have a manner *entirely too cordial to every
body!* I like to treat people with civility but not with *indiscrim-
inate* cordiality."[13]

The more King's travels kept him away from the plantation,
the greater were the cares borne by Mrs. King as the mistress of
more than a hundred slaves. It was in regard to the slaves that
she felt the greatest need of his presence. The misfortunes of a
neighboring planter, for instance, led him to offer for sale the
wife of Smart, one of the King slaves. She came to Mrs. King with
a request that she and her six children be purchased by the Kings.
Mrs. King, also laboring under financial difficulties, was unable
to find the $4,100 price. Another marriage outside the plantation
caused trouble for Peter, Lord King's personal servant. "Con-

trary to my expressed orders—he would take a wife at the Wylly's.
he [*sic*] was brought home a few hours ago severely injured by
one of the Wylly negro men."[14] A neighbor had fallen into evil
ways and was encouraging drinking and carousing among the
King Negroes. Mrs. King offered her son-in-law's suggestion that
her husband use his political influence to have the young man
replaced in his job of lighthouse keeper. She found the problem
he presented quite beyond her capabilities.

Mrs. King seldom wrote her husband without reporting on the
sick list at the plantation hospital. In a typical summary she recorded two confinements, one unspecified injury, "2 others I
cant find out exactly what ails them & 2 children with fever—
nothing that appears *alarming*."[15] For most illnesses she herself
prescribed the treatment, sending for a doctor only in emergencies. Even so, medical care was a considerable expense. "My doc-
tors bill for sick negros last year was $90—& I did not perceive the
patients were any the better for their attendance. . . ."[16] In her
accounts for 1857 she listed a drug bill of $351.97.[17] When sick-
ness was widespread the mistress of the plantation had no leisure.
"I was taken up pretty much all Sunday in weighing off Physic
for sick negroes," she once wrote her son who was attending the
University of Virginia.[18] The medical care she gave her slaves
amounted to more than mere dosing and hospitalization, as another letter to her son revealed:

We lost poor Annie last night. . . . We (Cousin & I) sat up with her
all Sunday night—was with her nearly all Monday & left her at 9 that
night apparently doing well. I left Pussy directions to call me if Anna
seemed at all worse.[19]

Doubtless Annie received special attention because she was the
only child of Mrs. King's personal maid, Rhina, but in at least
one other letter Anna King wrote of having kept another night-
long vigil. As part of her medical duties she kept a watchful eye
on the health of the whole neighborhood, in order to be prepared
for epidemics. Standing water was recognized as a health hazard
and was drained off by a system of ditches. Public health officer,
nurse, and physician—all these roles were included in the cares
of the mistress of a plantation.

King's absences from home threw upon his wife a heavy parental load. Their nine children ranged in age from the schoolboy
Cuyler to Hannah Couper, now ten years married. Even the eldest children remained within the family circle, and Hannah,

settled at nearby Hamilton, made constant demands upon her mother's time. Mrs. King attended her in her confinements and exercised a grandmother's care when the Couper children fell ill. With such a brood of children and grandchildren, Anna King could count on steady employment whenever mumps, measles, whooping cough, or other childhood diseases made the rounds of the neighborhood. She had to take over in other nursing crises, such as caring for Cuyler when his mechanical aptitude led him into danger. He and a young friend, after building a steam-driven toy sawmill, wired down the cork that served as a safety valve. The resulting explosion burned both boys seriously. King's share in such parental concerns was confined mainly to reading about them in his wife's letters.

On the subject of schooling for their children the two parents consulted often and at length by letter. For the boys there was a succession of preparatory schools and colleges. Butler never returned to the University of Georgia, but Lord finished at Exeter and Yale and went on to Harvard Law School. They, with their next brother, Mallery, had received instructions from tutors, but Mrs. King insisted that the two younger boys have the benefits of regular preparatory schooling. After the departure of their governess in 1854, the younger girls pursued their studies mainly under their mother's direction. From her, too, they received training in the domestic arts and social graces. Her many family cares prompted Anna King to express to her husband the wish that "Our dear children were all as they were years ago when I used to *count* them before going to bed every night. . . ."[20]

King's remoteness from domestic concerns was nowhere more apparent than in his relationship with his daughters, Georgia, Florence, and Virginia.[21] As children they had seen him only in the intervals when his public duties in Washington or San Francisco permitted him to spend some time on Saint Simons. While they grew to womanhood in the 1850's they saw less of him. It was mainly through correspondence with them and their mother that King followed the progress of his daughters to maturity. At home the girls shared the household duties of their mother. From time to time they took over the superintendence of domestic affairs, particularly when some entertainment was in prospect. Occasionally one would embark on a program of improving her knowledge of some domestic art, such as cooking or the canning of fruits. As they grew older they began to show some interest in cultivating the flower plots that their mother allotted them in her gardens. Saint Simons offered little in the way of community life, but on Sundays they drove to the north end of the island to church, where Georgia sometimes sang and played the melodeon for the services. For special occasions, such as Christmas or a visit by the bishop, the girls might help with the refurbishing of the church. Such was the homely round of daily existence which King's daughters knew while he travelled about on the business of the Southern Pacific Railroad Company.

Although the social opportunities open to young ladies on Saint Simons were limited, there was a small circle of neighbors with whom the three King girls exchanged afternoon calls and tea. The coming of a visitor or the return of one of the men of the family was made into an occasion for formal dinner parties and evening entertainments, with theatricals, charades, dancing, and music. Since an evening of dancing sometimes did not break up until two in the morning, or even dawn, Mrs. King occasionally found herself provoked by her daughters' entertaining. "When my patience is nearly exhausted by their love of company," she wrote her husband, "I have to think of my *young days* & can now appreciate the annoyance I must have given to my sainted Mother."[22] The wedding of an acquaintance could set off a whole round of parties which might encompass the neighboring islands and require the services of whatever brothers were at home as sailing masters.

Formal entertainments were the exception, not the rule. For everyday society the King girls turned to a smaller circle of families that included the Hugh Fraser Grants and the Stephen Clay Kings on the mainland. With these friends and relatives, among whom were companions of the same age, visits were exchanged frequently and informally. One such visit began with the unexpected debarkation of a party of young Grants on the beach in front of Retreat, giving the Kings barely time enough to dress properly. After a hastily improvised dinner party and a carriage drive along the beach at low tide, Georgia, Florence, and Virginia returned to the mainland in the boat with the Grants. Within this circle of intimates, visits were often measured in days or weeks, rather than hours.

Pleasant as the society of the neighborhood might be, it afforded only a small field for the activities of three marriageable young ladies. In order to widen the social opportunities of her daughters, Mrs. King in the winter of 1855 arranged a visit of several weeks to Savannah. There, under the tutelage of their mother, the girls paid and received formal calls and attended the theater. Sundays brought them the chance to attend the services at the Independent Presbyterian Church or to hear Bishop William Elliott preach at Christ Church. Town life provided other activities, occasionally exciting, that were lacking on the island; Florence and Virginia had some dental work done, and Georgia narrowly escaped stepping into the line of fire while a street brawl was in progress. The next year, the King girls enjoyed another season in town, when their married sister, Hannah, played hostess to them in her new home.

Although he seldom saw his daughters, Thomas Butler King was not unmindful of their welfare. On a brief visit to Retreat in 1856 he promised them a trip to the Virginia springs that summer. When this excursion failed to materialize, he consoled them with the gift of a pair of ponies to be used in their drives along the beach. But he did not forget the promise of a trip, and although they did not have a chance to pass the season at the spas, the two elder daughters enjoyed a visit to Washington and Philadelphia during the winter. Virginia, whose mother referred to her as "our bookworm," elected to pursue her education further at Madame Dupres' school in Charleston. Along with two of Hugh Fraser Grant's daughters, she enrolled at Madame Dupres', but they found the place not up to their expectations and left after only five days. When the fortunes of the Southern Pacific Railroad looked brightest in the summer of 1857, young Butler took his sisters to Virginia for three weeks of the gay season at the White Sulphur and Sweet Springs. From the resort area the girls went on to New York, where their father was struggling with railroad problems on the eve of the great financial panic. In New York Georgia received and rejected a proposal of marriage, thus matching the record of her sister Florence, who had previously refused the suit of a neighbor at Retreat.

For Georgia, Florence, and Virginia, the visit to the North in 1857 long remained their greatest venture into the society of the outside world. They returned to their familiar tranquil round of daily life at Retreat. In the mornings the ladies of the family would gather in one room to sew, while Georgia or visiting Aunt Louisa read some elevating work, such as Anne Manning's *The Household of Sir Thomas More,* or perhaps Thomas Butler King's latest railroad report. There were always absent members of the family to write to. Afternoons were generally devoted to long walks, rides, or drives along the beach when the tide permitted.

Often there were young nieces and nephews to be entertained, perhaps with an excursion to the wharf to catch crabs or to the beach to hunt for turtle eggs. In the evenings the family gathered in the parlor, where the girls sang duets with their brothers, or played at charades and tableaux, or simply passed a quiet evening reading. For a while they took up the fad of table-tipping, but they soon became skeptical.

Thomas Butler King had a closer relationship with his five sons than with his daughters. Masculine pursuits and interests led more easily to companionship, particularly with the two elder boys, Butler and Lord, who entered business and professional life during the 1850's. In addition, social conventions of the times permitted King's sons, but not his daughters, to travel alone to New York or Washington to meet their father when he visited those cities. King accepted certain responsibilities as a father to his sons, and even in the midst of his financial adventures he tried to give each of them the benefit of his companionship as the young men finished their schooling. Thus, Butler became his assistant in San Francisco, while both Lord and Mallery traveled with him on his business journeys for the Southern Pacific company.

All the boys except Butler attended school or college during the 1850's. A chronicle of the lives of the younger boys would recount little out of the ordinary. They usually spent their vacations at Retreat, where they assumed some of the duties of overseeing the plantation. Mallery, for instance, not only helped supervise the field work, but also put his engineering studies to work at improvements of the buildings and grounds. Cuyler excelled at running and repairing the gins. Aside from these duties, all the boys took advantage of the hunting and fishing that the island offered, coupling the pleasure of sport with the providing of wildfowl, fish, and venison for the larder. Similarly, alligator hunting supplied exciting moments and carried the utilitarian justification that it reduced the inroads on the plantation swine. Boating was both a commonplace necessity and a time-consuming sport for island dwellers. Besides these diversions, the King boys joined, sometimes reluctantly, in the social activities of their sisters.

Among them, the King boys attended a large number of educational institutions. In 1853 Floyd King went north to a preparatory school; the following year he enrolled in the Georgia Military Institute. A succession of illnesses kept him at home during the winter and spring of 1855, but with the coming of summer he entered Francis R. Goulding's school at Kingston, Georgia. Although he showed interest in a military career, Floyd was disappointed in his hopes that he might secure an appointment to West Point. Not until he reached the University of Virginia did Floyd begin to justify his parents' hopes that he would apply himself to his studies and pick a profession. In a long letter of advice about professional training, King assured Floyd that he had confidence in his ability to make up for wasted years of preparatory schooling, and that the funds would be available for further professional preparation. If Floyd aspired to a political career, King continued, he advised law rather than engineering as a background. He cautioned Floyd that politics had many drawbacks as a profession, among them the need of a full purse. "A man who enters the political field should either possess a fortune or remain a bachelor."[23]

The school career of Cuyler, the youngest son, paralleled that of his brother Floyd. Cuyler attended a succession of schools in Savannah, Roswell, and Marietta, Georgia, and the Bloomfield Academy near Charlottesville, Virginia. Nearly always he was located near one of his elder brothers, to whom he could look for guidance and companionship. Like Floyd he failed to apply himself to his studies as his parents felt he should. Some of the educational deficiencies of these younger boys might be attributed to the fact that they grew up during the years when their father was often absent from home. King felt it necessary to try to exonerate himself of any guilt as a negligent father. In a letter to his son Mallery he insisted that he had given all his children an opportunity to acquire a good education and that the two youngest could still make up for lost time if they would put forth *"one half* the *mental* and *physical* exertion applied to the *construction* and *sailing* of useless canou [*sic*] boats. . . ."[24]

Mallery King, the third son, gave his parents more cause for satisfaction. He stood high scholastically, both at the northern preparatory school that he attended and at the Georgia Military Institute. He showed a sense of responsibility by submitting careful accounts of his school expenditures and by keeping an eye on his two younger brothers at a nearby school. Ambitious to become an engineer, Mallery looked forward to working for a railroad company upon the completion of his studies at the Georgia Military Institute and the Poughkeepsie Collegiate School. King was quick to appreciate his son's ambition and in the winter and

spring of 1857 took him on a field survey of the line of the Southern Pacific Railroad. Father and son consulted with the engineers
and directors and hunted with parties of gentlemen along the
route. This Texas trip was to be Mallery's closest approach to
professional engineering. He returned to Retreat to help Butler
manage the plantation, and more by default than by intention
became master in residence when Butler was called north to look
after his father during an illness. Not until war brought changes
to Retreat did Mallery escape from Saint Simons, although brother
Lord deplored his giving up his profession and sister Georgia
feared that he would be "sacrificed to that poor old plantation."[25]

The most promising of the King boys, and at the same time
the most trying, was Lord, the second son. Educated at Exeter,
Yale, and Harvard Law School, he spent his vacations in Pennsylvania with the childless uncle for whom he was named. He was
inclined to be extravagant, if the reproofs of his parents were
justified. Even to a mother's eye he showed a tendency to laziness.
When he finished his law studies in 1855, he returned to Retreat
and spent his time exercising, hunting, reading, and helping his
sisters entertain their guests. Mrs. King looked forward to the
end of the social season on the island, when company would no
longer distract Lord from his preparations for the Georgia bar.
Exasperated, she wrote her husband: "He wants energy and a
determination to face the foe."[26] Eventually, Lord made arrangements to read law in the office of a Savannah attorney, and by the
end of the year had earned a letter of praise from his father. King
encouraged him to persevere in his work and studies: "What I
desire and hope to see is my sons stepping forth into the World,
high toned, prudent, temperate, industrious gentlemen!"[27] King
approved of his son's decision to begin his practice by following
the circuit court in the spring of 1856, and he supplied the names
of old friends who would receive his son kindly.

When the prospects of the Southern Pacific seemed brightest
in 1857, General Superintendent King appointed his son Lord as
his private secretary, and for six months they travelled together
on company business. In Austin, Lord watched his father push
measures through the Texas legislature. The inner mysteries of
lobbying elicited from him some youthful philosophy: ". . . with
a woman you may understand "yes" for "no" and return to the
charge, but with Legislation, if you let it floor you, you have to
stay down."[28] Lord's secretarial position disappeared with the reorganization of the company in the following spring, but he con-

tinued his close association with his father during the strenuous political campaign that King waged in Georgia in 1859.

King was closer to his eldest son, Butler, than to any of the other children. Together they had faced the problems of the collector's office in San Francisco; they had lived together and invested money in various California speculations, and they both held stock in the Pacific railroad venture. When King went abroad in 1853 he entrusted the management of all his affairs to Butler, and at Retreat the son became his father's chief deputy. Life on the island suited him to perfection, and while he was on the Pacific Coast he often wrote of his wish to return, declaring that "if I ever get money enough to buy a plantation and Negros St. Simons is the very spot I would live at."[29] When he had finished his California adventure, he began looking about for an establishment on the island where he might set himself up as a planter. Both his parents encouraged him in his ambition, and his mother in particular was anxious to have him settled on his own plantation nearby. For three years Butler's hopes of buying a place of his own centered on the neighboring estate of Hamilton. With the promise of financial aid from his parents he was several times on the point of reaching a purchase agreement with the agent in charge, but final terms could never be agreed on. Another islander offered a better price, and Butler had to turn his thoughts in other directions. Meanwhile, he had become engaged to Miss Lettie Shepard, and a separate establishment became the more desirable for the prospective bridegroom. A trip north in 1858 gave Butler an opportunity to buy an undeveloped tract on the mainland. After an examination of the land and consultations between Butler, his father, and the owner, a tentative agreement to buy was reached. Butler returned to Georgia to complete the arrangements for the transfer of the plantation.

In January 1859 the family was rejoicing in the return of King from his latest travels and in the prospect that was opening up for Butler. Their joy was turned to grief by the sudden illness and death of the eldest son. Mrs. King was prostrated, and King abandoned the business affairs that would have taken him from her side. The winter and spring became a period of mourning during which the Kings nursed their sorrow. The family, fortunate indeed to have remained so long unbroken, was drawn closer together by the death of Butler. With the coming of spring, however, the head of the family left the seclusion of Retreat to resume once more an active business and political life.

· X ·

Return to the Wars

BETWEEN 1849 and 1859 Georgia politics had taken their course with scarcely any participation by Thomas Butler King. The long struggle in Congress over the Compromise of 1850 had produced a party revolution in the state, which saw Alexander H. Stephens and Robert Toombs, King's Whig colleagues in Congress, join with the Union Democrat Howell Cobb to form the Constitutional Union Party, which was dedicated to upholding and defending the Compromise. This new alliance of moderates proved an unstable combination. In 1852 the Union Democrats returned to their old allegiance, but the Whigs were unable to regain the strength that had enabled them to win state elections during the previous twenty years. Many Whigs shifted to the Democratic Party, some joined the ranks of the Know-Nothings, and others dropped their old name and simply ran Opposition candidates in local elections. The net result was almost complete control of state politics for the Democrats after 1852.

For the political leaders of Georgia, this transitional era was a difficult one. Howell Cobb, who had led his followers into the Constitutional Union Party, managed to return to the Democratic party and even to hold national cabinet office. Toombs and Stephens made the shift from Whiggery to Democracy without having to give up their congressional seats, but they continually faced the problem of finding a place in the party which they had once regarded as the enemy. All three of these leaders of the 1840's had to bow to the nominal leadership of Herschel Vespasian Johnson, the Democratic governor from 1853 to 1857. In 1857 the stresses among the different leaders bearing the Demo-

129

cratic label opened the way for a new personality in state politics,
Joseph Emerson Brown. At the time Brown was a relatively obscure judge of the Cherokee Circuit, but the Democrats fixed on
him as a compromise candidate for governor. After his election
he caught the imagination of the voters with his able administration, his devotion to the cause of Southern Rights, and his championship of the common man. He remained a power in Georgia
politics for many years.

In the First Congressional District of Georgia the triumph of
the Democratic Party came early. When King resigned his seat
in 1850 his successor was a Savannah Democrat, Joseph Webber
Jackson. After one term Jackson gave way to James Lindsay
Seward of Thomasville, who belonged to the extreme Southern
Rights wing of the party. One of Seward's main themes in campaigning was the unjust domination of the First District by Savannah and the seaboard area; he himself gloried in the nickname
"the Wire-Grass Boy." With his back-country origin, his extreme
Southern Rights views, and his appeal to the common man, Seward resembled Governor Brown, whose political beliefs have been
described as "the social gospel of Jacksonian Democracy blithely
astride the credo of John C. Calhoun."[1] Twice Seward won re-
election to Congress in King's old district, and he was the incumbent congressman when King made his decision to reenter
politics.

During the same ten years King's own political allegiance went
through rapid changes. He had been the acknowledged leader of
the Whig Party in California and its candidate for the United
States Senate. In 1852 he supported the Whig candidate for the
presidency, General Winfield Scott. For the next three years his
railroad interests took him out of the field of open political activity, although he was constantly involved in the political aspects
of railroad building. In January 1855 a group of his old political
friends in Glynn County proposed his name as a candidate for
Congress from the First District of Georgia, but he was at the
time preoccupied with the organization of the Texas Western
Company, and nothing came of this move.[2] Instead, after a summer spent on Saint Simons he announced his candidacy for the
Senate of Georgia in the columns of the *Savannah Republican,* a
Know Nothing newspaper. Immediately, his opponents brought
up all the charges that had been levelled against him at the time
of his California mission, and to them added an accusation that
he had mishandled the county school funds which had been en-

trusted to him in 1832. As a Know Nothing candidate for state office, therefore, King entered into a defense of his entire political career. He published a long explanation of his activities in California, demanded an audit of the old accounts, and canvassed the county for votes. Despite these efforts, he was defeated by an Independent Democrat, T. T. Long.[3] Essentially, King's unsuccessful candidacy for the Senate in 1855 was an episode between journeys on the business of the Texas Western Railroad Company. Yet the experience showed what obstacles King would face if he tried to resume his political career in Georgia. The investigation of the charges of mishandling the school funds brought him a small financial windfall, for a balance was found to be due him on the old account.[4] That ghost, at least, had been put to rest.

With this campaign King brought to an end his brief excursion into the Know Nothing camp. For the past two years his business associations had been largely with prominent Democrats, and his old Whig associates in Georgia were also turning Democratic. King followed them into the party that he had once anathematized, and capped the change by attending the Democratic National Convention in Cincinnati in 1856. He held no official status as a delegate, but his interest in a transcontinental railroad made his presence understandable. One of his closest associates in the railroad was Robert J. Walker, and there is one vague hint that at Cincinnati King was part of a coterie working for Walker's nomination for the presidency. In New York a month later he declared publicly his support of the Democratic nominee, James Buchanan.[5]

For the next three years King was more involved in Texas politics as a lobbyist than in Georgia politics as a candidate; not until 1859, when the personal tragedy of his son's death had kept him at home for several months, did he once more show an interest in the contest for office. In March of that year he embarked on an intensive campaign to secure the nomination as the Democratic candidate for the First District congressional seat. With his son Lord, he travelled about the area, renewing old political ties and speaking frequently at public gatherings. The cordiality with which he was received pleased him and encouraged him to continue his efforts. To his wife he wrote jubilantly: ". . . my old friends *go for me* as well as the entire body of the democratic party."[6] After a month's tour that covered seven counties Lord King reported optimistically that his father's "energy and ability are truly wonderful," and that "he leaves the most favorable im-

pressions wherever he goes."[7] The campaigning continued into
April, when King invaded the back-country stronghold of the incumbent congressman, James L. Seward. The *Wire Grass Reporter* dragged out the old charges that he had been responsible
for the anti-slavery clause in the California constitution and that
he had handled funds improperly. To refute these accusations
King returned to Retreat and drafted a pamphlet reply. He published a collection of letters from associates in California in 1849
to prove that he had nothing to do with the movement for the
formation of that state, including the anti-slavery clause in the
constitution. He also defended at length his handling of various
funds.[8] Through an old political friend he secured a mailing list
of the voters of the district, and he arranged for the pamphlet to
be distributed at public places throughout the area. After a brief
rest at home toward the end of May, King and his son again set
out on a campaign tour, this time in the northern counties of the
district, near Savannah.[9]

The First District Democratic Convention to nominate a candidate for Congress met in Waresboro, Georgia, July 13, 1859.
Over one hundred delegates attended from twenty-five of the
twenty-eight counties. Despite the rural setting, the convention
was a full-dress performance, complete with caucuses among the
delegates. A city reporter satirized the little knots of politicoes
". . . scattered for a quarter of a mile up and down the road. . .
four men with their right legs thrown over a stump—two whittling
together mounted on a pile of boards—three squatted in the middle
of the road. . . ."[10] The sectional cleavage within the district was
clearly marked. Seward, the incumbent, appealed for renomination frankly on the grounds that for twenty years previous to his
election either Savannah or Brunswick had monopolized the office.
However, at the time of his nomination in 1857 Seward had
agreed to throw his influence at the next election behind the candidate of the Chatham County (Savannah) delegation. Since
Savannah offered no local resident as a candidate, Seward felt that
he was not bound by his earlier pledge. Even so, he had to deal
with William H. Stiles, whose strength lay in the northern part of
the district, and King, who held the allegiance of the southeast.
When the convention moved toward the adoption of a rule requiring the nominee to receive the support of two-thirds of the
delegates, Seward announced that he would not seek renomination, apparently preferring to withdraw gracefully rather than
suffer a possible defeat. The four names put into nomination were

King, Stiles, Powhatan B. Whittle, and Peter Early Love. Love was assailed as a mere catspaw because he was Seward's law partner, but Seward's support made him the strongest candidate. He led on the first ballot, while King, Stiles, and Whittle divided the other votes. King's supporters watched his bloc dwindle from 14½ to eleven through five roll calls, and on the sixth they attempted to lead a break to a dark-horse candidate, Alexander S. Atkinson. When their move failed they joined in the nomination of Love by acclamation on the seventh ballot.[11]

In his bid for the nomination King failed signally to capture the vote of Savannah and the northern part of the district, formerly centers of his strength. The loyalty of Glynn and the adjoining counties proved him to be still a political force in the state, although far weaker than he had been in the 1840's. Nor could King ascribe his failure to want of energy or publicity; he had made his views widely known and had campaigned vigorously. Few of his previous campaigns had been so bitterly fought, and in this one, as in the election of 1844, he felt that an opponent had impugned his honor. William H. Stiles, writing under the name "Philippi" in the *Southern Georgia Watchman*, repeated the charge that King was responsible for the anti-slavery clause in the California constitution and implied that King had mishandled funds when he served as Collector of San Francisco. King demanded that Stiles publicly retract his charges, and after further exchanges of correspondence he sought satisfaction on the field of honor. When Stiles refused to meet him in a duel, King denounced him "as a malicious slanderer and a coward."[12] This unsuccessful bid for the nomination to Congress, with its bitter rivalry and unhappy conclusion, would have convinced a less determined man that his political star had set.

Whatever disappointment the failure to be nominated may have brought to King, it was eclipsed by the personal tragedy that assailed him. On August 22, 1859, occurred the death of Anna Matilda King, his wife of thirty-five years. She had been unable to reconcile herself to the loss of her son Butler, and the twice-bereaved family attributed her death directly to her grief. Yet it may have been some consolation to King that in their common suffering in the months before her death, he and his wife had found another bond of affection and regarded one another with increased tenderness.[13]

The death of Anna King brought about many changes at Retreat. Georgia, the eldest unmarried daughter, tried to fill her mother's place both as mistress of the plantation and as center of the family. Now it was Georgia King, not Anna, who had to make decisions on all the daily activities of the plantation—gardening, dairying, preserving fruits, conserving supplies, managing the servants. She treated illnesses among the slaves, planned wardrobes for her schoolboy brothers, and kept the absent members of the family informed on developments at home. To her brother Cuyler, when she informed him of the death of their "inestimable servant" Quamina, she confessed: "I feel sometimes as tho' I shall grow old very fast now."[14] In addition to supervising the household, Georgia King tried to supply her father with companionship, and she sometimes acted as his secretary.[15]

While Georgia managed the housekeeping, her younger brother Mallery conducted the planting operations, having succeeded, unintentionally, to the position once occupied by Butler. Under Mallery's direction Retreat prospered, and the cotton crop of 1859 was the largest that had been harvested for several years. But even the return of $11,000 which this crop brought on the Savannah market failed to lift all indebtedness from the plantation. With more than $7,000 debt remaining to be paid, Mallery determined to expand the planting area by reclaiming a marsh. For the summer of 1860 he planned an experimental reclamation project of between sixty and seventy acres, with more to follow if this was successful. "We must have new lands," explained Georgia King to her brother Lord; "these old ones are so worn out, that we cannot expect to make good crops."[16]

After Anna King's death a legal division of her property took place. Retreat and its slaves had been secured to Mrs. King's children by her father's will, and her death brought about an accounting of the family finances. After the crop of 1859 had been sold the estate was appraised and the 139 slaves were apportioned among the surviving children. The debt of the plantation was similarly divided. In actuality, this division of the property took place only on paper, and the estate continued to operate as a unit. By agreement among themselves, King's children deeded their father a half interest in their individual shares of their mother's property. To her brother Floyd, Georgia explained:

. . . of course we all felt, as you do, that Father is master and all ours was his. . . . To settle everything properly for Father, Lord prepared the paper sent to you, giving Father a half-interest in the share of each of us, so our husbands, if any, won't expect more than half our shares.[17]

A balance sheet of King's financial status in 1860 would have shown only this half-interest in Retreat as a solid asset. He had hopes, besides, of returns from a legal action and of some profits from his stock in the Southern Pacific Railroad.[18]

With two of his children taking up the responsibilities of the plantation, King turned his energies once more to politics and promotion. He announced for the Senate of Georgia and was chosen over a fellow Democrat in the October elections.[19] It was in the lesser arena of the Georgia legislature, rather than in Congress, that he renewed his career in elective office.

King met a warm reception when he returned to the legislative halls at Milledgeville. Even after the passage of a decade, many of his colleagues in the Senate were old acquaintances from his earlier political career. Of particular importance to King was his meeting and reconciliation with Governor Joseph E. Brown, who in 1850 had led the movement in the legislature to censure King for his activities in California. The Governor was already secure in the leadership of the Democratic party that was to name him governor for four terms; his friendship or enmity could prove decisive in the Democratic Party of the state. In the 1859 session of the legislature the rapprochement between the two men bore fruit in their joint efforts to pass legislation to aid railroad construction in the state.[20]

Governor Brown called on the legislature to foster the building of new lines of railroad by extending the credit of the state to such projects. He pointed with pride to the success of the state-owned Western and Atlantic and to the existing privately owned railroads. Yet he felt that the benefits of the transportation system should be spread more widely over the state and that healthy competition should be encouraged. To accomplish these ends he recommended a general law permitting the state to endorse the bonds of railroad companies.

From the Committee on Internal Improvements Chairman Thomas Butler King brought in two reports: the majority recommended inaction; the minority, of whom King made himself the spokesman, endorsed the policy of general grants of credit. The supporting arguments pointed out the key position of Georgia as a transportation link between the Atlantic and inland cotton areas, emphasizing the desirability of competition to keep rates low. The building of competing lines between Georgia ports and connections in western states would secure to Georgians the profits from the transportation of the bulk of the American cotton crop.

State aid would enable railroad companies to complete links with western roads and extend their lines into sparsely settled areas. As an example of the latter type of development, King pointed to the Savannah, Albany and Gulf road, which had doubled the value of taxable property in its vicinity. A similar result from roads built under the proposed measure would more than repay the state for extending its aid to new lines generally. The Committee concluded that the state needed three more railroads leading from the coast to the interior. If proper safeguards were provided, no one could seriously doubt the financial prudence of the plan. The bill accompanying this report followed closely the recommendations of Governor Brown and set the amount of the loan credits at $7,000 per mile.[21]

As Chairman of the Committee on Internal Improvements, King led the legislative battle over this measure. Against considerable opposition he succeeded in bringing his state aid bill to the floor of the Senate for debate. After speaking briefly in its favor he surprised observers by calling for a vote on the previous question, thus cutting off further discussion. The bill passed the Senate, sixty-one to forty-nine. The following day opponents moved for a reconsideration of the measure and launched an attack on specific provisions of the bill. Experience had proved the system unworkable, according to one critic, and if it did work it would promote useless short lines, benefit the low country to the detriment of the mountainous regions, and lead to unsound financial operations. King replied that the safeguards in the act would protect the state from losses. He denounced the Central and the Georgia railroads as monopolistic enterprises which had profited from state aid in the past and now sought to forestall the building of competitive lines. He pointed to the exorbitant freight rates charged by the two companies where they had monopolistic control of the traffic of an area. The state could rid itself of this evil by encouraging competitive lines. King's forces maintained their majority on the motion to reconsider.[22]

The railroad question arose in several guises during the session, and from the debates and votes it is clear that King gave leadership to the back-country representatives who opposed the influence of Savannah and Augusta and of the two railroad lines originating in those cities. The vote on the state aid bill shows a pronounced geographical breakdown. The senators from the northern portion of Georgia were almost unanimous in their approval, and they were joined by a bloc of nine senators from southeastern counties.

Some strong support came from southwestern Georgia, and a few senators from midstate gave the bill their vote. The proponents of the bill came from roadless sections or from mountainous or swampy areas where railroad building presented difficult engineering problems and higher costs. In general, the seacoast and midstate areas, already served by existing rail lines or by sea and river transport, opposed state aid. King's principal opponent in the Senate debate was Alexander R. Lawton of Savannah; when the bill reached the floor of the House, Julian Hartridge, another Savannah resident, led the opposition. King's chief supporters in the discussion of the bill were Philemon Tracy of Macon and James Lindsay Seward of Thomasville. When a bill was presented to permit the Central Railroad to absorb a short subsidiary line, Tracy proposed an amendment requiring the Central to charge uniform freight rates on long and short hauls. James L. Seward even suggested that monopolistic control promoted such high charges that the legislature should assume general rate-making powers.[23]

As King had expected, his measure met defeat in the House of Representatives. But the setback in the lower house did not discourage him at all, he informed his son. "As you have seen, our measure in favour of State ade [sic] was lost in the House. *It can be carried next year.* The foundation of success has been laid."[24] On that optimistic note, the matter rested until the next session of the legislature.

King's leadership of the internal improvement forces in the Senate was reminiscent of his early career in state politics. Similarly, he showed enthusiasm about the movement for direct trade between Georgia and Europe, another subject of interest when he had formerly held a Senate seat. Between 1837 and 1839 he had been among the leaders of the commercial conventions that attempted to stimulate direct trade between Europe and the cotton ports of the South. By 1840 the commercial convention movement had withered away, but interest in the idea revived once more in the 1850's.[25] On December 9, 1859, King laid before the Senate a series of resolutions empowering the governor to appoint a commissioner to accompany the representatives of the Cotton Planters Association abroad and report on the possibilities of direct trade. By this maneuver King, who was already contemplating a trip to Europe on railroad business, may have been making a bid for the official standing that the appointment might have given him, but nothing more came of the resolutions after they were buried in

committee. Later, he lost confidence in this particular project for
direct trade and abandoned his tentative plans for a journey.

In addition to their legislative duties, the assembled politicians
were already looking forward to the national presidential contest
of the next year. Howell Cobb, the Georgian who was Secretary
of the Treasury in President Buchanan's cabinet, had been suggested as a possible successor to Buchanan, but an almost manda-
tory requirement for his candidacy would be the united support
of his home state's delegation at the national nominating convention. The Democratic members of the legislature obligingly re-
solved themselves into a Democratic caucus to name delegates to
the Democratic convention scheduled to meet in Charleston the
following April. Proponents of Cobb as the choice of Georgia's
Democrats were selected for the Charleston meeting by the caucus,
which also wrote resolutions endorsing the Buchanan administration. King spoke in favor of the resolutions endorsing Cobb, and
he was named as an alternate delegate to the convention.[26] But
Cobb's supporters in the legislature found that they had adopted
an unpopular course. The cry for a regular state convention, led
by anti-Cobb factions, became too strong to resist. At the convention to choose delegates to Charleston, Cobb's enemies managed
to name a different slate of representatives who were less sympathetic toward the ambitions of the Secretary of the Treasury. Disturbed over the prospect of contesting groups vying for Georgia's
seats at the convention, compromisers within the party arranged
for a merging of the two lists of delegates. The final roster contained approximately equal numbers of pro- and anti-Cobb members, and King was dropped from the list of alternates. Cobb, thus
deprived of the wholehearted support of his own state, saw his
hopes of nomination disappear.[27]

King the railroad promoter could hardly be expected to disregard the measures being advocated by King the legislator at
Milledgeville. Early in 1860 the senator from Glynn joined forces
with a group who were promoting a railroad line from central
Georgia to Brunswick. After one abortive beginning as the Fort
Valley Railroad Company, this project took form as the Macon
and Brunswick Railroad Company. It was envisioned as a com-
petitor with the Central Railroad for the traffic of central Georgia.
Local investors subscribed to enough stock to begin building the
first forty-seven miles of road. Obviously, if King could bring
about the passage of his railroad bill at the next session of the
legislature, the prospects of the company would be improved.

However, the promoters were unwilling to rely wholly on such a contingency, and they planned an elaborate scheme by which they hoped to secure capital in Europe. To present their project to European investors at some unspecified future time, they chose Thomas Butler King.[28]

Along with his involvement in local Georgia railroading, King retained an interest in the transcontinental project, although he had dropped out of the leadership of the Southern Pacific Railroad Company after the sale of the road in May 1858. In April 1859 a truce was effected between the rival claimants of the Southern Pacific assets, and Jeptha Fowlkes led a movement for still another reorganization. The various issues of stock, estimated to amount to $2,500,000, or double the value of the assets, were called in for reissue on a one-for-two basis. Salaries were to be reduced, dividends were to be foregone until one hundred miles of road were in operation, and all former transactions of the company were to be reviewed by a special board. Fowlkes gave place to J. Edgar Thompson, president of the Pennsylvania Railroad Company, as the leader of the reorganized corporation.[29] King had been following these moves with the deepest interest, for his financial hopes depended on the success of the company. Besides the stock which he had managed to retain, he held a note from Fowlkes acknowledging the indebtedness of the company to King for $32,500. If Congress should pass favorable legislation, his own prospects would rise with those of the Southern Pacific. Therefore, King journeyed to Washington to use his influence in support of a bill before Congress granting government aid to the Southern Pacific. Fowlkes was confident that the Senate would pass the bill, but doubtful about its success in the House. All possible pressure was needed, and timely action was essential. "The great point," wrote Lord King to his father, "is to get it up and passed if possible before the Charleston Convention for not one of the Presidential aspirants dares to oppose it."[30]

In 1860 the battle over routes continued to block the passage of any Pacific railroad bills in Congress. The principal railroad measure of the session was the Curtis Bill, which provided federal aid for a central route that split into two eastern branches. Andrew Jackson Hamilton, a Texas Democrat, protested against the Curtis Bill on the grounds that it discriminated against the South. He pointed out that the House had already passed the Morrill tariff and a homestead bill, both considered inimical to the interests of the South. If a third discriminatory bill was passed, he asserted, he would favor the secession of the Southern states from the Union. Recommitted, the Curtis Bill was amended to include Hamilton's provisions for aid to a Southern road, and the Southern Pacific was the only likely candidate for the aid that was proposed. While the fight over this bill was at its height, King was in Washington making "efforts among Southern men . . . to secure the passage of the Pacific Railroad bill. . . ."[31] Dr. Fowlkes was also actively engaged in lobbying, and one observer has left us a graphic picture of "the Doctor carrying all the while, at Washington and elsewhere, a hatful of stock, which he would transfer according to emergencies, saying 'there's enough for all, go in and work for the bill.' "[32] Even this openhanded policy failed to secure all the votes needed.

In April many of the congressmen packed their bags for the trip to Charleston, South Carolina, where the Democratic National Convention was scheduled to take place. With them went King, still the lobbyist for the transcontinental railroad. In Charleston he worked "to secure, in the Platform of the party, a resolution in favour of government aid to the P[acific] R[ail] R[oad] Co[mpany]—This I have done—"[33] The adoption of a Pacific railroad resolution by the Democrats augured well for some sort of railroad measure from the next Congress, for the Republicans, who controlled the House, were already on record as favoring such aid.[34]

King's pleasure over his success as a lobbyist was tempered by his alarm over the disruption of the Democratic party that began in Charleston. "I believe that the *safety of the Union* depends on the preservation of the *National* Democratic party," he asserted in a letter prepared for publication in Georgia; ". . . I can see no hope . . . except in the reunion and patriotic efforts of the Democratic party."[35] Privately, he was even more gloomy about the political future. He declined to predict what would happen, but he expressed the belief that the quarrels within the party might be patched up. Explaining their father's views to her younger brother, Georgia King wrote: "Father fears that the division at Charleston is but a prelude to a disunion of the States, worked by ambitious politicians—who forget the good of our country in trying to gain notoriety for themselves."[36] Since he entertained these views, it was logical that he should try to help lead those Georgians who favored the reassembling of the Democratic National Convention. Eventually, he served as one of the Georgia delegation to the Baltimore Convention that nominated

Breckinridge, but illness prevented his taking an active part in the proceedings. Illness likewise interrupted any plans he might have had for campaigning, but he did take time out from a visit to Newport, Rhode Island, to prepare a Democratic address. Stressing the economic interdependence of the sections, he praised the Union under which the states had so far lived in prosperity, but he insisted that it must remain the constitutional Union of former days, not the consolidated government advocated by the Republicans.[37]

For King the election-year summer was full of sorrows. Plagued by recurrent illness, he visited his ailing brother Henry in Pennsylvania. From there he was called to the sickbed of his brother Andrew in New York, where his own illness again prostrated him. When he and Andrew regained some measure of health, they went together to Saratoga to convalesce and to taste the pleasures of resort society, and from Saratoga, they went on to Newport, Rhode Island. Hardly had they settled once more in their New York hotel quarters, when Andrew King suffered a relapse and died. On the eve of the national election King was preoccupied with the duties of attending his dying brother, and making funeral arrangements and plans for Andrew's widow. These private cares continued to overshadow political developments until the time for the meeting of the Georgia legislature.[38]

The legislative session of 1860 in Milledgeville was a momentous one, for it would decide the state's course in the secession crisis. The people of Georgia were far from unanimous in their feelings about secession, and the leading political figures stood as far apart on the question as the unionist Alexander H. Stephens and the fire-eating Robert Toombs. Within the legislature the diversity of views was as great. Georgia King, who acted as her father's secretary for the session, wrote to her brother Floyd:

There will be a heavy battle & fight—Some men are for secession disunion—without deliberation—others, for *submission* to all things—You know dear Father takes the medium and calm course—Mr. Toombs is here—& also Gov. Johnson. I believe the former is for the most immediate and violent action. Mr. Styles (Wm. Carey) arrived yesterday—I saw him last night—he is for *revolution*—no convention—"break up the government"—march fifty men into Sav[annah]—seize the Custom House—march to W. seize the treasury—&c &c &c &c &c. These extreme men are to be managed on one side—and on the other there are some you can [']t *move*—they think any act on *our* part will be *unconstitutional*—[39]

To this divided body Governor Joseph E. Brown gave strong
leadership down the road to secession. In his annual message he
reviewed the measures taken during the past year to strengthen
the defenses of the state, and he recommended further military
preparations. In a special message he indicted the federal government for its aggression against the South, listed the injuries in-
flicted on Georgia, and recommended legislation empowering him
to call a convention on secession. He left no doubt about his own
views. With the election of the Black Republican ticket, he declared, the time has come for action. "The argument is exhausted."[40]

Like Brown, King was a seccessionist, although more moderate
in his views. In this crisis he acted the part of mediator and man-
ager, rather than prime mover. After the delivery of the special
message on the calling of a secession convention, King proposed
that the subject be referred to a special joint committee of the
House and Senate. To this committee, headed by King, were referred all the various resolutions on secession. On November 17,
1860, King presented the report of his committee, with legislation instructing the governor to call a convention which should
decide whether Georgia was to secede.[41]

Among the measures which Governor Brown proposed to the
legislature was one which was to affect King's life deeply during
the next fifteen months. On November 8, 1860, Brown strongly
recommended the establishment of a line of steamships between
Savannah and some important European port. He had been given
to understand that a company in Belgium had five steamers ready
to begin the run immediately if they should be guaranteed five
per cent on their capital investment. He asked for legislation
authorizing the guarantee and for power to appoint a commissioner to conclude an agreement with the company. A special
committee endorsed the recommendations, and the legislature
unanimously adopted the resolutions. It was clear from this action that most of the members expected a dissolution of the
Union to occur shortly.

Governor Brown, like the legislature, acted as if secession was
a foregone conclusion. On January 2, 1861, he gave the order for
state troops to seize Fort Pulaski, the principal fortification on the
Savannah River. On the same day he offered to King the appointment to arrange for direct steamship service between Savannah
and the Old World. This appointment was comprehended in a
broad commission to represent the State of Georgia in the courts

of Europe. Indicating his willingness to accept, King set about arranging his personal affairs for the trip abroad.[42]

To his past roles as politician, planter, lobbyist, and promoter, King now added a new part: would-be diplomat. There is no indication that the representative of the independent State of Georgia hesitated to choose the way of disunion. In the events at Charleston in the preceding summer he had seen signs of a dissolution of the Union, yet in the final attempt to patch up party differences he chose to go with the minority who rejected Stephen A. Douglas as the party candidate. Perhaps he hoped, like others, that secession would end in reunion, or that if persisted in it would be accomplished peacefully. No statement survives to show exactly when or why he took the path of secession. His plans throw no more light on the decision. His business schemes were based on the assumption that secession, if it occurred, would take place peacefully, yet before he left home he arranged for the evacuation of Retreat. He also refused to allow his daughter to accompany him, partly on the grounds that hostilities might begin.[43] From his plans and actions, the inferences are that in the summer of 1860 he reluctantly acquiesced in a course that he judged would lead to secession; thereafter, he hoped for peace but prepared for war.

For two years King's life had been full of personal losses, financial disappointments, and political setbacks. Financially and politically, gains offset many of the losses. His new connection with a railroad company in Georgia held a promise of substantial profits, and the signs of recovery of the Southern Pacific Railroad had once more raised his hopes for his investment in that company. Politically, he had tested his strength and defended his record in the First District, where he had found a surprising residue of his old political power. His failure to secure the nomination for Congress had been counterbalanced in part by his election to the state Senate. He had effected a reconciliation with the most powerful political figure in the state and had worked with him for the development of a system of state aid for railroads. He had charted a safe course through the political shoals of the election year, and in the legislature had helped guide the members toward united action. From Governor Brown he had received the appointment to a post of honor. It remained to be seen how well he could play the diplomat.

· XI ·

A Confederate in Europe

THE DULLEST prophet could have foretold that for Americans 1861 would be an eventful year. One by one the states of the deep South were declaring their withdrawal from the Union. If the leaders of secession had solemn thoughts about the gravity of their decisions, they must have felt equally a sense of high adventure, for they were undertaking to create a new nation. Until a confederacy of their own design took form, each state took up the powers, once assigned to a central government, to manage its own foreign relations, defense, and other affairs. It was in this interim, after Georgia seceded and before the Confederacy took shape, that Governor Brown appointed Thomas Butler King as a commissioner to Europe. Probably the closest parallel for the position he held was to be found in the colonial agencies of the pre-Revolutionary era. If the seceding states established themselves and formed a new government, King's appointment opened up for him the possibility of an entirely new career as the Laurens, or Adams, or Franklin of the new nation.

The swift movement of events precluded such a development. King's letters of appointment as representative of Georgia to the courts of Europe were issued on January 30, but within the week representatives of the seceding states had gathered in Montgomery, Alabama, to bring into being the Confederate States of America. King joined the move to Montgomery, and remained until the new government had begun operations. His chief concern, he wrote his son Mallery, was the passage of a postal bill for Atlantic steamers.[1] The act which the provisional Congress passed greatly resembled the one which King had sponsored twenty years before in the United States Congress. Under the law of March 1, 1861, the Confederate Postmaster General was authorized to contract with any line of steamers for transportation of the mails from the Confederate States of America to foreign ports. Compensation was to be limited to actual postage revenues, and postal rates were not to exceed those currently in force under the laws of the United States.[2] Obviously, this mail subsidy was aimed at accomplishing on the national level the same transatlantic steamer service which Governor Brown and the Georgia legislature had tried earlier to encourage.

While Georgia and the other Southern states were taking their first steps towards forming a confederacy, war was still only a possibility. Lincoln was inaugurated in Washington, and still no warlike action ensued. Meanwhile, the daily affairs of life went on, and King, despite a bout of illness, prepared for his journey to Europe. In addition to his official business, he had the private affairs of the Macon and Brunswick Railroad to promote. King and his associates in this company envisaged their line as a rival to the Central Railroad for the cotton traffic of central Georgia. Through local subscriptions they had obtained enough capital for the first forty-seven miles of road. The work was under way, and the initial section was expected to be completed by autumn. In order to complete the remaining 138 miles of track of their main line, they needed capital. The possibilities were limited: state aid, of the kind that King had sponsored in the legislature; bankers in the north, particularly New York; or foreign investment. In the existing political situation, neither state aid nor the New York money market could be counted on. King and his associates therefore prepared to float a loan of $5,000,000 abroad, in return for which they would repurchase shares of stock in Georgia and deliver control of the road to European investors. In addition, the promoters had an even more lucrative transaction in view. One fourth of the capital was to be invested in yellow pine timber lands in Georgia near the line of the railroad. The possession of these reserves, together with judicious purchases of existing stocks of yellow pine lumber, would give them a virtual monopoly on this valuable material, producing large immediate profits. King was designated as the agent to arrange for the loan, and to purchase iron rails for the completion of the section of road then being built, with a commission of five per cent on all transactions.[3]

When King left New York aboard the *Adriatic* on March 13,

1861, part of his commission was already outdated. He had been
instructed to ascertain if England, France, and Belgium would
recognize the sovereign State of Georgia before the formation of
a Southern confederacy, and the Confederate States of America
was already functioning as a government. Yet his instructions had
been broadly conceived as embracing "timely explanations" to
the "Governments, Bankers, Merchants, and Manufacturers of
Europe" on the significance of events in America "to the end that
prompt measures may be taken to conduct trade into its new
channel. . . ."[4] How and where this mission should be performed
was left up to the agent. As soon as the *Adriatic* docked in Southampton, King hurried up to London. Opinion in the English
capital was generally favorable to the Confederacy, he found, for
the prospect of free trade with the cotton states was enticing. "If I
had authority to negotiate," King wrote his son, "I think I could
have the Government of the Confederate States acknowledged in
ten days."[5] Lacking authority to speak for the Confederacy, he
soon left London and travelled to the Continent to pursue the
varied commissions, public and private, that had been entrusted
to him.

The speculative scheme of the Macon and Brunswick Railroad
came first, or at least furnished the opportunity for approaching
influential people. In Paris, King established contact with the
head of the banking house of Bellot des Minieres, Freres et Com-
pagnie. The choice was a logical one, for Minieres was currently
engaged in negotiations with the Southern Pacific Railroad Company for building new sections of road, negotiations that King
may very well have known of from his connection with the company. In addition, Minieres had become involved in other investments in the South, notably the James River and Kanawha
Company of Virginia. Minieres expressed great interest in the
Macon and Brunswick venture, but he did not commit himself
to the scheme. The encouraging letter embodying his views, it
might be noted, antedated the news of the bombardment of Fort
Sumter. This opening gambit with the French firm, however,
provided King with letters of introduction to important governmental circles in Belgium, to which country he now turned his
steps.[6]

In Belgium King sought out the company which had been suggested by Governor Brown as the recipient of the state subsidy for
establishing steamer service between Georgia and Europe. In
authorizing the offer the legislature had acted on the assumption

that the company was eager to begin direct trade, but their commissioner met a refusal when he tried to conclude an agreement.
King reported his failure in noncommittal words:

But the Belgians are a manufacturing, not a commercial people, and
while the Company are most anxious to send us their merchandise . . .
they have but little practical knowledge of, or experience in ocean
navigation, and especially the management of steamships.[7]

However, King reported that he was well received, and that public opinion in Belgium favored the Confederacy. What he did
not mention, although it was very much to the point, was the
fact that Confederate batteries opened fire on Major Anderson's
troops in Charleston harbor three days before King arrived in
Brussels. The news of this event, which probably reached Belgium
while he was consulting with financial leaders, could hardly fail
to put a completely different complexion on the question of
direct trade.

Unsuccessful in Belgium, King returned to Paris, which remained his headquarters for his stay in Europe.[8] Current developments in French politics made it possible for him to hope that he
might best achieve his ends in France. To carry out the aggressive
new commercial policy of Napoleon III, the French Corps Legislatif and Imperial Council had authorized the building of additional steamers for the existing subsidized French steamship lines
to New York and the West Indies. If King could bring about a
change of the termini of these routes to Southern ports, his mission would be more than successful, but it was a task that would
challenge the most adroit and experienced lobbyist.

Confronted with a general ignorance of American affairs, King
embarked on a campaign to educate the leaders of public opinion
in France. Gathering what statistics he could find, he produced
a memoir on steam navigation addressed to the Comte de Morny,
French Minister of Commerce. To accompany this memoir he
composed for the minister a letter in which he invited the French
to take the lead in securing the commerce of the Southern states.
He managed to have copies of the memoir in English and French
placed in the hands of the Emperor.[9] The French translation,
together with the letter to the Comte de Morny, was printed in
pamphlet form, and then distributed widely. Among the recip-
ients of this brochure King listed the members of the Imperial
Council, the Senate, and the Corps Legislatif; newspaper editors,
Chamber of Commerce, insurance companies, and leading French

manufacturers; members of the German Commercial Union; and the diplomatic corps in Paris.

King's letter to Morny was aimed specifically at securing the establishment of a French-subsidized line of steamships to Savannah and the extension of a French-West Indies line to New Orleans. He dwelt in glowing terms on the possibilities open to French enterprise. The passenger fares alone he estimated at more than $5,000,000 yearly. To this would be added the mail subsidies for all postal service between the Confederacy and Europe. He pointed out the ease with which existing lines of communication in both France and the Confederacy could be integrated into a system under French control. Most of all, he emphasized the new opportunities in international trade. The South had espoused free trade and had opened her coasting trade to foreigners. A total export trade which he estimated to be worth $300,000,000 was seeking a new channel. Simply by changing the termini of the French steamship lines to New Orleans and Savannah, France could secure the commercial leadership in the two leading cotton ports of the Confederacy. "Cannot France be persuaded to take the lead and reap the advantage?"[10]

Whether it was due to King's plea or not, the French transatlantic steamer policy was changed. The Corps Legislatif approved the extension to New Orleans of the established Bordeaux-West Indies run. The committee considering the steamship subsidy recommended further that in the light of American developments either Norfolk or Savannah be chosen as the terminus of the line of steamships from Le Havre. This change was also accepted, without debate, by the legislators.[11] In the final analysis, since Napoleon III was unwilling to break the blockade to enforce such a trade, this minor change in the French subsidy system can hardly be regarded as important; nevertheless, King's persuasiveness must receive some of the credit for bringing about one of the few official actions in Europe that looked to the establishment of the Confederate States of America.

While King was at work on the Continent, the official Confederate commissioners arrived in England. William Lowndes Yancey, Pierre Adolphe Rost, and Ambrose Dudley Mann, "armed with a dissertation on state sovereignty in their right pockets, and a sample of New Orleans middling upland cotton in their left,"[12] made their first bid for recognition by Queen Victoria's government. Although they had interviews with Lord John Russell, official channels remained closed to these "diplomatic representatives" of an unrecognized government. Yet King lacked even the dubious status that a Confederate appointment would have conferred. His daughter Georgia went so far as to draft letters to Jefferson Davis, Alexander H. Stephens, and Robert Toombs, appealing to them to give her father some sort of appointment under the Confederate government which would regularize his position abroad.[13] Her plea, if it reached them, fell on deaf ears; King remained only a commercial agent and an emissary from Georgia to the courts of Europe.

Nebulous as King's diplomatic appointment was, he exploited it to the full in presenting the case of the Confederacy to European governments. To Edouard-Antoine Thouvenel, French Minister of Foreign Affairs, King wrote a long public letter. Government, he argued, is based on the consent of the governed, and the people of the South no longer consented to the government in Washington. The Union had been a compact among the states, and the seceding states were merely resuming the sovereign powers which they had delegated to the federal government. The government in Washington was now waging "a war of conquest and subjugation on the absurd pretext of preserving the Union."[14] King then launched an attack on Abraham Lincoln and accused the President of duplicity. By his violation of the Constitution and of the pledges he had given, Lincoln had forfeited all claims to the sympathy of Europeans. In a more telling economic argument, King sought to arouse Thouvenel to the threat which the blockade of the South constituted for French interests. He warned that the cotton crop would soon be arriving at the ports of the Confederacy. Cotton "is as necessary to the working of the spindles and looms of France and England as bread is to feed those who operate them. Has Mr. Lincoln a right to forbid the supply of either?"[15] The war had originated in the attempt of people of the Northern states to force a high tariff on the South, and this Northern policy, he assured Thouvenel, was aimed at world supremacy in commerce and manufacturing. "This war is, consequently, a war on the industry of France and England, under false pretenses."[16] In this letter King presented Thouvenel with arguments emphasizing the recurrent themes of Confederate diplomats: that secession was legally and morally justified and that France, from self-interest alone, should maintain trade relations with the South.

Far more elaborate was the letter which the diplomatic representative of Georgia wrote to Lord John Russell, Queen Victoria's Secretary of State for Foreign Affairs. Like the letter to Thouvenel, this was designed for public circulation rather than as a bona fide bid for the recognition of Georgia. King began with a brief history of the formation of the Constitution of the United States, in order to prove his contention that secession was a legal right of the Southern states. They exercised this right, he asserted, only as a last resort, the final answer to repeated aggressions on the part of the Northern states. The political separation grew out of the differences in the economic interests of the sections. This line of argument led to an outline of the development of manufacturing, particularly in the northeastern United States, and a sketch of the tariff policies of the federal government since the War of 1812. King denounced the policy of tariff protection, and emphasized the role of the South in resisting the protectionists for over thirty years. With the election of the candidate of the protectionist party, the South, "finding it useless to prolong the contest, has withdrawn from the Union."[17]

Having explained the principles and causes of secession, King proceeded to an analysis of the economic resources and relationships of the two sections. Using tables of figures derived from the 1850 census and estimates for 1860, he touched briefly on the relative state of manufacturing, commerce, and agriculture in the North and the South, and arrived at the conclusion that the economy of the United States rested on the agricultural wealth of the South. The shipping tonnage of the nation, for example, had kept almost exact pace with the increase of the cotton supply. The South was the producing section; the North derived its economic existence from carrying Southern produce and supplying Southern needs for manufactured products. Resorting once more to tables of statistics, King arrived at the figure of $213,000,000 in yearly profits wrested by the North from the South. Now that the South had seceded, this profit lay waiting for the enterprise of European merchants, carriers, and manufacturers.[18]

King continued his letter to Russell with an almost lyrical disquisition on cotton—the nature of the plant, the productivity of slave labor, the improvements that had taken place in cultivation, and the capability of the South to supply the expanding demand for cotton indefinitely. After a recapitulation of the economic resources of the South, he repeated his direct appeal:

This vast commerce . . . is now offered to the manufacturing and commercial nations of Europe. Will they accept it, or will they permit Mr. Lincoln's blockading squadron to forbid the intercourse?[19]

He followed this question with a pointed warning that if Europe was to receive any of the cotton crop of 1861, commercial relations must be established immediately.

In conclusion, King assured Russell of the falsity of Federal representations that the South could not maintain its independence. He had indicated in his letter the economic strength of the Southern states. He needed only to add that the Confederacy contained more than a million and a quarter men between the ages of eighteen and forty-five, enough to withstand the assault of any number of Federal troops that Lincoln might send against them.

In addition to these appeals to governmental officials, which served merely as propaganda vehicles, King employed his time in preparing other articles for newspapers. Of these, only one, entitled "The American Blockade," survived in draft form among his papers.[20] It reads like an international lawyer's brief, beginning with a technical discussion of what constituted contraband of war, together with a brief history of the policy of the United States. King came to the conclusion that the United States had heretofore always adhered to the principle of "liberty of commerce to neutrals except in places invested, besieged and blockaded."[21] He then proceeded to the definition of a blockade and cited writers on international law to prove that a blockade must be a fact, not a mere proclamation. This requirement, he pointed out, had been reaffirmed by a congress of European nations in the Declaration of Paris in 1856. He then applied the principles of the foregoing section to the conditions existing in American waters in 1861 and showed that the blockade proclaimed by President Lincoln did not conform to the rules of international law. By this illegal blockade, European countries were being deprived of their rights as neutrals, and some of their citizens were suffering hardships as a consequence. Because of the interruption of the cotton supply from the South, some districts of England and France already faced distress, and desolation was in prospect. Quoting French newspapers of September and October 1861, King pointed to the signs of depression in the textile centers of France and England, Lyons and Manchester. Mills in the English city had found it necessary to adopt a three-day week to conserve the supply of cotton. According to King's estimates, between 130,000

and 140,000 French workmen were affected by the cotton shortage; in England, he estimated the number indirectly touched
would exceed four million. The inescapable conclusion was that
neither England nor France could afford to allow such important
segments of industry to come to grief because of an illegal
blockade.

By the publication of these articles and letters, the Commissioner from Georgia had assumed the role of a Confederate
propagandist rather than a commercial agent for his state. It
would be hard to justify his activities except in the broadest
interpretation of his instructions. Yet in his propaganda efforts
King was attempting in some measure to fill the vacuum left by
a decision of the official Confederate commissioners. Shortly after
their arrival in London, Yancey, Rost, and Mann decided that
they could best serve the Confederate cause by refraining from
open attempts to influence public opinion through the daily
press. When Rost arrived in Paris to take up his duties there,
King tried to persuade him that the official commissioners should
undertake propaganda efforts. Rost informed the Georgian that
he had neither instructions nor funds to carry on such work.
Furthermore, he took the position that Napoleon III was an ab-
solute monarch who would make his decisions without regard for
public opinion.[22] King disagreed decidedly. He, too, was without
specific instructions and funds, but he made good use of the resources available to him. He kept in touch with other Confederate
sympathizers and propagandists as far away as Moscow and Lis-
bon.[23] He argued forcefully and planned the distribution of his
writings where they might exert a wide influence. He extolled the
commercial opportunities presented by a new nation pledged to
free trade principles, and he attacked the enemy on a vulnerable
point, the doubtful legality of the blockade. Whether European
public opinion could have been won to the side of the South is
an unanswerable question; certainly it was not to be won by inaction. In comparison with the official representatives, King
showed great initiative and energy.

Insofar as public opinion can be gauged, sympathy for the Confederacy and antagonism toward the United States grew during
the months that King was active in the propaganda field. In
France the change was particularly noticeable in official circles.
The Emperor moved from vaguely pro-Union views to such definite pro-Confederate leanings that in July he suggested to Lord

Cowley that he was ready to intervene if the British would support him.[24] No doubt the progress of events in America and other considerations determined this shift of opinion, but some credit may be allowed to the Southerners abroad who argued the case for recognition.[25]

In a sense, every Confederate in Europe was a representative of his country, and by his conduct could engage the sympathies of his hosts and associates. Henry Adams, a member of the staff at the American legation in London, expressed the concern he felt over the situation in England. Every Southerner abroad, he wrote to his brother Charles Francis, "is inspired by the idea of independence and liberty, while we are in a false position. . . . They have an object and they act together."[26] Confederates in Europe won so much sympathy that the Lincoln administration organized a group of distinguished private citizens to try to counteract the Confederate propaganda, and John Bigelow was made consul in Paris primarily to take charge of the battle for European sympathy.[27] Thomas Butler King, as one of the earliest and most active advocates of the cause of the South, deserves to share the credit for the successes that even the enemies of the Confederacy acknowledged.

King pursued his independent course and wrote as he pleased. He was answerable only to Governor Brown and the legislature of Georgia for the fulfillment of his mission. On the practical side, however, he was also answerable to the printers and translators of his pamphlets for services that had never been contemplated in his commission. Originally, King had expected to remain in Europe about three months, defraying his expenses and taking a fee for his services from the $3,000 which the legislature had appropriated, the greater part of which he converted into negotiable form before he left New York. At the end of June, when he had already exceeded his planned stay by several weeks, he considered drawing on his own resources for additional funds, but he found that drafts on firms in the Confederacy were not being accepted by the usual sources of credit. By this time his first publishing bills had been presented, both of them for relatively small printings. In July the demands of creditors were becoming insistent, and a suit was being threatened over one bill. Finally, King resorted to an unauthorized draft on Governor Joseph E. Brown of Georgia for another $2,500, which the Governor was generous enough to honor out of his contingent fund. Perhaps King's move at the end of September from the Hotel Montaigne to a furnished apartment was an attempt to cut his expenses; at any rate, his bill for lodging was lowered to less than half the former cost.[28]

By the middle of October, King had still not carried out the specific instructions to conclude an agreement for a subsidized line of steamers between Europe and Georgia. When his negotiations with the Belgian-American Company failed, he had seized the opportunity to influence the plans of the French government and had brought about a significant change in the future projects of the subsidized French companies. In addition, he canvassed other possibilities by opening a correspondence with English steamship companies. Finally, on November 1, 1861, he concluded a contract with the Liverpool firm of Frederick Sabel and Company to establish regular weekly steamship service between Liverpool and Savannah within six months after the removal of the blockade, with a subsidy from the state of Georgia not to exceed $100,000 yearly for five years.[29] A month later King went aboard a vessel in Southampton, England, outward bound for Cuba, where he would take passage for his blockaded homeland.

King arrived in Cuba in December 1861, and waited approximately a month for a ship which would take him to the Confederacy. He left Havana on January 20, 1862, aboard the *Calhoun,* a light-draft steamer bound for New Orleans with a cargo of coffee, powder, medical supplies, and firearms. The *Calhoun* had seen service as a Confederate naval vessel, but had been converted to blockade running, carrying false registry papers as the *Cuba.* At daybreak of the third day of the run from Havana, as the *Calhoun* was standing into the delta of the Mississippi, she was sighted by a ship of the blockading fleet, the *U.S.S. Colorado.* The *Calhoun* headed for shoal water in East Bay where the *Colorado* could not follow, but Captain Bailey of the blockading frigate ordered two schooners to give chase. With the benefit of a strong northerly wind, the *Samuel Rotan* pulled alongside the *Calhoun* within an hour. By that time most of the firearms had been jettisoned, and the passengers and crew had taken to the boats, leaving the steamer on fire in two places. Boarding parties from the *Samuel Rotan* succeeded in putting out the fires before they damaged the remaining cargo materially. Besides the valuable goods that were saved, Captain Bailey could report the capture of the baggage and papers of Thomas Butler King, a Confederate commissioner. His men gave chase to the fleeing passengers and crew, but failed to overtake them.[30]

The differences that twelve months had wrought in King's personal fortunes were striking. In January 1861 he was a Georgia planter and railroad promoter, preparing to leave a country uneasily at peace; he reached the Confederacy a year later a fugitive from Federal guns. His Sea Island home had been abandoned to the mercies of military action, and a new plantation awaited him in the wire-grass region of the mainland. His children, united at home in 1861, were now scattered over three states; his four sons were in the army, and his daughter Georgia had married a soldier without waiting for his consent. His nephew James, with whom the two younger daughters were staying, urged their father to come to Linda Plantation after the labors of the past year, but for King personal comfort had to wait. From New Orleans, where the fleeing passengers of the *Calhoun* found refuge, he journeyed directly to Richmond. Of his activities in the Confederate capital he wrote only vaguely: "My stay here has been much longer than I intended, but as I had suggested to the Government very important measures I have been detained to make explanations . . . ."[31] Undoubtedly, he was using his experience in Europe to give weight to his counsels to Confederate leaders, and it seems likely that the important measures were concerned with the need to publicize the Confederate cause. In April, Secretary of State Judah P. Benjamin wrote to John Slidell, the new Confederate Commissioner in Paris: ". . . it becomes absolutely essential that no means be spared for the dissemination of truth, and for a fair exposition of our condition and policy before foreign nations."[32] Edwin de Leon, with whom King had been in contact in France, was designated the official propagandist for the Confederacy in Europe.[33] It is possible that King used a part of his time in Richmond to seek a position of honor in the permanent government that was inaugurated in February. If so, he kept his own counsel and revealed no feelings of dejection over his failure to receive an appointment. With the approach of summer he turned his steps toward Georgia and the new plantation in Ware County which he had not yet seen.[34]

· XII ·

The Last Battle

NOT UNTIL he returned to Georgia late in the spring of 1862 did the full impact of the war touch Thomas Butler King. Home was no longer the plantation house on Saint Simons, but rather the cottage in Ware County to which the planting operations had been moved during his absence in Europe. In the winter of 1860-61, King had foreseen the possibility that the family would be forced to abandon Retreat. His acquaintance with naval affairs, the vulnerability of the Georgia coast, the location of Retreat—all made him appreciate the threat of hostile action in case of war. While he made preparations for his diplomatic venture, therefore, he corresponded with his eldest son about the necessity of transporting the family and slaves to the mainland if military action threatened.[1] Although no definite place of refuge was picked before he left, the choice of Mallery King fell upon the same area that he and his father had visited the preceding year in search of new cotton land.

With careful planning, the younger Kings accomplished their removal from Saint Simons gradually. With the news of the bombardment of Fort Sumter, Florence, Virginia, and Georgia King began packing their belongings. Valuables were buried, pictures and books were shipped to Savannah for storage, and the three Misses King, together with the children of the slaves, crossed over to the mainland plantation where their sister, Hannah King Couper, resided.[2] Even the Couper home was too close to the sea to afford any real security, and the arrival of a blockading vessel off the coast set Florence and Virginia King once more on the move. They took refuge with their cousin James King and with friends at Tebeauville, some sixty-five miles inland near the new plantation.

Of all this moving, and the concurrent activities of his sons in the army, King received only fragmentary reports while he was in Paris. He did learn, by her own hand, why Georgia did not accompany her sisters to Tebeauville. Among the young West Pointers who had resigned their commissions in the United States Army to cast their lot with the Confederacy, she had met one, Major William Duncan Smith, whom she found to be "a very noble hearted, generous man."[3] She had accepted his proposal of marriage, and despite the failure to receive any approving words from her father the couple went ahead with their plans for an early wedding. From Paris, King did send them his blessing, but it was many months later that Georgia King Smith heard of the missing letter. She was the first of his daughters to see King upon his return, when she went to Richmond to take care of him while he recovered from an attack of food poisoning. Her husband, they discovered, was the nephew of one of King's oldest personal and political friends, F. M. Robertson of Charleston, South Carolina. By the first of May, King had recuperated enough to make the journey to Tebeauville, and Georgia rejoined her husband, now Brigadier General Smith, at his new command in Charleston.[4]

Regarding the new plantation at Tebeauville, King had received conflicting reports. Mallery King, who had borne the responsibility for management of the slaves during the past three years, thought that the land was good, "tho' I don't suppose we will be able to make more than provisions the first year."[5] Lord King was more enthusiastic after spending a long convalescent leave there:

In comparison with other planters, and especially considering that we are all in the army, I think we have been very fortunate. . . . All our negroes are well housed and there is a fair prospect of making provisions the present year. . . . Mall deserves the credit firstly Wm Couper & the Girls next.[6]

At least there were sure to be congenial neighbors, for Tebeauville was the refugee area for many of the planters of the Altamaha. Hannah King Couper, whose husband was trying to supervise both his own and the Kings' removal to Tebeauville, was more aware of the drawbacks to their new situation:

there are hundreds now without meat & worse with *no salt*—And here are thousands of negros run away from the coast into these woods—

who cant possibly make any thing like provisions enough for another
year.[7]

The King slaves seemed content with their new quarters and
were behaving well "& there was not one who did not eagerly ask
'When are we to see Mausa?' "[8]

It was to this new establishment that King turned his steps
after his illness in Richmond. A small cottage had been built near
the railroad line from Tebeauville to Waresboro, and here his
eldest unmarried daughter, Florence, kept house for him. To the
great satisfaction of his daughters, he took up the challenges presented by the new situation and began to show an interest in
making the new plantation pay for itself. Some of the hands were
already at work cultivating provision crops; King now sent others
out into the extensive pine forests of the neighborhood to produce turpentine. He anticipated that this would prove to be a
marketable crop in a Confederacy short of manufactured products, but the demand for the naval stores turned out to be very
uncertain, and the returns did not match the income that the
Kings were accustomed to receive on their usual cotton crop. In
the face of war-imposed difficulties, King failed to salvage even
a living from his "planting" operations.[9]

The following year saw one more step in the breakup of the
King menage as an economic unit. To provide a cash income,
King turned to the practice of selling the labor of the slaves, like
other slaveowners who had sought refuge in the Tebeauville area.
In August 1863 he suspended turpentine production and hired
twenty-two hands to the government. He engaged a farmer of the
neighborhood to live on the place and supervise the production
of a corn crop, "and (which is very important) begin a regular
system of spinning and weaving clothes for the negros."[10] By hir-
ing a slave to the government, Georgia King Smith explained to
her brother, "we can get $25 pr month & have him fed—& then if
he runs to the Yankees get $2500 from the Government—"[11]The
$6,600 yearly income from this arrangement was expected to sup-
ply the cash to maintain the family and the slaves who remained
at Tebeauville. Under the impact of war, the way of life that
King had known at Retreat had disappeared.

By the end of the summer of 1862 King felt that he could leave
his new home for a trip to the Madison Springs resort, before
going on to see Governor Brown. There was still the unfinished
business of a report to the governor and the legislature on the

results of his trip to Europe, and he no longer held a seat in the Senate which would enable him to look out for his own interests. Governor Brown, however, endorsed his report, and in November recommended that King be relieved of the unexpected additional expenses that his prolonged stay in France had entailed. The Governor's recommendations were referred to a special committee headed by King's friend A. E. Cochran, who had succeeded him as senator from Glynn County. Cochran's committee issued a report that complimented King highly for the carrying out of his mission. The contract which King had made with Sabel and Company of Liverpool was regarded as a complete fulfillment of his instructions, but was rejected by the legislature because of the praiseworthy change which had been effected in French steamship policy. The Commissioner's triumphs over difficulties were recounted in brief but glowing terms, and the highest praise was reserved for his propaganda efforts. His publications, the committee declared, "have done more to place the real political and commercial resources of this country before the European people than any acts or papers which have fallen under their observation during our troubles."[12] The appropriation for additional funds went through without opposition, and shortly before Christmas Cochran was able to write King the good news that $2,900 now stood to his credit in the treasury, adding:

Mr. Hester in the House & Mr. Seward in the Senate made speaches ... to the effect that your services to the country in Europe had been of more value than all which had been done by the representatives of the Confederacy. I heard Ex Gov. Johnson & Vice President Stephens say as much. . . .[13]

Such expressions of appreciation from former rivals in politics would have been gratifying, if they had not arrived in the wake of bad news from the battlefront.

With the outbreak of the war, all four of King's sons had volunteered for service in the Confederate armies, and still another soldier was added to the family by Georgia's marriage to General William D. Smith. None of the Kings had been badly injured in the early engagements in which they participated, but death struck quickly in the second year of the war. First came the news that General Smith was dead, felled not by bullets, but by a long illness. Then, in December the casualty lists from Fredericksburg bore the name of Henry Lord Page King, killed while carrying dispatches as a member of General McLaws's staff in the fighting for Marye's Heights. His body was brought back to Georgia by his servant, and on Christmas Day 1862 was laid to rest in the graveyard at Christ Church.[14] From the burial, King went on to Richmond to collect the effects of his dead son, and to catch a glimpse of his son Floyd, who managed to get a ten-day leave from his duties. Floyd was shocked by the change in his father's appearance since they had last seen one another, and wrote warningly to Mallery King that their father was "breaking fast."[15]

Despite his grief, King found the air of the Confederate capital stimulating. Old friends, along with some old enemies, sat in the seats of power, and he made new acquaintances. To the distinguished visiting Guards officer, Colonel Fremantle, he appeared "very agreeable and well informed."[16] The two men met by chance at the hotel, and King introduced the visitor to the social circle that revolved about Mrs. Robert C. Stanard, whose house in Richmond was "one unremittent salon."[17] But surely this bustling capital would be even more enjoyable if he, too, held an official position. By June King had decided to seek a seat in Congress, much to the distress of his widowed daughter, who thought it unsuitable for her father to enter the lists against "a young man scarcely tried. . . ."[18] King was not swayed by her protest.

The first task of the prospective candidate was to place his name before the public for nomination. During the last week in June the *Savannah Republican* carried in its columns an exchange of public letters. Representative citizens of ten counties of the First District wrote to King, asserting that the country needed his experience to help guide its destinies and requesting permission to propose his name at any convention that might be held. With a faint show of reluctance, their correspondent agreed to the suggestion. The following day the same group of men issued an invitation to the voters of the district to send delegates to a convention to be held July 23, 1863, at Blackshear, Georgia. This move was quickly countered by the incumbent of the First District seat, Julian Hartridge. He made public a letter declaring himself a candidate and opposing the call for a convention. The exigencies of the times and the absence of many voters on army duty made a convention impracticable, he contended. He proposed to make no campaign, but he agreed to render a public account of his services to any voters who invited him to address them.[19]

During the ensuing month the supporters of the two candidates took up the cudgels for the man of their choice. Some backers of King attacked Hartridge for evading the traditional nominating convention and for speaking throughout the district when he had declared that the times would not justify a campaign. A defender of Hartridge, on the other hand, decried the convention because it was inspired by King and favored only by his supporters. County meetings that endorsed Hartridge passed resolutions against the convention, while most of the counties that appointed delegates to the convention expressed a preference for King.[20]

Since Hartridge's supporters boycotted the convention, King's unanimous nomination at Blackshear could hardly be called surprising. The platform of the convention, embodied in an address to the people of the district, accused the incumbent, Hartridge, and the Confederate Congress generally with "criminal neglect or bungling mismanagement."[21] The first charge against the Congress was its failure in the realm of finances; until recently, no taxes had been levied to give stability to the currency. As a result, inflation had raised the cost of government and the cost of living, yet speculators in cotton had profited enormously. To remedy the previous failures, the writer of the address proposed a government monopoly on the cotton crop. After this opening criticism, the address listed other deficiencies of the Congress: its weak naval policy, the practice of keeping secret the sessions of the House of Representatives, and the inadequate pay scale for the army. The broadside closed with a tribute to King, emphasizing his twenty years of legislative experience.

Despite the difficulties of wartime, the campaign was waged with enthusiasm at the hustings and in the press. King and Hartridge were joined by another candidate, Charles H. Hopkins, who made his bid for election mainly on the question of raising the pay of soldiers. All three candidates publicly answered a series of involved questions propounded by "A Citizen." In simplified form, these inquiries were: whether the country should continue the war or seek an early peace, whether the pay of the soldier should be increased, and whether an alternative to the independence of the Confederacy or submission to the United States should be considered. In posing the last question, "A Citizen" seemed to have had in mind some attachment to England or France in a dependent or protectorate status. Each of the candidates rejected the third question as ridiculous or irrelevant and advocated an increase in the pay of the soldier. On the question of continuing

the war, some differences of attitudes appeared. Hopkins declared
himself in favor of the earliest possible peace with honor, without
amplifying his stand. Hartridge called for the aggressive prosecution of an offensive war as the only way to an honorable peace.
King favored a cessation of hostilities, but at the same time emphasized the need for a vigorous prosecution of defensive warfare
until the Lincoln government sought peace.[22] In addition to an-
swering these questions, both King and Hartridge spoke widely
throughout the district, each appealing for votes on the record of
his past services to the state. Even though bad health forced King
to interrupt his canvass, his daughters expressed increasing confidence in his success during the last six weeks before the election.[23]

The final returns of the October election were delayed more
than two weeks, awaiting the arrival of all the absentee votes of
the soldiers. On the face of the first returns, Hartridge seemed
sure of reelection, since he had carried Chatham County by a
margin of eight to one, and Chatham accounted for nearly one-
fourth of the total vote. It soon became apparent that King had
won a majority of the counties of the interior of the district, and
Hartridge's victory became more doubtful. The vote for Hopkins
was negligible. When the last of the absentee votes from the
armies in Tennessee and Virginia had been counted, Hartridge's
majority was reduced to fifteen votes out of a total of more than
six thousand ballots.[24]

King's ambition and temperament alike precluded his accept-
ing meekly a defeat by such a narrow margin, particularly when
ample grounds appeared for a contest of the election. At its next
session the Chatham County grand jury denounced "the practice
of buying and selling votes at elections, a practice which is said
to have been not uncommon in years past, but which this Grand
Jury believed was carried on, with scarce an attempt at conceal-
ment, at the State election in October last."[25] Announcing that
open bribery was practised, with the price ranging between five
and ten dollars a vote, the Grand Jury returned several indict-
ments. King, who had amassed a heavy majority outside of Chatham, could hardly fail to profit from a successful prosecution of
these cases. However, a contest would have to await the meeting
of the next Congress, and he bided his time until the spring of
1864. Meanwhile, he had shown some of his old power as a vote-
getter, and his name would be kept before the public by the
senatorial election that was scheduled to take place when the
legislature met in November.

More than once when he was a congressman, King had cast a longing eye in the direction of Senator John M. Berrien's seat in the United States Senate, but he had never dared openly to challenge the elder statesman of the Whig Party in Georgia. Now, when he himself had taken on an elder statesman role, King's earlier ambition entered the realm of possibility. Herschel V. Johnson, whose term was expiring in 1863, had originally accepted the senatorship reluctantly and had served unenthusiastically.[26] Yet he consented to stand again for election, and his known political following made him the favored candidate. State sectionalism, as was so frequently the case, found an outlet in the senatorial selection. Both Johnson and Benjamin H. Hill, the other Georgia Senator, represented the upcountry agricultural interest; the seaboard area, in the opinion of residents, deserved a representative of its own. The *Savannah Republican* proposed the name of a man whose wisdom, the editor felt, fitted him to be Johnson's successor, whose experience in business and naval matters had prepared him to represent the commercial interests of Savannah— Thomas Butler King.

In accordance with the usual custom, King and the other senatorial hopefuls were invited to take seats on the floor of the legislature, and some of them addressed that body unofficially. In the balloting that took place November 25, 1863, the votes were divided among eight candidates. Herschel V. Johnson led the first ballot with seventy-nine adherents, but Robert Toombs, Lucius J. Gartrell, and Thomas Butler King all showed substantial strength. On the second ballot Johnson increased his lead over the other candidates, and on the third he received a majority of the votes cast, most of King's original supporters acquiescing in the majority choice. Even so, King could derive satisfaction from the knowledge that he could make a respectable showing in a contest with some of the foremost political leaders of Georgia and far surpass the once popular Howell Cobb.[27]

Defeated in his bid for the Senate, King reverted to the earlier plan of contesting the election of Hartridge the preceding October. With the evidence of corruption already before the courts, he might have been successful, but before the battle was joined he found himself engaged with a more deadly enemy. In March, sickness forced him to postpone his journey to Richmond. After a partial recovery in April, he fell so gravely ill that his son Floyd applied for compassionate leave to go to his father's bedside. Once more King began to recuperate, only to suffer another relapse. On

May 10, 1864, he died at his home in Waresboro, Georgia. His last hours were peaceful ones, and he was able to speak consoling words to the daughters who nursed him and to leave his blessing for his absent sons.[28]

So died Thomas Butler King, planter, promoter, and politician. With his boyhood in Massachusetts, his youth in Pennsylvania, and his activities in Georgia, California, and Texas, King typified the restless American who pushed into new areas to give political and economic organization to a continental domain. At the same time that the industrial revolution altered the economy of King's native state, the rise of cotton culture based on slavery fixed the course of development in his adopted home, Georgia. Steam power worked another revolution in transportation, and rails came to replace waterways as the carriers of passengers and goods. King's business affairs and his public career kept him in the forefront of these economic developments. Political parties took form and disintegrated, and King the State Rights man, the Whig, the Know Nothing, and the Democrat had a voice in governmental decisions for three decades. When the Southern states seceded and tried to establish a new nation, King the Georgian reported the resolutions calling for the secession convention and then served as his state's representative in Europe. Into whatever role he played he poured his best energies, his considerable talents, and his unquenchable spirits.

As a planter, King was a significant figure less for what he did than for what he was: one of that extremely small group of slave-owners who counted their dependents in the hundreds. He was the head of a large plantation, the ultimate expression of the cotton economy at its fullest development. Socially and economically he stood at the top of a complex organization that ranged down from himself through his family, the tutor and governess, the overseer, the house servants, and the driver, to the field hands. Under his supervision the interdependent members of this economic unit supplied themselves with the necessities of life and produced the cotton crop which would bring in the cash for additional needs or desires. The principal beneficiaries of the system, of course, were the owner and his family, and the Kings in many ways embodied a way of life which was regarded as the ideal of the plantation South. The large family remained a closely knit group, dependent on one another for amusement and society, working at their assigned supervisory tasks within the framework of the family. They enjoyed abundance and leisure, but their activities were simple and close to the land which nourished them, rather than luxurious and carefree. For the most part, they lived in rural isolation, save for summer visits to resorts in the South, or "at the North." The master, on the other hand, mixed freely in the affairs of the outside world, pursuing his business interests or holding public office. Towards the other members of the economic unit, particularly the slaves who performed the basic labor, the Kings maintained an attitude compounded of several elements, two ingredients being a sense of responsibility and a feeling of affection.

King's planting experiences over forty years illustrate some of the characteristics of the plantation system, especially its wastefulness and tendency to expand. When he first undertook the management of Retreat in the 1820's, he embarked on a program of expansion. Over the course of ten years he added to his holdings until he owned some 20,000 acres and 355 slaves. Few planters of the time could match him in the scope of his operations, and it was fitting that at the end of the 1830's he should emerge as a spokesman for planters. The master of Retreat and Waverley plantations and the owner of the Middleton Barony took the lead in seeking to alter the cotton marketing system by promoting direct trade with Europe and by changing the system of credit and sale. The proposals which he and other planters put forward, along with their prosperity, disappeared in the depression that followed the Panic of 1837. Even after the heavy financial losses that he suffered, King still belonged to the class of large planters, since he remained the supervisor of his wife's estate. Under his direction, Retreat continued for twenty years to supply the needs of some 150 people.

Although he was no agricultural reformer, King was alert to the need for diversified farming and careful husbanding of resources. He eagerly adopted new methods and improvements which would increase the productivity of the plantation. According to the census records of 1850 and 1860, Retreat was the most productive of the Saint Simons cotton plantations, yet at the same time it was well balanced with livestock and products for home consumption. The Retreat orchards were well known locally. Nevertheless, the exhaustion of the soil and the increasingly inferior position of this "old" plantation in competition with newer and more fertile lands were revealed as the years passed. In their efforts to increase production, the Kings in the 1850's acquired more land on the island, and they seriously considered moving west. The Civil War merely hastened the death of Retreat as a plantation, and King's war-time experience on the mainland showed how completely the society and economy in which he had lived was disintegrating under the impact of war.

King the promoter was a pioneer in the development of railroads. The Brunswick and Altamaha Canal and Railroad Company and the Brunswick and Florida Railroad were typical of the wild expansion of the Jacksonian era that ended in the financial debacle of 1837. To these schemes King contributed an enthusiastic leadership and a talent for publicity. He added refinements to the projects for exploiting a natural advantage, and he attracted outside capital to the development of Brunswick. His financial misfortunes resulted from a combination of unsound financing and the downfall of the general economy. His companies suffered from the basic instability that characterized the railroad and banking mania of the 1830's.

King's later financial adventure with the Southern Pacific Railroad had a curiously repetitive quality. Once more he grasped the opportunity of exploiting a geographic advantage, the Thirty-second Parallel transcontinental rail route. Once more his chief contributions were enthusiasm and a talent for publicity. He repeated the financial errors of his earlier projects, building a structure of inflated values and high-sounding promises, rather than a sound transportation company. Once again his hopes were wrecked with the collapse of the general economy in the Panic of 1857. Yet the very scope of the Southern Pacific project illustrates how greatly King's economic vision had grown over the span of two decades. Inspired by the vision of a transcontinental railroad, he helped set up a $100,000,000 corporation, spread publicity on a national scale, and used his political experience to gain for his companies the governmental grants that were essential to success. The Southern Pacific scheme, with its irresponsible financing, its exploitation of natural advantages, and its alliance of business and government, gave a foretaste of the era of big business that was to follow after King had passed from the scene.

In his corporate ventures King was uniformly unfortunate. He lacked the administrative talent to translate his dreams into reality. With different associates, he might have made better use of his abilities as a publicist and lobbyist. Under other management both the Brunswick and Florida and the Southern Pacific projects were partially realized within twenty years after he envisioned them. As it happened, he went from one failure to another; his enthusiasm and persistence, his persuasiveness, and his vision only served to prepare the way for others to succeed.

It was as a politician that King achieved his greatest success and met his greatest disappointment. His political career spanned the era from Nullification to the last congressional election under the Confederacy. Over that period of thirty years his course often appeared inconsistent, but it closely reflected his economic background and his sectional views. As a State Rights advocate he served his apprenticeship in Georgia politics, sponsoring state aid to the economic development of his area. In Congress, he led his colleagues into the alliance that was the Whig party. His own shifting opinions well illustrate the increasing conformity of the Georgia Whigs with the national organization. From a nullifier and a spokesman against the tariff, King became a proponent of a national bank and a moderately protective Whig tariff. His sponsorship of the increase and reorganization of the navy and of a two-ocean network of subsidized mail steamship lines made him one of the most nationalistic of all the Southern Whigs. His advocacy of railroad grants and of federal expenditures for rivers and harbors placed him in the forefront of the Whigs who favored federal internal improvements.

In both his political and economic careers runs one thread of consistency. Whether in state politics or national, in Washington, Milledgeville, Austin, or San Francisco, he supported the alliance of business and government in the development of transportation facilities. His early measures in state politics and his legislative triumphs in Washington embodied the principle of government aid; his transcontinental railroad plans depended on government assistance; and when he returned to Georgia politics he took up once more the same theme. In the national legislature he also served as the special advocate of the commercial community of Savannah, the principal seaport in his state. In all his ventures he sought to establish that identity of interests that would ally men of wealth and talent with the established government, the same principle which Alexander Hamilton had championed in the first years of the republic. In his own person, King united two of the economic groups, the planters and improvers of trade routes—who joined with the manufacturers and merchants to give leadership to the Hamiltonian party of the 1840's, the Whigs.

At the same time, King was the heir by adoption of the State Rights philosophy which acknowledged Thomas Jefferson as its founder. The conflict between his Hamiltonian and Jeffersonian views pulled him first one way, then another. He favored land grants by Congress to aid the construction of railroads, but he followed State Rights doctrine by insisting that the grants be made to the states, not directly to the railroad companies. During one term in Congress he opposed the Independent Treasury on the grounds that it concentrated too much power in the general government; during the next, he advocated a national bank to preserve the commercial stability of the nation. He could denounce the tariff as a piece of legislation for special interests one term, and sponsor an $800,000 subsidy to steamship lines the next. During his years in Congress, he never solved the conflict in basic philosophies of government that produced these paradoxes. On the whole, his Hamiltonian views prevailed; he gave lip service to State Rights principles, but the outstanding measures that he sponsored tended to strengthen the general government.

As a veteran Whig in Congress, King became one of the leaders of the national party. He helped to unite the Northern wing of the organization behind the candidacy of Taylor in the campaign of 1848, but his ambition to become Taylor's Secretary of the Navy was thwarted by the opposition of his Georgia colleagues, Toombs and Stephens. Instead, he became Taylor's agent to carry out the President's policy in California, attempting at the same time to become one of the Senators of the new state. He was one of the few Southerners who remained faithful to Taylor when the President insisted on the admission of California to the Union as a state, but by this time King had abandoned his political base in Georgia. His administrative appointment in California was essentially a continuation of the political adventure begun in 1849. He introduced reforms at the Custom House, but his strict enforcement of the revenue laws made him unpopular. At the same time he used the San Francisco Custom House as a headquarters for building up the Whig Party in the state and as a springboard for his own attempts to become Senator from California in 1851 and 1852. He was torn between his desires to serve the administration, to serve his party, and to serve himself, and he ended by pleasing no one. The California adventure on which he based his hopes for political and economic advancement produced neither fortune nor place.

When King reentered the arena of Georgia politics in the late Fifties, he sounded the familiar theme of state aid to private transportation companies, but this time in opposition to the leading interests of Savannah. Although he did not regain his old seat in

Congress from the First District, he showed signs of recovering a place of leadership in state politics during a term in the Senate of Georgia. When the choice of secession was presented, he did not hesitate to go with his state down the road of disunion, in strong contrast with his actions ten years earlier in support of the Taylor administration. As a Confederate, he served his country in an anomalous diplomatic mission notable mainly for his strenuous propaganda efforts.

When all King's different political roles are assessed, it is clear that he reached his peak in his last two terms as a Congressman, when he was still closely attuned to the needs of his district and when his experience and seniority in the House of Representatives gave him the power to serve his constituency. By careful attention to the desires of his area, by party regularity, and by solid legislative achievements, he established himself as an outstanding Whig member of Congress in the 1840's. His hopes of becoming Secretary of the Navy or Senator were thwarted by his own deficiencies or the jealousy of others. For all his talents, energy, and ambition, he lacked the popular traits that raise a man to the first rank among politicians.

As King lay dying, the armies of the country that he had chosen had already begun their march toward final defeat. With him was dying also the whole economic and social order of which he had been a conspicuous leader, and during the war both King the promoter and King the planter had lost their occupations. Although King the politician had met rejection at the polls, with characteristic optimism he prepared to contest an election which denied him an opportunity to serve his country. To the end he remained an adventurer, eager to do battle for a place of honor. The news of his death brought to his family a letter from a long-time associate, J. L. Locke, who paid honor not to the achievements of a public man, but to the virtues of a friend:

He was very brave and manly—generous, liberal, with nice sensibility —courtly manners—and so many of those becoming graces with [which] Nature refuses to endow the mass of human beings.[29]

Locke's tribute would have made a fitting epitaph to be inscribed on the tomb of Thomas Butler King, in the burial ground of Christ Church, Saint Simons Island, Georgia.

Notes

1. Gravestone, Page-King burial plot, Saint Simons Island, Georgia; Henry G. Wheeler, *History of Congress, Biographical and Political: Comprising Memoirs of Members of the Congress of the United States, Drawn from Authentic Sources: Embracing the Prominent Events of their Lives, and Their Connection with the Political History of the Times* (New York, 1848), II, 9 (hereinafter cited as Wheeler, *History of Congress*); Sarah Harriet Butts, *The Mothers of Some Distinguished Georgians of the Last Half of the Century* (New York, 1902), p. 96.

2. Edward Elbridge Salisbury, *Family Histories and Genealogies. A Series of Genealogical and Biographical Monographs on the Families of McCurdy, Mitchell, Lord, Lynde, Digby . . . and a Notice of Chief Justice Morrison Remick Waite* (New Haven, 1892), I, 280-90 (hereinafter cited as *Family Histories*) ; Frances Manwaring Caulkins, *History of New London, Connecticut. From the First Survey of the Coast in 1612, to 1852* (New London, 1860), pp. 152-54, 235.

3. Josiah Howard Temple, *History of the Town of Palmer, Massachusetts, Early Known as the Elbow Tract: Including Records of the Plantation, District and Town, 1716-1889* (Springfield, 1889), pp. 30-32, 55-74, 140, 167-68, 496-99 (hereinafter cited as *History of the Town of Palmer*).

4. *Ibid.*, pp. 496-99; Salisbury, *Family Histories*, I, 280-90; Butts, *op. cit.*, p. 96; R. J. Massey, "Thomas Butler King," in *Men of Mark in Georgia*, ed. William J. Northen (Atlanta, 1907-1912), II, 366; Wayland Fuller Dunaway, *A History of Pennsylvania* (New York, 1948), pp. 135-36; George Peck, *Wyoming; Its History, Stirring Incidents, and Romantic Adventures* (New York, 1858), pp. 38-43.

5. Massey, "Thomas Butler King," *loc. cit.*, p. 366.

6. Thomas J. Abernethy, "A Brief History of Westfield Academy," an unpublished ms. in the Westfield Athenaeum, pp. 2-14.

7. Wheeler, *History of Congress*, II, 9; Massey, "Thomas Butler King," *loc. cit.*, p. 366.

8. Lois Kimball Mathews, *The Expansion of New England* (Boston, 1909), pp. 139 ff.

9. Wayne County, Georgia, Deed Book B, pp. 280-83; Glynn County, Georgia, Deed Book H, pp. 44-45, 437-46; Wheeler, *History of Congress*, II, 10; Wilson and Fiske, *Appletons' Cyclopaedia of American Biography*, III, 546-47.

10. Samuel Washington McCallie, *Physical Geography of Georgia* (Atlanta, 1925), pp. 19-24; *Executive Documents,* 24th Cong., 2nd Sess., No. 122.

11. The life of the Sea Islands is probably best known through the publication of Frances Anne Kemble's *Journal of a Residence on a Georgia Plantation in 1838-1839* (New York, 1863); Ellis Merton Coulter, *Thomas Spalding of Sapelo* (University, La., 1940) is a modern study of one of the leading planters of the islands. A more romantic approach is to be found in Caroline Couper Lovell, *The Golden Isles of Georgia* (Boston, 1932). Guion Griffis Johnson, *A Social History of the Sea Islands with Special Reference to St. Helena Island, South Carolina* (Chapel Hill, 1930) deals more with South Carolina than with Georgia, but extensive references to Glynn County planters are to be found on pp. 60-68.

12. Strictly speaking, Savannah has no harbor; only the depth of the river on which Savannah is located allowed the city to develop an ocean commerce. Darien, at the mouth of the Altamaha, offers no good deepwater anchorage. *Executive Documents,* 24th Cong., 2nd Sess., No. 122.

13. George Gillman Smith, *The Story of Georgia and the Georgia People, 1732 to 1860* (Macon, Ga., 1900), pp. 304-05; Ellis Merton Coulter, *A Short History of Georgia* (Chapel Hill, 1933), pp. 186, 221, 266-69.

14. Glynn County, Georgia, Deed Book A-B-E-F, pp. 269-75, 426-29, 517, 519; Deed Book G, pp. 24-25, 63-65, 127, 194, 219-20, 394-95, 410; Records of Christ Church, Frederica, Georgia, in possession of Mrs. Margaret Davis Cate, Sea Island, Georgia; Wheeler, *History of Congress,* II, 10.

15. William Page to Messrs. B. King & Co., June 9, 1823; B. King & Co. to Anna M. Page, July 16, August 18, 1823; Anna M. Page to B. King & Co., July 26, August 23, 26, 1823; John McNish to Anna M. Page, July 22, 1823, William Page Papers, Southern Historical Collection, University of North Carolina, Chapel Hill, N. C.

16. Glynn County (Georgia) Court of Ordinary, Wills and Appraisements, Book D, pp. 157, 209 ff.

17. Glynn County (Georgia) Court of Ordinary, Wills and Appraisements, Book D. pp. 209 ff.; United States Coast and Geodetic Survey Charts, 1856, 1867; interviews with Mrs. F. D. Aiken, Saint Simons Island, Georgia, July 16, 28, 1954. Mrs. Aiken, a granddaughter of Thomas Butler King who lived at Retreat in the 1870's, was able to identify buildings on coastal charts of the ante-bellum period and to relate some family traditions about the house and buildings. Remains of the tabby buildings and foundations of the main dwelling can still be observed on the grounds of the Sea Island Golf Course, Saint Simons Island.

18. Wayne County (Georgia) Deed Book B-C-D, pp. 189-93. Deeds for the Mineral Springs Academy and the Mineral Springs religious meeting ground give some ideas of the plan of the colony; hardly any traces remain at the site.

19. Memorandum of sale, June 1, 1830; Thomas Butler King to John G. Shoolbred, January 6, 1836, King Papers; Wayne County (Georgia) Deed Book B-C-D, pp. 218, 219, 236, 555; Wheeler, *History of Congress,* II, 11, recorded King's income from planting in the middle Thirties as about $20,000 yearly.

CHAPTER II

1. William Wigg Hazzard, "History of Glynn County," manuscript, Library, University of Georgia, Athens.

2. James Etheridge Callaway, *The Early Settlement of Georgia* (Athens, 1948), p. 54; Kenneth Coleman, *The American Revolution in Georgia, 1763-1789* (Athens, 1958), pp. 10, 227; Map of Brunswick, October 12, 1819, King Papers.

3. *Executive Documents,* 24th Cong., 2nd Sess., No. 130, p. 5; for further descriptions of the harbor, see *ibid.,* No. 122, No. 123.

4. *Executive Documents*, 24th Cong., 2nd Sess., No. 122; Margaret Davis Cate, *Our Todays and Yesterdays: A Story of Brunswick and the Coastal Islands* (Brunswick, 1930), pp. 161-64 (hereinafter cited as *Our Todays*).

5. *Acts of the General Assembly* (1826), p. 53. The incorporators were James Fort, John Burnett, Sr., John Burnett, Jr., James Gould, Daniel Blue, John Hardee, William B. Davis, Henry DuBignon, Stephen Clay King, and Thomas Butler King.

6. *Acts of the General Assembly* (1834), pp. 331-33; Glynn County, Georgia, Deed Book H, pp. 461-64. For further details on the Davis episode, see Fletcher Melvin Green, "Georgia's Board of Public Works, 1817-1826," *Georgia Historical Quarterly*, XXII (June 1938), 136-37, and Ralph Betts Flanders, "Planters' Problems in Ante-Bellum Georgia," *ibid.*, XIV (March 1930), 26-28.

7. *Executive Documents*, 24th Cong., 2nd Sess., No. 122, p. 19. The cotton traffic on the Altamaha was estimated at 70-80,000 bales annually.

8. *Ibid.*, p. 16.

9. Milton Sidney Heath, *Constructive Liberalism: The Role of the State in the Economic Development in Georgia to 1860* (Cambridge, 1954), *passim*; see especially Chapter X.

10. *Acts of the General Assembly* (1834), pp. 212-18.

11. *Executive Documents*, 24th Cong., 2nd Sess., No. 122. Baldwin's engineering report occupies the first twelve pages of this document.

12. Survey vouchers, King Papers, 1835-1836. Lack of dates and supplementary information impairs the usefulness of these papers for detailing the progress of the survey. Baldwin submitted a bill of $4,070 for his services. However, King later wrote that he shared the original expense with Abraham Colby, and that their contract with Baldwin was assumed by the company after its formation. King to Thomas Lamb, July 16, 1837, King Papers. See also, Cate, *Our Todays*, pp. 208-10.

13. *Acts of the General Assembly* (1835), pp. 187-93, 217.

14. *Acts of the General Assembly* (1836), pp. 40-42. The Bank of Brunswick was a later refinement of the Brunswick scheme, and the charter was secured after outside capital had been obtained. However, most of the charter associates can be identified as local residents.

15. Deed for 5,640 acres adjoining the town of Brunswick, October 13, 1836, King Papers.

16. *Acts of the General Assembly* (1835), pp. 54-55.

17. Glynn County, Georgia, Deed Book H, pp. 470-74, 501-09, 517-25; N. H. Ballard, *118th Annual Report of the Public Schools of Glynn County Georgia and the City of Brunswick* (Brunswick, 1906), pp. 64 ff.

18. T. B. King to Edward Eldredge, December 29, 1836, King Papers. Although the basic nature of the financing is simple, the existence of three companies with mutual stockholders, directors, and officers tends to confuse the records. Charles W. Cartwright of Boston was chairman of the board of directors of the land and railroad companies; King was president, Thomas Lamb was secretary, and William Hales, treasurer.

19. T. B. King to Henry K. Curtis, Nov. 7, 1836; T. B. King to B. F. Perham, Nov. 7, 1836; T. B. King to Thomas Lamb, April 3, 1837; Henry Curtis to T. B. King, April 18, June 16, 1837; B. F. Perham to T. B. King, June 16, 1837, King Papers. For further details of the Brunswick development, see the writer's "Flush Times in Brunswick, Georgia, in the 1830's," *Georgia Historical Quarterly*, XXXIX (September 1955), 221-39.

20. Edward Eldredge to T. B. King, March 25, April 10, 1837; Thomas Lamb to T. B. King, May 9, July 30, 1837, King Papers.

21. T. B. King to Thomas Lamb, Aug. 23, 1837, King Papers. King estimated his assessment at $6,875. According to the treasurer's report, Oct. 26, 1837, King's version of his debt was correct. The worst delinquents among the subscribers seem to have been Amos Davis of Bangor, Maine, and Abraham Colby of Boston.

22. T. B. King to Thomas Lamb, July 16, 1837, King Papers.

23. Thomas Lamb to T. B. King, July 30, 1837; Treasurer's Report, Brunswick and Florida Railroad Company, Oct. 26, 1837, King Papers.

24. Thomas G. Cary to T. B. King, May 1, 1839. See also, Cary to King, February 8, March 1, June 24, 1839, King Papers.

25. T. B. King to H. K. Curtis, Aug. 22, 1838; T. B. King to Thomas G. Cary, Aug. 23, 1838, King Papers. In discussing his trip to Philadelphia, King told his correspondents that he went by invitation and presented his scheme to "Mr. Biddle." Although it seems likely that this was Nicholas Biddle, no identifying name appears in King's correspondence, and he later corresponded with E. R. Biddle regarding the railroad.

26. T. B. King to E. R. Biddle, Oct. 19, 1838, King Papers. Apparently, working capital was to be secured through state aid, issue of bank notes by the Bank of Brunswick, and bond sales in England.

27. T. B. King to Thomas G. Cary, Aug. 23, 1838; Mitchel Young to T. B. King, Oct. 27, 1838; William Smith to T. B. King, Oct. 29, 1838; T. E. Blackshear to T. B. King, Nov. 15, 1838, King Papers.

28. T. B. King to H. K. Curtis, Aug. 22, 1838; T. B. King to Thomas G. Cary, Aug. 23, 1838; Moncure Robinson to T. B. King, Sept. 5, 1838; T. B. King to Joseph Lyman, Oct. 13, 1838; Joseph Lyman to T. B. King, Nov. 1, 1838, King Papers.

29. T. B. King to H. K. Curtis, Aug. 22, 1838; H. K. Curtis to T. B. King, Sept. 21, 1838, King Papers. Curtis was to contribute his notes on the original survey as well as his services.

30. T. B. King to Thomas G. Cary, Aug. 23, Nov. 10, 1838; E. R. Biddle to T. B. King, Sept. 28, 1838, and King to Biddle, Oct. 19, 1838; Joseph Lyman to T. B. King, Nov. 20, 1838, King Papers.

31. Joseph Lyman to T. B. King, Nov. 20, 1838, King Papers.

32. Thomas G. Cary to T. B. King, Nov. 10, 1838, March 10, May 10, 1839; James Hamilton to T. B. King, Jan. 19, Feb. 10, 1839, King Papers.

33. Thomas G. Cary to T. B. King, May 3, 1839; T. B. King to Benjamin A. Lincoln, Oct. 19, 1838, King Papers.

34. *Brunswick Advocate*, June 8, 1837, Nov. 1, Dec. 27, 1838.

35. *Senate Documents*, 23rd Cong., 1st Sess., No. 289, p. 295; *ibid.*, 26th Cong., 1st Sess., No. 577, p. 283.

36. Matthew Brown Hammond, *The Cotton Industry; An Essay in American Economic History* (Ithaca, 1897), pp. 360-61, interleaves.

37. M. Grace Madeleine, *Monetary and Banking Theories of Jacksonian Democracy* (Philadelphia, 1943), pp. 87, 99-103, 110-11.

38. Moncure Robinson to T. B. King, July 4, Aug. 18, 1839, King Papers.

39. A. L. King to T. B. King, Jan. 28, Feb. 13, 1841, King Papers.

40. George White, *Statistics of the State of Georgia . . .* (Savannah, 1849), p. 285. See also, *Executive Documents*, 24th Cong., 2nd Sess., No. 130; *Senate Documents*, 27th Cong., 3rd Sess., No. 247, p. 339.

CHAPTER III

1. The following summary is based primarily on Ulrich Bonnell Phillips, *Georgia and State Rights, A Study of the Political History of Georgia from the Revolution to the Civil War, with Particular Regard to Federal Relations* (Washington, 1902), pp. 96-142 (hereinafter cited as *Georgia and State Rights*); Paul Murray, *The Whig Party in Georgia, 1825-1853* (Chapel Hill, 1948), pp. 1-88; Helen Ione Greene, "Politics in Georgia, 1830-1854," unpublished doctoral dissertation, University of Chicago, 1946, pp. 52-73; Porter Lee Fortune, Jr., "George M. Troup, Leading State Rights Advocate," unpublished doctoral dissertation, University of North Carolina, 1949, pp. 298-314.

2. Murray, *The Whig Party in Georgia, 1825-1853*, p. 34.

3. *Senate Journal* (1832), pp. 115-16.

4. *Ibid.*, pp. 189-95, 206, 235-36.

5. *Ibid.*, pp. 220-44. For an account of the general movement, see Fletcher Melvin Green, *Constitutional Development in the South Atlantic States, 1776-1860. A Study in the Evolution of Democracy* (Chapel Hill, 1930), pp. 179, 187, 206-09, 233 (hereinafter cited as *Constitutional Development*).

6. *Journal of a General Convention of the State of Georgia to Reduce the Members of the General Assembly. Begun and Held at Milledgeville, the Seat of Government, in May 1833*, pp. 17-19, 22-27, 32-35, 48-49 (hereinafter cited as *Journal of a General Convention, 1833*). According to a tabulation supplied to the delegates, the population of Glynn in 1831 was: White, 622; Colored, 4,028; Representative, 3,039.

7. *Journal of a General Convention, 1833*, p. 46; Murray, *The Whig Party in Georgia, 1825-1853*, pp. 50, 52; Green, *Constitutional Development*, p. 236.

8. Murray, *The Whig Party in Georgia, 1825-1853*, pp. 59-61; *Savannah Republican*, Oct. 13, 29, Nov. 1, 1834. It is interesting to note that the *Republican* first used the term "Whig" to describe Georgia anti-Jacksonians in a discussion of the 1834 elections, Oct. 17, 1834.

9. James Graves was sentenced to death by the Georgia courts for his part in a violent episode in the Cherokee gold country. He appealed to the United States Supreme Court, which issued a writ of error summoning the governor of Georgia to appear before the Supreme Court, but the sentence of the state court was carried out.

10. *Senate Journal* (1834), pp. 90-94.

11. *Savannah Republican*, December 15, 1834.

12. *Ibid.*

13. *Ibid.*, December 16, 1834.

14. *Ibid.*, December 12 (quoting the Milledgeville *Georgia Journal*), 15, 16, 1834.

15. *Senate Journal* (1834), pp. 103-06. In three later trials of strength on issues related to the Graves case, King also stood with the State Rights minority. *Ibid.*, pp. 182, 260-63, 300-01.

16. *Ibid.*, pp. 241-56.

17. *Ibid.*, pp. 27, 119, 136, 267-68, 359-62. It may be recalled that King was just now gaining control of Davis's old enterprises in Brunswick.

18. *Senate Journal* (1835), pp. 60, 99, 129, 177, 263.

19. *Savannah Republican*, August 26, 28, Sept. 14, 1835.

20. *Senate Journal* (1835), pp. 12-14, 119-21, 326.

21. *Ibid.*, pp. 102, 352-57; *Savannah Republican*, Nov. 14, 25, Dec. 4, 1837, Jan. 5, 1838.

22. *Senate Journal* (1837), pp. 6, 8, 30, 44, 66, 71, 88, 105, 164, 218-19, 221-23, 228-29, 286.

23. *Senate Journal* (1837), pp. 10-11, 12-15, 105, 237, 239, 249-57, 268-69, 297-301; Thomas Payne Govan, "Banking and the Credit System in Georgia, 1810-1860," *Journal of Southern History*, IV (May 1938), 164-84.

24. *Senate Journal* (1838), pp. 97-100, 148-52, 156, 228, 264, 291.

25. *Ibid.*, pp. 103-06.

26. *Ibid.*, pp. 189-91.

27. *Ibid.*, pp. 163-65, 189-91, 301-04.

28. *Ibid.*, pp. 11-14, 67, 243, 263, 278-89, 301; *Savannah Georgian*, Oct. 4, 20, 1838; *Savannah Republican*, Nov. 19, 24, Dec. 3, 5, 1838. The *Republican* correspondent hints strongly that a deal arranged between King and the Central Railroad group broke down.

29. *Savannah Republican*, Aug. 28, Dec. 21, 1835; Nov. 17, 1836; March 9, April 14, 29, May 18, 1837.

30. *Savannah Republican,* Sept. 21, 1838. The technique of issuing personal platforms enabled the State Righters to exploit the strength of individual candidates, but it gave no guaranty of later harmony.

31. *Ibid.,* Oct. 22, 1838. The contest was extremely close. Only 3,000 votes separated William C. Dawson, who received the greatest number, from McWhorter, the Union Democrat who received the least.

32. *Brunswick Advocate,* Oct. 4, 1838. King received 105 votes, his opponents 17. In his simultaneous race for the Senate, King received 84 votes, opponents unrecorded.

33. Herbert Wender, *Southern Commercial Conventions, 1837-1859* (Baltimore, 1930), pp. 9-11; Weymouth T. Jordan, "Cotton Planters' Conventions in the Old South," *Journal of Southern History,* XIX (August 1953), 321-45.

34. *Savannah Republican,* Oct. 18, 20, 21, 1837. The limited co-partnership was designed to induce European firms to establish transatlantic branches. King sponsored such a law in the Georgia legislature.

35. *Ibid.,* April 4, 5, 6, 7, 1838; Wender, *Southern Commercial Conventions, 1837-1859,* pp. 19-21.

36. *Savannah Republican,* Oct. 26, 29, 31, Nov. 1, 1839; for a more detailed account of the convention and its plan, see Thomas Payne Govan, "An Ante-Bellum Attempt to Regulate the Price and Supply of Cotton," *North Carolina Historical Review,* XVII (October 1940), 302-12.

37. Madeleine, *Monetary and Banking Theories of Jacksonian Democracy,* pp. 110-11; Hammond, *The Cotton Industry,* pp. 360-61, interleaf; John Aiton Todd, *The World's Cotton Crops* (London, 1924), p. 145.

38. Govan, "An Ante-Bellum Attempt to Regulate the Price and Supply of Cotton," *loc. cit.,* p. 312.

CHAPTER IV

1. Anne Royall, *The Huntress,* March 7, 1840; see also T. B. King, Jr., to Anna M. King, March 4, 1851, King Papers. A portrait of King is to be found in the *American Review,* II (1848), 438-39, interleaf.

2. Francis Hobart Herrick, *Audubon the Naturalist; A History of His Life and Time* (New York, 1917), II, 11-12; Anne Royall, *The Huntress,* March 7, 1840.

3. For King's manner of speaking, see Wheeler, *History of Congress,* II, 62; Theodore Dehon Jervey, *Robert Y. Hayne and His Times* (New York, 1909), pp. 517-18; *Savannah Republican,* April 7, 1838; *Savannah Georgian,* Sept. 10, 1844, Oct. 2, 1848.

4. Anna M. King to T. B. King, Feb. 12, 1843; March 7, May 23, 1848; T. B. King to Anna M. King, Feb. 12, 1843, King Papers. The King correspondence reflects an unbroken mutual devotion between husband and wife. The Kings' eldest son, William Page, died at the age of six. Gravestones, King-Page burial plot, Saint Simons Island, Ga.

5. J. F. King to Lin Caperton, Feb. 19, 1866, King Papers.

6. Wheeler, *History of Congress,* II, 10; T. B. King to Anna M. King, Dec. 18, 1842, King Papers.

7. Henry S. McKean to T. B. King, June 2, July 3, 1842; James I. Kuhn to T. B. King, Dec. 4, 1841, King Papers.

8. Charles Grant to T. B. King, April 6, 1844; J. N. Reynolds to T. B. King, Aug. 5, 1846; Robert C. Schenck to T. B. King, May 6, 1846, King Papers; Wayne County, Georgia, Deed Book B-C-D, pp. 189-93; Herrick, *Audubon the Naturalist; A History of His Life and Time,* II, 11-12; Howard Corning, ed., *Journal of John James Audubon Made While Obtaining Subscriptions to his "Birds of America" 1840-1843* (Cambridge, 1929), pp. 64, 67, 75; *Brunswick Advocate,* July 27, Aug. 16, Sept. 13, 1838.

9. *Congressional Globe*, 26th Cong., 1st Sess., *Appendix*, p. 808.

10. T. B. King to Anna M. King, May 29, 1840, King Papers.

11. *Niles' National Register*, LVIII (March-September, 1840), 152. King was the only member of the Georgia congressional delegation who attended the Baltimore meeting.

12. Wheeler, *History of Congress*, II, 16 states that King "franked upward of forty thousand" documents in four months of this campaign. See also the draft of a letter, T. B. King to his fellow Georgians, May 29, 1840, King Papers, and *Savannah Republican*, May 4, 1840.

13. Arthur Charles Cole, *The Whig Party in the South* (Washington, 1913), pp. 56-61; Murray, *The Whig Party in Georgia, 1825-1853*, pp. 172 ff. The *Savannah Republican* began referring to King and his colleagues as Georgia Whigs in March, 1840, when it came out for Harrison for President.

14. A. L. King to T. B. King, June 2, 1840; B. H. Conyers to T. B. King, June 3, 1840; Thomas F. Hazzard to T. B. King, July 28, 1840, King Papers.

15. Murray, *The Whig Party in Georgia, 1825-1853*, p. 182; Wheeler, *History of Congress*, II, 16; *Savannah Georgian*, July 13, Aug. 6, 8, 1840.

16. Wheeler, *History of Congress*, II, 16; *Savannah Republican*, July 28, Aug. 5, 21, Oct. 3, Dec. 25, 1840.

17. William Y. Hansell to T. B. King, July 24, 1840. There is some evidence that the Rockwell note was involved in the purchase of a party organ for the State Rights party. Wheeler, *History of Congress*, II, 12; undated, unidentified newspaper clippings, King Papers; Iverson L. Harris to George W. Lamar, March 10, 1841, Iverson Louis Harris Papers, Southern Historical Collection, University of North Carolina, Chapel Hill, N. C.

18. R. R. Cuyler to T. B. King, March 23, 1840, King Papers. Cuyler, a prominent railroad promoter and politician in Savannah, was a personal friend for whom King named his youngest son.

19. A. L. King to T. B. King, Jan. 28, 1841; George C. Dunham to T. B. King, Feb. 8, 1841, King Papers. Dunham was one of King's overseers.

20. Notices of four suits at law, April, 1841, King Papers; W. W. Hazzard to T. B. King, Feb. 1, 1841; John W. Anderson to T. B. King, Feb. 4, 1841; L. McDonald to T. B. King, Feb. 15, 1841, King Papers.

21. *Savannah Georgian*, Oct. 22, 1840; Murray, *The Whig Party in Georgia, 1825-1853*, p. 184.

22. *House Journal*, 27th Cong., 1st Sess., pp. 328, 331, 344.

23. *Congressional Globe*, 27th Cong., 1st Sess., p. 302.

24. Charles Francis Adams, ed., *Memoirs of John Quincy Adams, Comprising Portions of his Diary From 1795 to 1848* (Philadelphia, 1874-1877), X, 512 (hereinafter cited as Adams, *Diary*).

25. *House Journal*, 27th Cong., 1st Sess., p. 325.

26. *Ibid.*, pp. 403, 409, 512.

27. *Executive Documents and Reports Committees*, 27th Cong., 1st Sess., No. 3.

28. *Congressional Globe*, 27th Cong., 1st Sess., p. 239.

29. *House Journal*, 27th Cong., 1st Sess., pp. 270, 311; *Senate Journal*, 27th Cong., 1st Sess., pp. 129-30.

30. *Congressional Globe*, 27th Cong., 1st Sess., p. 238. John Quincy Adams successfully blocked Wise's attempt to exclude steamers from the squadron.

31. Charles Lee Lewis, *Matthew Fontaine Maury the Pathfinder of the Seas* (Annapolis, 1927), pp. 32-41; John Walter Wayland, *The Pathfinder of the Seas; the Life of Matthew Fontaine Maury* (Richmond, 1930), pp. 41-51.

32. Henry King to T. B. King, July 30, 1841; Arthur St. C. Nichols to T. B. King, July 24, 1841; A. E. Brown to T. B. King, July 25, 1841; Samuel Lawrence to T. B. King, July 27, 1841, King Papers.

33. *Washington National Intelligencer*, Sept. 18, 1841.

34. Harold Hance and Margaret Tuttle Sprout, *The Rise of American Naval Power, 1776-1918* (Princeton, 1949), pp. 117-18.

35. *Congressional Globe*, 27th Cong., 1st Sess., p. 412.

36. *House Journal*, 27th Cong., 1st Sess., p. 235.

37. *Congressional Globe*, 27th Cong., 1st Sess., p. 99.

38. Adams, *Diary*, X, 512.

39. *House Journal*, 27th Cong., 1st Sess., p. 302.

40. *House Journal*, 27th Cong., 1st Sess., pp. 217-23; Adams, *Diary*, X, 539; Murray, *The Whig Party in Georgia, 1825-1853*, pp. 194 ff.; Raynor G. Wellington, *The Political and Sectional Influence of the Public Lands, 1828-1842* (Cambridge, 1914), pp. 98-102; Roy N. Robbins, *Our Landed Heritage; The Public Domain, 1776-1936* (Princeton, 1942), p. 83.

41. Henry King to T. B. King, Nov. 21, 1841, King Papers.

42. Duncan L. Clinch to T. B. King, Aug. 12, Dec. 23, 1841, King Papers.

43. George C. Dunham to T. B. King, Feb. 8, June 23, 28, Aug. 9, 14, 18, Sept. 18, 1841; John Dunham to T. B. King, July 29, 1841, King Papers.

44. Henry King to T. B. King, Nov. 21, 1841, King Papers.

45. T. B. King to his creditors (Draft), Jan. 17, 1842, King Papers; Wheeler, *History of Congress*, II, 11. The *Savannah Republican* of March 5, 1842, contains the notices of U. S. Marshal's sales of 246 slaves and nearly 20,000 acres in three counties to satisfy judgments against King. Later references in the King Papers make it clear that the sacrifice of this property still left King in debt.

46. S. T. Chapman to T. B. King, Feb. 20, 1842, King Papers.

47. Anna M. King to T. B. King, Aug. 11-12, 1842, King Papers.

48. Anna M. King to T. B. King, June 2, Aug. 11-12, Aug. 16, 1842; Sherrod Williams to T. B. King, July 16, 1842, King Papers.

49. Caleb S. Hunt to T. B. King, June 9, 1842; H. S. McKean to T. B. King, July 3, 1842; Anna M. King to T. B. King, Aug. 9, 11-12, 1842, King Papers.

50. James McIntosh to T. B. King, May 17, 1842, King Papers. See also Henry King to T. B. King, Dec. 22, 1841, King Papers.

51. Sprout, *The Rise of American Naval Power, 1776-1918*, pp. 124-26; Allan Ferguson Westcott, ed., *American Sea Power Since 1775* (Chicago, 1947), pp. 101-04.

52. *Savannah Republican*, October 13, 24, 1842; *Washington National Intelligencer*, Oct. 24, 31, 1842; *Niles' National Register*, LXIII (1842), 144.

53. *Savannah Republican*, Oct. 17, 19, 20, 22, 1842.

54. T. B. King to Anna M. King, Oct. 24, 1842, King Papers.

55. Murray, *The Whig Party in Georgia, 1825-1853*, pp. 101-05; *Savannah Republican*, June 16, 17, 1842; Committee of the nominating convention to T. B. King, June 16, 1842; Edward Hopkins to T. B. King, June 21, 1842, King Papers. Hopkins wrote King that the early declaration for Clay was designed to strengthen the state ticket, but expressed doubt that it would have much favorable effect.

56. *Savannah Georgian*, October 22, 26, 1842. Under the general ticket system of election, each candidate ran against the field, rather than contesting with a specific rival for the vote of a district. The election tested not only the strength of the parties, but the comparative drawing power of individual candidates throughout the state.

57. T. B. King to Anna M. King, February 12, 1843, King Papers.

58. T. B. King to Anna M. King, Jan. 14 [?], 1843, Feb. 12, 1843; William P. Molett to T. B. King, Feb. 4, 1843; R. W. Thompson to T. B. King, April 28, 1843; David Law to T. B. King, Nov. 9, 1843, King Papers. King even considered making a new start in the West and consulted with friends on the possibilities of Missouri and Iowa as future homes.

CHAPTER V

1. *Savannah Republican,* May 31, June 24, 26, 1843; Duncan L. Clinch to T. B. King, May 4, 1843; John M. Berrien to T. B. King, May 12, 1843; A. J. Miller to T. B. King, May 29, 1843; David Law to T. B. King, Aug. 7, 1843; W. C. Dawson to T. B. King, Aug. 8, 1843, King Papers.

2. T. B. King to Anna M. King, June 26, 1843; J. H. Steele to T. B. King, July 14, 1843; C. H. Hopkins to T. B. King, July 23, 1843; W. C. Dawson to T. B. King, Aug. 8, 1843, King Papers.

3. *Savannah Republican,* Aug. 30, Oct. 18, 27, 30, Nov. 25, 1843; John W. Hooper to T. B. King, Aug. 28, 1843, King Papers.

4. *Savannah Republican,* Oct. 14, Nov. 15, 1843; Murray, *The Whig Party in Georgia, 1825-1853,* pp. 105-06, 116; O. A. Luckett to T. B. King, Sept. 1, 1843, King Papers.

5. T. B. King to Anna M. King, May 11, 21, 1844, King Papers; *Savannah Republican,* May 7, 11, June 12, 1844; John C. Butler, *Historical Record of Macon and Central Georgia* . . . (Macon, 1879), p. 163.

6. The *Savannah Republican,* July 27, 1844, contains King's Address to the People of the First Congressional District, which formed the basis of his reported campaign speeches and debates.

7. *Savannah Georgian,* July 23, 1844.

8. *Ibid.,* Sept. 10, 1844.

9. *Savannah Republican,* Aug. 31, 1844.

10. *Savannah Georgian,* Oct. 15, 1844.

11. *Ibid.,* Oct. 17, 1844; Murray, *The Whig Party in Georgia, 1825-1853,* pp. 110-11. King defeated Spalding, 3,809 to 3,078.

12. James R. Harvey to T. B. King, Oct. 22, 1844; see also, S. T. Chapman to T. B. King, Aug. 30, 1844, King Papers.

13. Joseph H. Burroughs to J. M. Berrien, Jan. 10, 1845, transcript supplied through the courtesy of the late Mrs. M. D. Cate, Sea Island, Georgia; M. M. Mattox to T. B. King, Feb. 8, 1845; T. B. King to General [Charles L. Floyd ?], Feb. 15, 1845; F. S. Bartow to T. B. King, March 22, 1845, King Papers; *Savannah Republican,* Jan. 10, 1845.

14. John Dunham to T. B. King, Dec. 3, 1845; Henry King to T. B. King, Dec. 12, 1845; for agricultural experiments, see particularly the series of letters, John Couper to T. B. King, Aug. 8, 23, 24, Oct. 28, 1845, and James M. Sturtevant to T. B. King, June 13, 1845, King Papers.

15. J. W. Winter to T. B. King, Aug. 9, 1845, King Papers.

16. Winter to King, Nov. 4, 1845; see also, S. T. Chapman to T. B. King, Oct. 17, 1845, and Duncan L. Clinch to T. B. King, Oct. 26, 1845, King Papers; Murray, *The Whig Party in Georgia, 1825-1853,* pp. 123-24.

17. *House Journal,* 29th Cong., 1st Sess., p. 622; *Congressional Globe,* 29th Cong., 1st Sess., p. 1118.

18. *Ibid., Appendix,* p. 465.

19. *Ibid.,* p. 467.

20. *Ibid.,* pp. 247, 812, 963-64, 1146.

21. *Reports of Committees,* 29th Cong., 1st Sess., Vol. I, No. 144, Vol. III, No. 681. See also, John Ericsson to John O. Sargent, March 21, 1847, King Papers.

22. *Reports of Committees,* 29th Cong., 1st Sess., Vol. III, No. 685.

23. Francis Winter to T. B. King, April 12, 1846; J. C. Hall to T. B. King, August 8, 1846, King Papers.

24. *Ibid.; Savannah Georgian,* August 25, Sept. 12, 1846.

25. *Savannah Georgian,* July 18, 27; Aug. 5, 11, 13, 20, 22, 31; Sept. 3, 5, 10, 25, 28; Oct. 1, 1846.

26. Thomas Chambers to T. B. King, Aug. 3, 1846, King Papers.

27. Truman Smith to T. B. King, Sept. 16, 1846; J. H. C. Mudd to T. B. King, Oct. 13, Nov. 23, 1846; Thomas Corwin to T. B. King, Nov. 6, 1846, King Papers.

28. *Savannah Republican,* Sept. 2, 9, 14, 16, 21, 29; Oct. 2, 6, 15, 29, 1846.

29. Henry King to T. B. King, July 25, 1846; S. C. King to T. B. King, Dec. 15, 1846; John Dunham to T. B. King, Jan. 28, May 13, 1846; Thomas G. Cary to T. B. King, Nov. 9, 1846, King Papers.

30. *Congressional Globe,* 29th Cong., 2nd Sess., pp. 33, 54, 57, 140, 568-69.

31. *Ibid.,* pp. 574-75. John Haskell Kemble, *The Panama Route 1848-1869* (Berkeley, 1943) , devotes his first chapter to a detailed history of the contracts.

32. *House Journal,* 29th Cong., 2nd Sess., p. 404; Francis M. Blount to T. B. King, Jan. 11, 1847; J. L. Locke to T. B. King, Nov. 15, 1847; John W. Anderson to T. B. King, Dec. 18, 1847, King Papers.

33. *House Journal,* 29th Cong., 2nd Sess., pp. 347, 350, 502.

34. *New York Tribune,* March 18, 1847.

35. *Ibid.,* March 24, 1847.

36. Committee of Correspondence to T. B. King, May 1, 1847; R. R. Cuyler to T. B. King, April 13, 1847, King Papers. Cuyler, President of the Central Railroad, was a personal friend for whom King named his youngest son.

37. *Savannah Republican,* June 3, 1847; Daniel Webster, *The Writings of Daniel Webster* (Boston, 1903), IV, 96-103.

38. Anon., "The Chicago Convention," *American Whig Review,* VI (1847), 111-22; see also, Mentor L. Williams, "The Chicago River and Harbor Convention, 1847," *Mississippi Valley Historical Review,* XXV (1949), 607-26.

39. Daniel Webster to T. B. King, July 1, 1847, King Papers.

40. *Washington National Intelligencer,* July 15, 1847; *Savannah Republican,* July 21, 1847.

41. Andrew L. King to T. B. King, August 10, 1847, King Papers.

42. G. W. Anderson to T. B. King, November 19, 1847, King Papers.

43. *Congressional Globe,* 30th Cong., 1st Sess., pp. 73, 103, 177, 238, 400, 683, 838, 951.

44. *Ibid.,* pp. 82, 135, 197, 779, 831, 838, 925-26, 951.

45. *Ibid.,* pp. 167, 285, 431, 916, 944, 986-87; Milo Milton Quaife, ed., *Diary of James K. Polk During His Presidency, 1845-1849* (Chicago, 1910) , IV, 35, 53 (hereinafter cited as Polk, *Diary*) .

46. *Congressional Globe,* 30th Cong., 1st Sess., pp. 782, 792, 805, 982; Kemble, *The Panama Route, 1848-1869,* pp. 17-19, 28-29.

47. *Reports of Committees,* 30th Cong., 1st Sess., Vol. III, No. 596. King at the time was in close touch with W. H. Aspinwall and other promoters who held the Pacific mail contract and were planning to build a Panama canal or railroad. Aspinwall to King, June 27, 1848; W. McKnight to T. B. King, July 30, 1848, King Papers.

48. *Washington National Intelligencer,* May 13, 19, Aug. 18, Sept. 30, Oct. 3, 5, 12, 13, 19, 31, 1848; Robert Royall Russel, *Improvement of Communication with the Pacific Coast as an Issue in American Politics, 1783-1864* (Cedar Rapids, Iowa, 1948), p. 8 (hereinafter cited as *Improvement of Communication*) .

49. *Congressional Globe,* 30th Cong., 1st Sess., pp. 429, 459, 512; *House Journal,* 30th Cong., 1st Sess., pp. 777, 1104, 1130-32, 1332. The discussion of the bill in the *Savannah Republican,* March 3, 7, April 3, 17, 1848, leaves no doubt about the popularity of the proposal in Georgia.

50. Anna M. King to T. B. King, May 23, 1848; R. R. Cuyler to T. B. King, March 26, May 16, 1848; S. M. Bennett to T. B. King, March 11, 1848; J. L. Locke to T. B. King, April 7, 1848, King Papers.

51. Edward T. Sheftall to T. B. King, May 13, 15, 1848, King Papers; *Savannah Republican,* May 15, 23, June 1, 3, 5, 7, 12, 21, 28, 29, 1848.

52. W. W. Paine to T. B. King, June 6, 1848, King Papers.

53. Anna M. King to T. B. King, May 23, 1848, King Papers.

54. Lord King to T. B. King, June 16, 1848; see also, T. B. King, Jr., to T. B. King, Jan. 10, June 5, 1848, King Papers.

55. *Washington National Intelligencer*, Sept. 2, 19, 1848; *Savannah Georgian*, Sept. 16, 1848.

56. *Savannah Georgian*, Sept. 20, 21, 25, 26, 28, Oct. 2, 1848.

57. *Ibid.*, Oct. 7, 9, 27, Dec. 5, 1848; Murray, *The Whig Party in Georgia, 1825-1853*, p. 139.

58. *Congressional Globe*, 30th Cong., 2nd Sess., pp. 423, 427, 430, 465-67.

59. *Reports of Committees*, 30th Cong., 2nd Sess., Vol. I, No. 26.

60. *Congressional Globe*, 30th Cong., 2nd Sess., pp. 40, 382-83. Aspinwall was not very hopeful about federal aid, but he thought King's plan offered the best chance for obtaining it. Aspinwall to King, June 27, 1848, King Papers.

61. Ulrich Bonnell Phillips, *Correspondence of Robert Toombs, Alexander H. Stephens, and Howell Cobb, American Historical Association Annual Reports* (1911, Vol. II), pp. 139-42 (hereinafter cited as Phillips, *Toombs-Stephens-Cobb Correspondence*); Benton, *Thirty Years' View*, II, 733-36; Murray, *The Whig Party in Georgia, 1825-1853*, pp. 140-41.

62. *Savannah Georgian*, Feb. 6, 1849; *Raleigh Register*, Jan. 27, Feb. 14, 1849; Benton, *Thirty Years' View*, II, 733-36; Phillips, *Toombs-Stephens-Cobb Correspondence*, p. 141.

CHAPTER VI

1. S. L. Smith to T. B. King, April 28, 1846, King Papers.

2. Henry King to T. B. King, June 22, 1846, King Papers.

3. John O. Sargent to T. B. King, April 4, 1848; see also, Sargent to King, May 5, 1848, King Papers.

4. S. Draper to T. B. King, Feb. 11, 29, 1848, King Papers.

5. John O. Sargent to T. B. King, April 22, 1848, King Papers.

6. James Walker to T. B. King, May 16, 1848, King Papers.

7. R. R. Cuyler to T. B. King, March 26, 1848, King Papers.

8. W. B. Hodgson to T. B. King, May 15, 1848, King Papers.

9. *Washington National Intelligencer*, June 9, 10, 12, 1848; Holman Hamilton, *Zachary Taylor, Soldier in the White House* (Indianapolis, 1951), pp. 89-97; Allan Nevins, *Ordeal of the Union* (New York, 1947), I, 201.

10. Thurlow Weed to T. B. King, July 15, 1848, King Papers.

11. *Savannah Georgian*, Sept. 21, 1848; *Washington National Intelligencer*, Sept. 19, 1848; *Washington Daily Union*, Sept. 2, 26, 1848; Hamilton, pp. 114-15, concludes that the Albany "revolt" was a cleverly managed act to quiet Clay supporters.

12. *Savannah Republican*, Sept. 18, 20, 21, 28; Oct. 2, 3, 19, 25, 27; Nov. 24, 1848.

13. *Savannah Republican*, Feb. 9, 1849; *Washington Daily Union*, Nov. 19, 25, 26, 1848.

14. R. R. Cuyler to T. B. King, Nov. 13, 1848, King Papers.

15. Hamilton, *Zachary Taylor, Soldier in the White House*, p. 136.

16. Woodburne Potter to T. B. King, Dec. 12, 18, 1848, King Papers.

17. Hamilton, *Zachary Taylor, Soldier in the White House*, pp. 136, 139.

18. John O. Sargent to John Jordan Crittenden, Feb. 6, 1849, Crittenden Papers, Manuscripts Division, Library of Congress.

19. *Ibid.*

20. Hamilton, *Zachary Taylor, Soldier in the White House*, p. 145.

21. J. L. Locke to T. B. King, Nov. 14, 1848, King Papers.

22. Alexander H. Stephens to John Jordan Crittenden, Jan. 17, 1849, Alexander H. Stephens Papers, Duke University, Durham, N. C. See also Stephens to Crittenden, Dec. 6, 1848, and Robert Toombs to Crittenden, Jan. 9, 1849, Crittenden Papers, Manuscripts Division, Library of Congress.

23. Hamilton, *Zachary Taylor, Soldier in the White House,* p. 152.

24. A. H. Stephens to J. J. Crittenden, Jan. 17, 1849, Alexander H. Stephens Papers, Duke University, Durham, N. C.

25. See the cryptic note, J. M. Berrien to Governor [George W.] Crawford, November 9, 1846, Berrien Papers, Manuscripts Division, Library of Congress, which indicates that Berrien and Crawford both regarded King with some antagonism.

26. Anna M. King to H. L. P. King, April 5, 1849, King Papers.

27. *Savannah Republican,* March 16, 1849.

28. *Congressional Globe,* 30th Cong., 1st Sess., p. 1007; Nevins, *Ordeal of the Union,* I, 23; Richard Harrison Shryock, *Georgia and the Union in 1850* (Durham, 1926), pp. 158-59.

29. John Middleton Clayton to John Jordan Crittenden, Dec. 13, 1848, John Jordan Crittenden Papers, Manuscripts Division, Library of Congress; John Jordan Crittenden to John Middleton Clayton, Dec. 19, 1848, Jan. 7, April 11, 1849, John Middleton Clayton Papers (hereinafter cited as Clayton Papers, Manuscripts Division, Library of Congress); Coleman, *Life of John J. Crittenden,* I, 335; Phillips, *Toombs-Stephens-Cobb Correspondence,* p. 139.

30. Ulrich Bonnell Phillips, *The Life of Robert Toombs* (New York, 1913), pp. 61-62.

31. *House Journal,* 30th Cong., 2nd Sess., pp. 539-40; Hamilton, *Zachary Taylor, Soldier in the White House,* p. 143.

32. Polk, *Diary,* IV, 375-76.

33. Cole, *The Whig Party in the South,* p. 155.

34. *Executive Documents,* 31st Cong., 1st Sess., Vol. V, pp. 9-11.

35. *Ibid.,* pp. 11, 12, 743, 946-48; Thomas Ewing to Adam Johnson and Ewing to John Wilson, May 23, 1849, King Papers.

36. T. B. King to John Middleton Clayton, April 27, 1849, Clayton Papers; see also, Anna M. King to Henry Lord Page King, May 22, 1849, King Papers.

37. Hubert Howe Bancroft, *History of California* (San Francisco, 1882-1890), VI, 278-79; Hallie Mae McPherson, "William McKendree Gwin, Expansionist," unpublished doctoral dissertation, University of California, 1931, p. 98; *Washington Daily Union,* Jan. 30, 1850; T. B. King to Anna M. King, June 28, 1849, King Papers; T. B. King to John Middleton Clayton, June 20, 1849, Clayton Papers.

38. *Executive Documents,* 31st Cong., 1st Sess., Vol. V, pp. 785-92, 941-43; Vol. VIII, Doc. 59, p. 6.

39. T. B. King to John Middleton Clayton, July 22, 1849, Clayton Papers; see also Bayard Taylor, *Eldorado,* p. 208.

40. *Executive Documents,* 31st Cong., 1st Sess., V, 952; VIII, No. 59, p. 6; Thomas ap Catesby Jones to Anna M. King (copy), Sept. 1, 1849, King Papers; *San Francisco Pacific News,* August 25, 28, 30, Oct. 4, 13, 27, 1849.

41. T. B. King to George Washington Bonaparte Towns, Sept. 29, 1849, printed in the *Savannah Republican,* Dec. 24, 1849.

42. William Tecumseh Sherman, *Memoirs* (New York, 1891), I, 106; see also Taylor, *Eldorado,* p. 208. An excellent case, based only on speculation and hints, can be made out for the contention that King's assignment in California was to win the senatorship for the Whigs. William M. Gwin and David C. Broderick, both Democrats, were known to have emigrated to California with the avowed intention of returning to Washington as senators. It is almost inconceivable that the administration should have neglected to provide a candidate to increase Whig representation if Congress should admit the new state that might be formed. It may be remembered that King had had a hand in a similar scheme when Iowa was admitted to the Union. The rumor was abroad in Georgia as early as August, 1849, that King was to be one of the new senators from California, and Howell Cobb later wrote his wife that King went to seek the senatorship. Mrs. King wrote that her husband spoke of his mission as "a bold stroke for fortune." Strong

confidence in King's vote-getting ability might account for Clayton's cryptic note to Crittenden: "the states will be admitted free and Whig." As for the "free" in that statement, even Robert Toombs admitted that there was no likelihood of California's being a slave state. See William Ellison, ed., "Memoirs of the Hon. William M. Gwin," *California Historical Society Quarterly*, XIX (1940), 1-26, 157-84, 256-77, 344-67; Jeremiah Lynch, *A Senator of the Fifties: David C. Broderick, of California* (San Francisco, 1911), pp. 34, 38; Cole, *The Whig Party in the South*, p. 155; Phillips, *The Life of Robert Toombs*, pp. 60-61; George Fort Milton, *The Eve of Conflict; Stephen A. Douglas and the Needless War* (Boston, 1934), p. 49, footnote; *Savannah Georgian*, Aug. 12, 1849; Anna M. King to Henry Lord Page King, May 22, 1849, King Papers.

43. *San Francisco Pacific News*, Aug. 25, 28, 30, Oct. 4, 13, 23, 27, Nov. 6, 1849. The editors of the *News* were avowed Democrats.

44. *Senate Journal*, 1849-1850, pp. 24-25.

45. *Washington Daily Union*, Jan. 30, 1850.

46. *Baltimore Sun*, quoted in *Savannah Daily Morning News*, Jan. 26, 1850.

47. George Rawlings Poage, *Henry Clay and the Whig Party* (Chapel Hill, 1936), pp. 194, 204 ff.; Phillips, *The Life of Robert Toombs*, pp. 65 ff.; Hamilton, *Zachary Taylor, Soldier in the White House*, pp. 229 ff.

48. Richardson, *Messages and Papers*, V, 18.

49. *Ibid.*, V, 29-30.

50. *Washington Daily Union*, Jan. 26, 1850.

51. *Congressional Globe*, 31st Cong., 1st Sess., pp. 337-40.

52. *Washington National Intelligencer*, Feb. 25, 1850.

53. *Executive Documents*, 31st Cong., 1st Sess., Vol. VIII, No. 59, p. 5.

54. *Congressional Globe*, 31st Cong., 1st Sess., *Appendix*, p. 349.

55. Thomas Butler King, *Address of the Hon. T. Butler King to the People of the First Congressional District, May, 1859* (Savannah, 1859), *passim*.

56. *Ibid.*, pp. 24-25.

57. T. J. Green to T. B. King, April 13, 1855, T. J. Green Papers.

58. Sherman, *Memoirs*, I, 106-07.

59. *Executive Documents*, 31st Cong., 1st Sess., Vol. VIII, No. 59, pp. 1-32. This document also had a commercial edition as a pamphlet entitled *California: The Wonder of the Age.*

60. William L. Hodge to T. B. King, April 10, 1850; C. W. Denison to T. B. King, May 6, 1850; Peterson Thweatt to T. B. King, June 13, 1850, King Papers; *Savannah Daily Morning News*, April 17, 1850, quoting *Baltimore Sun.*

61. T. B. King, Jr., to Anna M. King, July 23, 1850, King Papers.

62. Helen Ione Greene, "Politics in Georgia, 1830-1854," unpublished doctoral dissertation, University of Chicago, 1946, pp. 75, 195-96, 211-13.

63. Peterson Thweatt to T. B. King, June 13, 1850, King Papers.

64. J. N. Johnson to T. B. King, January 30, 1850, King Papers.

CHAPTER VII

1. T. B. King, Jr., to Anna M. King, Oct. 14, Nov. 21, 24, 25, 1850, King Papers.

2. Same to same, Nov. 27, Dec. 16, 1850, Nov. 30, Dec. 4, 1851, King Papers.

3. T. B. King, Jr., to Anna M. King, Jan. 8-11, 1851, King Papers.

4. *Ibid.*

5. T. B. King, Jr., to Anna M. King, March 30, April 1, 28, 1851, King Papers. Patrick, another Negro who accompanied the Kings, proved to be overfond of drinking; he was given a job as messenger at the Custom House. T. B. King, Jr., to Anna M. King, May 31, 1852.

6. *San Francisco Alta California*, Feb. 5, May 15, Sept. 30, 1851; *San Francisco Daily Herald*, July 19, 1850; Bancroft, *History of California*, VI, 675; J. H. C. Mudd,

Special Treasury Agent, to Thomas Corwin, Feb. 15, 1851, Letters from Collectors, Jan., 1850 to Dec., 1852, San Francisco, Treasury Department, National Archives; *Senate Documents,* 32nd Cong., 1st Sess., Vol. X, No. 103, pp. 1-3.

7. Thomas Corwin to T. B. King, Nov. 15, 1850, Treasury Department Letterbooks J, No. 1, Collectors California; T. B. King to Thomas Corwin, April 30, 1851 (two reports), Letters from Collectors, San Francisco, 1849-1851, Treasury Department Records, National Archives; *Senate Documents,* 31st Cong., 1st Sess., Vol. XIV, No. 82; *Court of Claims Reports,* 35th Cong., 2nd Sess., No. 198; *San Francisco Alta California* and *Daily Evening Picayune* discuss the issues in great detail.

8. Treasury Department Letterbooks J, No. 1; Letters from Collectors, San Francisco, 1849-1851, Treasury Department Records, National Archives, Washington, D. C.; *San Francisco Alta California,* Sept. 22-Oct. 31, 1851; *San Francisco Daily Evening Picayune,* Sept. 25-Oct. 1, 1851.

9. *San Francisco Daily Herald,* March 24, 25, 26, 1851; *San Francisco Alta California,* March 22, 23, 24, 25, 1851; *San Francisco Pacific Daily News,* March 24, 1851; E. Carey to T. B. King, March 28, 1851; S. Lamb to T. B. King, March 29, 1851, Letters from Collectors, San Francisco, 1849-1851, Treasury Department Records, National Archives; T. B. King to Thomas Corwin, Dec. 18, 1850; J. H. C. Mudd to Thomas Corwin, March 31, 1851, Thomas Corwin Papers, Manuscripts Division, Library of Congress.

10. T. B. King, Jr., to Anna M. King, May 11, 1851, King Papers. The original spelling and punctuation are reproduced in the quotation.

11. *San Francisco Alta California,* May 5, 6, 7, 14, 15, 1851.

12. *San Francisco Daily Herald,* May 29, 1851; similarly, *San Francisco Alta California,* May 29, 30, 1851.

13. T. B. King to Thomas Corwin, May 31, July 14, 1851, Letters from Collectors, San Francisco, 1849-1851, Treasury Department Records, National Archives; T. B. King, Jr., to Anna M. King, July 15, 1851, King Papers; Hubert Howe Bancroft, *Popular Tribunals* (San Francisco, 1887), I, 346.

14. T. B. King, Jr., to Anna M. King, March 14, 1852, King Papers. The spelling and punctuation of the original are reproduced. See also letters from Butler King to his mother, Nov. 30, Dec. 15, 1851; Jan. 1, 13, 1852; T. B. King to Anna M. King, April 4, 1852, King Papers.

15. Robert Ernest Cowan, "The Leidesdorff-Folsom Estate," *California Historical Society Quarterly,* VII (1928) , p. 105-11; T. B. King, Jr., to T. B. King, Feb. 23, 25, 1853; account of T. B. King as agent, April 2, 1853, King Papers.

16. T. B. King to Anna M. King, April 4, 1852, King Papers.

17. T. B. King to J. H. C. Mudd, May 5, 1852; T. B. King to [Thomas Corwin?], May 15, 1852, Corwin Papers; Thomas Corwin to T. B. King, Oct. 2, 1852, Treasury Department Letterbooks J, No. 1, Treasury Department Records, National Archives.

18. San Francisco *Alta California,* Nov. 12, 1852.

19. T. B. King to Thomas Corwin, Nov. 15, 1852, Corwin Papers.

20. *Senate Documents,* 31st Cong., 1st Sess., Vol. XIV, No. 82; *House Executive Documents,* 33rd Cong., 1st Sess., Vol. II, No. 3, pp. 446-47; Vol VIII, No. 60; Vol. IX, No. 64; *House Miscellaneous Documents,* 37th Cong., 2nd Sess., Vol. I, No. 49, p. 3. For special treatment of the collectorship as a political office, see Leonard D. White, *The Jacksonians: A Study in Administrative History, 1829-1861* (New York, 1954), pp. 174-78.

21. Allan Nevins, *Fremont, Pathmarker of the West* (New York, 1939) , pp. 388-96; Cardinal Leonidas Goodwin, *John Charles Fremont, An Explanation of his Career* (Stanford Univ., Calif., 1930) , pp. 187-89; Charles Wentworth Upham, *Life, Explorations and Public Services of John Charles Fremont* (Boston, 1856), pp. 302, 309-10, 321-22.

22. *San Francisco Alta California,* Jan. 23, 1851.

23. *San Francisco Pacific Daily News,* Jan. 24, 1851.

24. *San Francisco Daily Herald,* Feb. 3, 1851.

25. T. B. King to Thomas Corwin, Jan. 15, April 30, 1851, Corwin Papers; Treasury Department Letterbooks, Letters from Collectors, San Francisco, Jan. 1850 to Dec. 1852, National Archives; J. H. C. Mudd to Millard Fillmore, March 2, 1851; J. H. C. Mudd to Truman Smith, Dec. 4, 1851, Millard Fillmore Papers, Buffalo Historical Society, Buffalo, N. Y. (hereinafter cited as Fillmore Papers).

26. *San Francisco Pacific Daily News,* Jan. 24, 1851; see also, *ibid.,* Feb. 13, 14, 1851, and *San Francisco Daily Herald,* Feb. 6, 12, 19, 1851.

27. *San Francisco Pacific Daily News,* Feb. 18, 1851.

28. *Ibid.,* Feb. 26, 27, March 1, 1851; California *Legislative Journals* (1851), pp. 1225-74, 1286-88.

29. *San Francisco Daily Herald,* July 31, 1851; see also, *ibid.,* March 4, 11, May 27, 1851; J. H. C. Mudd to Millard Fillmore, March 2, 1851; J. H. C. Mudd to Truman Smith, Dec. 4, 1851, Fillmore Papers; P. P. Hull to Thomas Corwin, Dec. 15, 1851, Corwin Papers. Crane, the first Whig editor on the Pacific Coast, had been sent out by the National Committee; after the election his government printing contracts were withdrawn.

30. *San Francisco Daily Herald,* May 30, 1851; Daniel I. Lisle, *A Circumstantial Statement* (San Jose, 1851), *passim.* Lisle's work is a brief contemporary account of the first organization of the Whigs. See also, William McKendree Gwin, "Memoirs of the History of the United States, Mexico, and California, 1850-1861" (MS), Bancroft Library, University of California, Berkeley, p. 73.

31. *San Francisco Daily Herald,* May 27, 1851.

32. *Ibid.,* May 26, 31 [misdated May 30], June 3, July 31, August 8, 1851; *San Francisco Alta California,* Aug. 1, 2, Dec. 20, 1851.

33. *Ibid.,* August 27, 28, 1851; *San Francisco Daily Herald,* Aug. 27, 30, 1851.

34. T. B. King, Jr., to Anna M. King, Sept. 15, 1851, King Papers.

35. John Wilson to Thomas Corwin, Sept. 30, 1851, Corwin Papers.

36. George B. Tingley to Thomas Corwin, July 14, 1852; see also, Resolutions of the Whig General Committee of San Francisco, May 15, 1852, Corwin Papers.

37. Files of the Solicitor of the Treasury, Judicial Records *(U. S. v. King),* National Archives, Washington, D. C. The history of this case is quite involved. In April 1855, the Solicitor of the Treasury instituted a civil suit against King, mainly to recover sums which had been exacted as penalties against importers and later distributed among the enforcing officers. No charges of corruption were involved, and the case was never finally decided, simply being marked "Closed" in 1878.

CHAPTER VIII

1. Memoranda of agreements, July 6, Oct. 14, 1852, undated, 1853; T. B. King, Jr., to Anna M. King, Oct. 31, 1852, Aug. 8, 1853; T. B. King, Jr., to T. B. King, Jan. 30, 1853; T. B. King, Jr., to J. W. Allen, April 2, 1853; T. B. King to J. P. Scriven, Sept. 3, 1853, King Papers.

2. Prospectus of the Atlantic and Gulf of Mexico Railway, 1853; T. B. King to————, draft, July 8, 1853; T. B. King to J. P. Scriven, Sept. 3, 21, 1853; T. B. King to Nelson Tift, Sept. 6, 1853; T. B. King to Sir Joshua Walmsley, Sept. 12, 1853, King Papers.

3. Charles Frederick Carter, *When Railroads Were New* (New York, 1909), pp. 227-28; George Rogers Taylor, *The Transportation Revolution, 1815-1860,* p. 86; Robert Edgar Riegel, *The Story of the Western Railroads* (New York, 1926), pp. 11-12; Robert Spencer Cotterill, "Early Agitation for a Pacific Railroad, 1845-1850," *Mississippi Valley Historical Review,* V (1919), 396-414; Margaret Louise Brown, "Asa Whitney," *Mississippi Valley Historical Review,* XX (1933), 209-24.

4. Lewis Henry Haney, *A Congressional History of Railways in the United States,*

1850-1887 (Madison, Wis., 1908), pp. 49-52; Allen Marshall Kline, "The Attitude of Congress toward the Pacific Railway, 1856-1862," *American Historical Association Annual Report, 1910,* pp. 191-96.

5. Russel, *Improvement of Communication,* pp. 95-103; Cotterill, "Early Agitation for a Pacific Railroad, 1845-1850," *loc. cit.,* pp. 398-407; Kline, "The Attitude of Congress toward the Pacific Railway, 1856-1862," *loc. cit.,* pp. 189-96; John Bell Sanborn, "Railroad Land Grants," *Wisconsin Academy of Science, Arts, and Letters Transactions,* XII (1898), 306-16; Edward Gross Campbell, "Railroads in the National Defense, 1829-1848," *Mississippi Valley Historical Review,* XXVII (1940), 361-78.

6. *Senate Journal* (1853), pp. 828-29, 1092; *Assembly Journal* (1853), pp. 1683-84; Andrew F. Muir, "The Thirty-Second Parallel Pacific Railroad in Texas to 1872," unpublished doctoral dissertation, University of Texas, 1949, pp. 25-26, 29; Russel, *Improvement of Communication,* p. 98; *Congressional Globe,* 32nd Cong., 2nd Sess., pp. 315-16.

7. T. B. King, Jr., to Anna M. King, Sept. 18, 27, Dec. 5, 1853; Henry King to T. B. King, Dec. 1, 1853, King Papers.

8. McKitrick, *The Public Land System of Texas, 1823-1910,* pp. 53-62; Louis J. Wortham, *A History of Texas, from Wilderness to Commonwealth* (Fort Worth, 1924), IV, 234; Edmund Thornton Miller, *A Financial History of Texas* (Austin, 1916), pp. 86-89, 110-11, 133; Aldon Socrates Lang, *Financial History of the Public Lands in Texas* (Waco, Texas, 1932), pp. 23, 104, 127-28, 132; Charles William Ramsdell, "Internal Improvements in Texas," *Proceedings of the Mississippi Valley Historical Association,* IX (1917), No. 1, 101-02.

9. T. B. King, "Address Delivered in Austin, Texas, Dec. 24, 1853"; Anna M. King to H. L. P. King, Dec. 25, 1853, King Papers; Austin *Texas State Times,* Jan. 7, 1854; Muir, p. 39.

10. McKitrick, *The Public Land System of Texas, 1823-1910,* pp. 60-65; Alexander Deussen, "The Beginnings of the Texas Railroad System," *Texas Academy of Science Transactions,* IX (1907), 42-74.

11. Extracts of the minutes of the Atlantic and Pacific Railroad Company, Nov. 1853 (dated June 28, 1854) ; Memorandum, T. B. King to Levi S. Chatfield, Jan. 25, 1854; T. B. King to Robert J. Walker (Draft), April 24, 1854; T. B. King, Jr., to Anna M. King, July 12, 1854; T. B. King, Jr., to T. B. King, Aug. 1, 1854; Contract between Governor Pease and Walker, King and their associates, Aug. 31, 1854, King Papers; Cornelius Glen Peebles, *Exposé of the Atlantic and Pacific Railroad Company (Extraordinary Developments)* (New York, 1854) , pp. 9-11 (hereinafter cited as Peebles, *Exposé); Circular to the Stockholders of the Atlantic and Pacific Railroad Company* (1855), *passim;* Muir, pp. 31-32, 40, 43-55.

12. *Circular to the Stockholders of the Atlantic and Pacific Company* (1855), *passim; Charter of the Texas Western Railroad Company* (1855), *passim;* Muir, pp. 62-64.

13. Andrew B. Gray, *Texas Western Railroad. Survey of Route, Its Cost and Probable Revenue, in Connection with the Pacific Railway; Nature of Country, Climate, Mineral and Agricultural Resources, etc.* (Cincinnati, 1855) , pp. 3-101, (hereinafter cited as Gray, *Survey of Route).*

14. *Circular to the Stockholders of the Atlantic and Pacific Railroad Company* (1855), pp. 8-16; *Charter of the Texas Western Railroad Company* (1855), pp. 3-11.

15. T. B. King, Jr., to T. B. King, Dec. 10, 1855; Samuel Jaudon to T. B. King, Dec. 19, 1855; D. W. Brown to S. Waggoner, Nov. 13, 1855; C. Bradley to T. B. King, Nov. 14, 1855; Leslie Comes to T. B. King, Nov. 16, 1855, King Papers; *Charter of the Texas Western Railroad Company* (1855), pp. 39-40; *Circular to the Stockholders of the Texas Western Rail-Road Company, Issued by Authority of the Executive Committee, New York, June, 1856,* pp. 27-28 (hereinafter cited as *Circular, June, 1856).*

16. Jeptha Fowlkes to Thomas Jefferson Green, March 7, July 22, 1855; W. R. D. Ward to Thomas Jefferson Green, Nov. 2, 1855, Thomas Jefferson Green Papers, Southern Historical Collection, University of North Carolina, Chapel Hill (hereinafter cited as T. J. Green Papers); Samuel Jaudon to T. B. King, Dec. 19, 1855, King Papers; Muir, p. 79.

17. Gray, *Survey of Route, passim; Charter of the Texas Western Railroad Company* (1855), pp. 31-36; *Circular, June, 1856*, pp. 3-26.

18. Minutes of the Executive Committee of the Texas Western Railroad Company, excerpt, Nov. 12, 1855; T. B. King to H. L. P. King, Dec. 31, 1855, King Papers; *Senate Journal* (1855-1856), pp. 151-54, 230-36; *House Journal* (Adjourned Session, 1856), pp. 21-25; Charles Shirley Potts, *Railroad Transportation in Texas* (Austin, 1909), p. 98.

19. T. B. King to H. L. P. King, Feb. 18, 1856, King Papers. Drafts of laws and amendments in King's handwriting are preserved in the King Papers.

20. T. B. King to H. L. P. King, May 5, 1856, King Papers. A committee of Texans examined the books of the company and issued a cautious endorsement of the management.

21. Wortham, *A History of Texas, from Wilderness to Commonwealth* IV, 234; John Henry Brown, *History of Texas, from 1685 to 1892* (St. Louis, 1892-1893), II, 366-69; Deussen, "The Beginnings of the Texas Railroad System," *loc. cit.*, p. 51; McKitrick, *The Public Land System of Texas, 1823-1910*, p. 69; H. McLeod to T. J. Green, Oct. 23, 1854, T. J. Green Papers. McLeod explains Governor Pease's opposition to the Texas Western on the grounds of state sectionalism.

22. Transcripts of the minutes of the Executive Committee of the Texas Western Railroad Company, Nov. 12, 1855, June 16, 1856; Muir, pp. 80-82.

23. *Senate Journal* (Adjourned Session, 1856), pp. 86-88, 99-105, 112-13, 206; *House Journal* (Adjourned Session, 1856) pp. 21-25, 416; T. B. King to H. L. P. King, August 10, 1856, King Papers.

24. Merger agreement between T. B. King and James W. Throckmorton and others, Aug. 23, 1856; T. G. Wright to T. B. King, Nov. 6, 1856, King Papers. The directors of the rival company rejected this particular agreement, but left the door open for a similar merger.

25. Transcript of the minutes of the Southern Pacific Railroad Company, Oct. 1, 1856, Jan. 17, 22, 1857; T. B. King to H. L. P. King, Dec. 14, 1856, King Papers.

26. *New Orleans Daily Picayune*, March 3, 18, 21, 22, 24, 25, 27, 29, 31; April 3, 5, 7, 9, 11, 14, 15, 25, 1857.

27. T. B. King to Anna M. King, April 9, 1857, King Papers.

28. *New Orleans Daily Picayune*, April 11, 25, 1857, June 26, 1858.

29. Transcript of the minutes of the Executive Committee of the Southern Pacific Railroad Company, Jan. 22, 1857; T. B. King to Mallery King, March 11, 1857; T. B. King to Anna M. King, April 29, 1857, King Papers; Muir, p. 92. The contract for laying the track and for grading forty-two additional miles was let to John T. Grant and Company of Atlanta, June 13, 1857.

30. T. B. King, Jr., to T. B. King, July 2, 1857, King Papers.

31. E. A. Blanch to George S. Yerger, Aug. 25, 1857; Agreement between Jeptha Fowlkes and the Southern Pacific Railroad Company, Sept. 10, 1857; C. A. Harper to T. B. King, Sept. 19, 1857; George C. Laurason to T. B. King, Sept. 26, 1857, inclosing resolutions of the board of directors, King Papers.

32. W. C. Laurason to T. B. King, Sept. 5, 1857, inclosing a report by Blanch; R. W. Loughery to T. B. King, Sept. 21, 1857; C. A. Harper to T. B. King, Sept. 19, 1857, King Papers.

33. E. A. Blanch to George S. Yerger, Aug. 25, 1857, King Papers.

34. *Ibid.*

35. R. W. Loughery to T. B. King, Sept. 21, 1857, King Papers.

36. W. C. Laurason to T. B. King, Sept. 5, 1857, King Papers.

37. R. W. Loughery to T. B. King, Sept. 21, 1857, King Papers.

38. Joseph Taylor to T. B. King, Dec. 9, 1857, King Papers.

39. R. W. Loughery to T. B. King, Nov. 22, 1857, King Papers.

40. Jeptha Fowlkes to T. B. King, Jan. 7, 1858, King Papers. The punctuation of the original is reproduced.

41. "Memorandum handed to Powell," Feb. 8, 1858, King Papers.

42. *Ibid.;* Lord King, when writing of the activities of his father and himself in Austin, expatiated on the use of the sectional argument, calling it "the sheet anchor of our hopes." H. L. P. King to T. B. King, Jr., Jan. 31, 1858, King Papers.

43. *New Orleans Daily Picayune,* June 16, 26, 1858; Muir, p. 98. Yerger admitted that he had drafted the bill for Wigfall.

44. Muir, pp. 97-100; Anna M. King to J. F. King, June 12, 30, July 4, 10, 1858, King Papers.

45. Jeptha Fowlkes to the Opponents of the S. P. Railroad of Texas, July 15, 1858; Jeptha Fowlkes to T. B. King, Aug. 7, 9, 16, 17, Sept. 9, 1858; D. P. Henderson to T. B. King, Sept. 24, Oct. 13, 1858; Thomas B. Lincoln to T. B. King, Oct. 9, 14, 20, 1858; *Louisville Journal,* Aug. 26, 1858, King Papers.

46. T. B. King to T. B. King, Jr., Dec. 15, 1858, King Papers.

47. After King left the active management of the Southern Pacific, in June 1858, the company went through a two-year period of reorganization and legal battles, essentially a struggle between Texans and outsiders for the control of the railroad. The details of the litigation indicate that neither side had very clean hands, and the State of Texas entered the contest as a third party with a suit to bring about forfeiture of the charter. In August 1860 the stockholders outside of Texas, led by Jeptha Fowlkes, secured control. See Muir, pp. 102-46.

CHAPTER IX

1. Except as otherwise noted, all statements in this chapter about the management of Retreat and the details of domestic life are drawn from the extensive correspondence among the various members of the King family for the years 1850-1860.

2. Anna M. King to T. B. King, Feb. 14, 1856, King Papers.

3. *Seventh Census, Slave Inhabitants, Georgia,* Vol. 3 (Glynn Co.), pp. 767-70; *Eighth Census, Slave Inhabitants, Georgia,* Vol. 3 (Glynn Co.), pp. 4, 8, Marshal's returns, National Archives; list of slaves, 1859, King Papers.

4. Anna M. King to T. B. King, Feb. 14, 1856, King Papers.

5. T. B. King, Jr., to T. B. King, Feb. 28, 1858, King Papers.

6. Anna M. King to T. B. King, Dec. 15, 1853, King Papers.

7. Anna M. King to T. B. King, Aug. 28, 1854, King Papers.

8. Anna M. King to T. B. King, Sept. 22, 1856, King Papers. Since Retreat had been left in trust to Anna and her children, she and her husband kept separate accounts, but this seems to have been largely a legal fiction.

9. Anna M. King to T. B. King, Dec. 21, 1858, King Papers.

10. Anna M. King to T. B. King, Sept. 7, 1854, King Papers.

11. Anna M. King to T. B. King, March 8, 1857, King Papers. Among the fruits mentioned more than once in family letters were three varieties of figs, strawberries, melons, peaches, oranges, and tomatoes. There are single references to muskmelons, silverseeds melons, and blueberries.

12. The flocks furnished 640 chickens for the family table in less than four months in the summer of 1857. Anna M. King to H. L. P. King, Aug. 20, 1857, King Papers. Ducks and turkeys are mentioned in other letters.

13. T. B. King to Anna M. King, June 7, 1857, King Papers.

14. Anna M. King to H. L. P. King, Dec. 4, 1854, King Papers.

15. Anna M. King to T. B. King, Oct. 12, 1858, King Papers.

16. Anna M. King to T. B. King, Sept. 11, 1858, King Papers.

17. Photostat of Account Book of Anna M. King, in possession of the Sea Island Corporation, Sea Island, Ga.

18. Anna M. King to J. F. King, Aug. 3, 1858, King Papers.

19. Anna M. King to J. F. King, Oct. 6, 1858, King Papers.

20. Anna M. King to T. B. King, June 29, 1857, King Papers.

21. In 1853 Georgia was 20 years old, Florence 18, and Virginia 17. The eldest daughter, Hannah Page, had been the mistress of her own household since her marriage at 19 to William Audley Couper eight years earlier.

22. Anna M. King to T. B. King, June 5, 1856, King Papers.

23. T. B. King to J. F. King, Dec. 5, 1859, King Papers.

24. T. B. King to Mallery King, July 20, 1860, King Papers.

25. Georgia King to H. L. P. King, Oct. [n. d.], 1859, King Papers.

26. Anna M. King to T. B. King, May 21, 1855, King Papers.

27. T. B. King to H. L. P. King, Dec. 31, 1855, King Papers.

28. H. L. P. King to T. B. King, Jr., Jan. 31, 1858, King Papers.

29. T. B. King, Jr., to Anna M. King, April 1, 1851, King Papers.

CHAPTER X

1. Horace Montgomery, *Cracker Parties* (Baton Rouge, 1950), p. 235. Montgomery's work, the most detailed study of Georgia politics from 1850 to 1860, served as the basis for the foregoing summary. Other books that are particularly helpful for background material on the period are Phillips, *Georgia and State Rights;* Percy Scott Flippin, *Herschel V. Johnson of Georgia, State Rights Unionist* (Richmond, 1931); and Herbert Fielder, *A Sketch of the Life and Times and Speeches of Joseph E. Brown* (Springfield, 1883).

2. Resolutions of a public meeting in Brunswick, Ga., Jan. 9, 1855, King Papers.

3. *Savannah Republican,* Sept. 21, Oct. 4, 1855; Albert Virgil House, *Planter Management and Capitalism in Ante-Bellum Georgia* (New York, 1954), pp. 122-23.

4. Anna M. King to H. L. P. King, Sept. 24, 1855, King Papers.

5. *Greensborough* (N. C.) *Patriot,* July 4, 1856. The *Patriot* noted the obvious relationship of King, Walker, the railroad, and national politics.

6. T. B. King to Anna M. King, March 10, 1859, King Papers.

7. H. L. P. King to Georgia King, April 16, 1859, King Papers.

8. Thomas Butler King, *Address to the People of the First Congressional District, May, 1859;* T. B. King to the editors of the *Wire Grass Reporter,* April 28, 1859, King Papers.

9. Anna M. King to J. F. King, May 30, 1859; H. L. P. King to Anna M. King, June 12, 1859, King Papers.

11. *Savannah Republican,* July 14, 1859.

11. *Savannah Republican,* June 3, 14, July 14, 15, 20, 1859.

12. T. B. King to the Public (untitled broadside), July 27, 1859, King Papers.

13. T. B. King to Anna M. King, Feb. 4, 6, April 7, July 9, 1859; Anna M. King to T. B. King, March 20, 1859; Anna M. King to John Floyd King, April 5, May 10, 30, 1859, King Papers.

14. Georgia King to R. C. King, March 26, 1860, King Papers.

15. Georgia King to J. F. King, Nov. 11, 1860; Georgia King to R. C. King, Nov. 13, 1860, King Papers.

16. Georgia King to H. L. P. King, July 12, Aug. 2, 1860, King Papers.

17. Georgia King to J. F. King, Feb. 16, 1860, King Papers. The Glynn County (Ga.) Court of Ordinary, Wills and Appraisements, Book G, pp. 48-50, lists the value of the estate at $115,000.

18. Georgia King to J. F. King, Feb. 16, May 14, 1860; Georgia King to H. L. P. King, Aug. 2, 1860; undated fragment [1859-1860], King Papers.

19. *Savannah Republican,* Oct. 6, 1859. King won by a majority of forty.

20. Florence King to J. F. King, Nov. 11, 1859; Georgia King to J. F. King, Nov. 13, 1859; Georgia King to R. C. King, Nov. 17, 1859, King Papers; *Savannah Republican*, Oct. 19, Nov. 12, 1859.

21. *Senate Journal* (1859), pp. 28-32; draft of a railroad bill, King Papers.

22. *Senate Journal* (1859), pp. 173, 183-84; *Savannah Republican*, Nov. 23, 24, 26, 1859.

23. *Senate Journal* (1859), pp. 256, 261-62; *Savannah Republican*, Dec. 2, 9, 1859.

24. T. B. King to H. L. P. King, Dec. 16, 1859, King Papers.

25. Herbert Wender, "The Southern Commercial Convention at Savannah, 1856," *Georgia Historical Quarterly*, XV (1931), 173-91; Laura A. White, "The South in the 50's," *Journal of Southern History*, I (1935), 29-48.

26. *Savannah Republican*, Dec. 10, 1859; Montgomery, *Cracker Parties*, p. 237.

27. Montgomery, *Cracker Parties*, pp. 237-38.

28. T. B. King to H. L. P. King, Dec. 16, 1859; King Papers; Henry G. Wheeler to T. B. King, Jan. 2, 1861; James R. Butts to T. B. King, March 27, 1861, undated memorandum [1861?], papers of T B. King, Case of the *Calhoun*, Judicial Records, Admiralty, 1862, National Archives; Phillips, *A History of Transportation in the Eastern Cotton Belt to 1860*, pp. 291, 359.

29. *New Policy of the Southern Pacific Railroad Co.*, [April 12, 1859], King Papers. The stock exchange was a complicated one. Holders of Atlantic and Pacific stock were given sixty days in which to exchange their stock according to former arrangements, receiving the newest issue at one for two. Holders of Southern Pacific stock were to receive one for two, unless they had failed (a) to subscribe fifty cents a share, or (b) to exchange stock at one for two under a previous reorganization; these holders were to receive stock on a one for three basis. See D. C. Wilder, Secretary-Treasurer, to Stockholders of the Southern Pacific Railroad Company, May 1, 1859; circular letter to stockholders of the Southern Pacific Railroad Company, May 30, 1859, King Papers; Russel, *Improvement of Communication*, p. 270; Muir, pp. 140-42.

30. H. L. P. King to T. B. King, Feb. 19, 1860, King Papers.

31. T. B. King to J. F. King, May 1, 1860, King Papers. See also *Congressional Globe*, 36th Cong., 1st Sess., pp. 2445-48; Russel, *Improvement of Communication*, pp. 283-85.

32. Horace Smith Fulkerson, *Random Recollections of Early Days in Mississippi*, p. 113. Fulkerson was the New Orleans agent for the Southern Pacific Railroad.

33. T. B. King to J. F. King, May 1, 1860, King Papers.

34. Russel, *Improvement of Communication*, p. 286. The platforms of Lincoln, Douglas, and Breeckinridge all favored some kind of aid to a Pacific railroad.

35. T. B. King to Robert Collins, May 11, 1860, King Papers.

36. Georgia King to R. C. King, May 11, 1860, King Papers.

37. Address to the citizens of Rhode Island, King Papers. Only an incomplete draft of this speech is to be found.

38. T. B. King to Mallery King, July 20, 1860; T. B. King to Georgia King, July 23, 1860; Diary of H. L. P. King, May-Nov., 1860, King Papers.

39. Georgia King to J. F. King, Nov. 11, 1860, King Papers.

40. Fielder, *A Sketch of the Life and Times and Speeches of Joseph E. Brown*, p. 166; Coulter, *A Short History of Georgia*, p. 297; T. Conn Bryan, "The Secession of Georgia," *Georgia Historical Quarterly*, XXXI (1947), 89-111; Louise Biles Hill, *Joseph E. Brown and the Confederacy*, pp. 36-47.

41. *Senate Journal* (1860), pp. 53, 97-98; Georgia King to J. F. King, Nov. 11, 1860; Georgia King to R. C. King, Nov. 13, 1860, King Papers.

42. T. B. King to H. L. P. King, Jan. 5, 1861; H. L. P. King to T. B. King, Jan. 16, 1861, King Papers. For King's commission, see *The Confederate Records of the State of Georgia*, II, pp. 21-24.

43. Georgia King to H. L. P. King, March 16, 1861, King Papers.

CHAPTER XI

1. T. B. King to Mallery King, March 5, 1861, King Papers.

2. *The Statutes at Large of the Provisional Government of the Confederate States of America* . . . (Richmond, 1864), p. 44.

3. T. B. King to H. L. P. King, Jan. 5, 1861; H. L. P. King to T. B. King, Jan 16, 1861; T. B. King to Mallery King, March 5, 1861, King Papers; Henry G. Wheeler to T. B. King, Jan. 2, 1861; James R. Butts to T. B. King, March 27, 1861; Bellot des Minieres to T. B. King, April 16, 1861; undated memorandum [1861], papers of T. B. King, Case of the *Calhoun*, Judicial Records, Admiralty, 1862, National Archives.

4. *The Confederate Records of the State of Georgia*, II, 23.

5. T. B. King to H. L. P. King, March 25, 1861, King Papers.

6. Muir, pp. 148-50; Wayland Fuller Dunaway, *History of the James River and Kanawha Company* (New York, 1948), pp. 195-202; Bellot des Minieres to T. B. King, April 16, 1861, papers of T. B. King, Case of the *Calhoun*, Judicial Records, Admiralty, 1862, National Archives.

7. *Papers Relative to the Mission of the Hon. T. Butler King, to Europe* (Milledgeville, Ga., 1863), p. 5. This pamphlet contained King's report to Governor Brown and the report on the mission by a legislative committee.

8. Hotel bills and correspondence indicate that King resided first at the Hotel du Louvre, then at the Hotel Montaigne, and finally at a furnished apartment, 29 Rue de Ponthieu. He arrived in Paris March 27 and left on his return journey October 30. He interrupted this seven-month stay by trips to Brussels (April 16-27) and to London (toward the end of August). One note suggests that he may also have made a brief visit to London in June. He left Southampton for Havana on December 2, 1861. Papers of T. B. King, Case of the *Calhoun*, Judicial Records, Admiralty, 1862, National Archives.

9. *Papers Relative to the Mission of the Hon. T. Butler King, to Europe*, p. 6; Georgia King Smith to H. L. P. King, July 21, 1861, King Papers. How King obtained access to Napoleon III remains obscure. One of his correspondents referred to the cooperation of Michel Chevalier, whose calling card is among King's papers. Chevalier was a senator, a leading free trade advocate, and the architect of current French commercial policy. John Slidell later made use of him to plant documents where they would come to the Emperor's notice. Papers of T. B. King, Case of the *Calhoun*, Judicial Records, Admiralty, 1862, National Archives; Arthur Louis Dunham, "Chevalier's Plan of 1859: The Basis of the New Commercial Policy of Napoleon III," *American Historical Review*, XXX (1924), 72-76; Henry Beckles Willson, *John Slidell and the Confederates in Paris (1862-1865)* (New York, 1932), p. 110.

10. *Papers Relative to the Mission of the Hon. T. Butler King, to Europe*, p. 14.

11. *Le Moniteur Universel*, June 20, July 17, 1861.

12. Frank Lawrence Owsley, *King Cotton Diplomacy; Foreign Relations of the Confederate States of America* (Rev. ed., Chicago, 1959), p. 56.

13. Undated drafts of letters to Davis, Stephens, and Toombs, by Georgia King Smith, King Papers.

14. *Papers Relative to the Mission of the Hon. T. Butler King, to Europe*, p. 16.

15. *Ibid.*

16. *Ibid.*, p. 16.

17. *Ibid.*, p. 8.

18. *Ibid.* King copied or paraphrased about one fourth of his letter from Thomas Prentice Kettell's *Southern Wealth and Northern Profits* . . . (New York, 1860).

19. *Papers Relative to the Mission of the Hon. T. Butler King, to Europe*. p. 13.

20. T. B. King, "The American Blockade" (draft), King Papers. Internal evidence indicates that this article was composed in Oct. 1861.

21. *Ibid.*

22. W. L. Yancey, P. A. Rost, and A. D. Mann to Secretary of State Robert Toombs, June 1, 1861, Confederate States of America, State Department Papers, Manuscripts Division, Library of Congress; Paul Pecquet du Bellet, "The Diplomacy of the Confederate Cabinet of Richmond and its Agents Abroad; Being Memorandum Notes Taken in Paris During the Rebellion of the Southern States from 1861 to 1865," pp. 14-16, Confederate States of America, Miscellany, Manuscripts Division, Library of Congress.

23. J. L. O'Sullivan to T. B. King, Aug. 25, 1861; F. S. Claxton to T. B. King, Sept. 1, 9, 1861, as printed in the *Washington National Intelligencer,* April 25, 1862. The *Intelligencer* devoted nearly four columns to the printing of some of King's correspondence which was captured.

24. Frederick Arthur Wellesley, *Secrets of the Second Empire. Private Letters from the Paris Embassy; Selections from the Papers of Henry Richard Charles Wellesley, First Earl Cowley. Ambassador at Paris 1852-1867* (New York and London, 1929), p. 220; Warren Reed West, *Contemporary French Opinion of the American Civil War* (Baltimore, 1924), pp. 26, 28, 30; Owsley, *King Cotton Diplomacy . . . ,* pp. 179-201.

25. Thomas Le Grand Harris, *The Trent Affair, Including a Review of English and American Relations at the Beginning of the Civil War* (Indianapolis, 1896), pp. 75-76, singles out King's letter to the Comte de Morny as a particularly effective propaganda article.

26. Henry Adams to Charles Francis Adams, Oct. 25, 1861, as printed in Worthington Chauncey Ford, ed., *A Cycle of Adams Letters, 1861-1865* (Boston, 1920), I, 61.

27. Margaret Antoinette Clapp, *Forgotten First Citizen: John Bigelow* (Boston, 1947), pp. 150-51; Thurlow Weed, *Autobiography of Thurlow Weed,* pp. 634-41; Bancroft, *The Life of William H. Seward,* II, 220-21; John Herbert Kiger, "Federal Governmental Propaganda in Great Britain during the American Civil War," *The Historical Outlook,* XIX (1928), 204-09.

28. Meredith Calhoun to T. B. King, June 28, 1861; Robert Mitchell to T. B. King, July 31, 1861, as printed in the *Washington National Intelligencer,* April 25, 1862; Dubuisson et Cie. to T. B. King, June 18, 1861; undated bill of Robert Mitchell; C. Haussoullier to [King?], July 31, 1861; Bills from Hotel Montaigne to T. B. King, Aug. 5, 1861, and Leroy et Cie., Sept. 30, 1861, papers of T. B. King, Case of the *Calhoun,* Judicial Records, Admiralty, 1862, National Archives; *The Confederate Records of the State of Georgia,* II, 322-23.

29. *Papers Relative to the Mission of the Hon. T. Butler King, to Europe,* p. 6. *The Confederate Records of the State of Georgia,* II, 116, 323, 325.

30. *Official Records of the Union and Confederate Navies in the War of the Rebellion,* Ser. I, Vol. XVII, pp. 72-75; statements of Joseph W. Tuck and John A. Rogers, March 11, 1862, Case of the *Calhoun,* Judicial Records, Admiralty, 1862, National Archives; *Savannah Republican,* Jan. 27, 29, Feb. 4, 8, 1862; *New York Times,* Feb. 28, 1862. "Jaque," the *Times* correspondent, allegedly took part in the capture.

31. T. B. King to R. C. King, March 14, 1862, King Papers.

32. J. P. Benjamin to John Slidell, April 12, 1862, Confederate States of America, State Department Papers, Manuscripts Division, Library of Congress.

33. J. P. Benjamin to Edwin de Leon, April 14, 1862, Confederate States of America, State Department Papers, Manuscripts Division, Library of Congress; Edwin de Leon to T. B. King, undated, papers of T. B. King, Case of the *Calhoun,* Judicial Records, Admiralty, 1862, National Archives.

34. S. W. Lawrence to Florence King, May 2, 1862; Georgia King Smith to Florence King, June 22, 1862, King Papers.

CHAPTER XII

1. H. L. P. King to T. B. King, Jan. 16, 1861, King Papers.
2. Georgia King to H. L. P. King, April 19, 1861, King Papers.
3. Georgia King to T. B. King, May 30, 1861, Case of the *Calhoun,* Judicial Records, Admiralty, 1862, National Archives.
4. Georgia King Smith to T. B. King, Feb. 10, 24, 1862; Georgia King Smith to Florence King, June 22, 1862; T. B. King to Florence King, April 5, 1862; S. W. Lawrence to Florence King, May 2, 1862, King Papers.
5. Mallery King to T. B. King, March 16, 1862, King Papers.
6. H. L. P. King to T. B. King, April 3, 1862, King Papers.
7. Hannah King Couper to T. B. King, April 8, 1862, King Papers.
8. *Ibid.*
9. Mallery King to T. B. King, July 1, 1862; Georgia King Smith to T. B. King, June 28, 1863; Georgia King Smith to J. F. King, Aug. 25, 1863, King Papers.
10. Georgia King Smith to J. F. King, Aug. 25, 1863, King Papers.
11. *Ibid.;* for the experience of other planters in the area, see [Richard W. Corbin], "Letters of a Confederate Officer to his Family in Europe during the Last Year of the War of Secession," *The Magazine of History With Notes and Queries, Extra No. 24* (1913), pp. 90-96.
12. *The Confederate Records of the State of Georgia,* II, 327; for further progress of this matter through official channels, see *ibid.,* II, 322-28, *House Journal* (1862), 97, 113, 142-44; *Senate Journal* (1862), p. 189.
13. A. E. Cochran to T. B. King, Dec. 18, 1862, King Papers.
14. *Savannah Morning News,* Dec. 16, 25, 1862; *Official Records,* Series I, Vol. 21, p. 582; Charles Edgeworth Jones, *Georgia in the War, 1861-1865* (Atlanta, 1909), p. 94. Saint Simons Island had been evacuated by the planters in the face of the enemy blockade, but had not yet been taken over by Federal forces.
15. Floyd King to Mallery King, Jan. 19, 1862 [1863], King Papers.
16. Arthur James Lyon Fremantle, *Three Months in the Southern States: April-June, 1863* (New York, 1864), pp. 216-17.
17. Mary Newton Stanard, *Richmond, Its People and Its Story* (Philadelphia, 1923), p. 187.
18. George King Smith to T. B. King, June 28, 1863, King Papers.
19. *Savannah Republican,* June 25, 26, 1863.
20. *Savannah Republican,* June 26, 30, July 6, 10, 11, 13, 16, 17, 1863.
21. *Address to the People of the First Congressional District of Georgia* (no facts of publication). Internally, this broadside carries the date of July 23, 1863, and, according to his daughter, it was written by King to give more respectability to a weak convention. Georgia King Smith to J. F. King, Aug. 13, 1863, King Papers.
22. *Savannah Republican,* Aug. 10, Sept. 4, 5, 7, 10, 15, 24, 29, Oct. 1, 1863.
23. Florence King to Floyd King, Aug. 18, 1863; Georgia King Smith to Floyd King, Aug. 25, 1863; Georgia King Smith to T. B. King, Sept. 30, 1863, King Papers. This campaign produced a curious sequel some six months later in the Northern states. A letter purporting to be from King and advocating peace and a reconstruction of the Union appeared in newspapers as far apart as New York and Louisville. Although later exposed, this hoax served as ammunition for the peace advocates in the North, who used it to snipe at the Lincoln administration. See the *Louisville Journal,* Jan. 9, 1864, and the *New York Tribune,* Feb. 19, 1864. For the *Tribune* reference, the writer is indebted to Mr. J. E. Missemer, San Diego, California, who is engaged in an attempt to unravel this complex deception, as well as a number of other Civil War forgeries.
24. *Savannah Republican,* Oct. 12, 14, 20, 28, 31, 1863; *Savannah Morning News,* October 28, 1863. For an explanation of Hartridge's majority, the writer is inclined to look to the legislature of 1859-1860. At that time, King proposed a bill for state

aid to railroad companies, and the supporters of the bill attacked the Central Railroad and Banking Company of Savannah as a "monopoly," "a soulless corporation," and "a bloody juggernaut." In the House, Julian Hartridge led the apologists of this powerful Savannah enterprise, and King bore the brunt of the Savannah-led counterattack. The *Republican,* August 10, 1863, stated obliquely that much of King's opposition in 1863 came from Savannah residents who thought him to be opposed to the interests of the city.

25. *Savannah Republican,* Jan. 18, 1864.

26. Flippin, *Herschel V. Johnson of Georgia, State Rights Unionist,* pp. 230 ff.

27. *Savannah Republican,* Nov. 4, 1863; see also *ibid.,* Nov. 16, 1863, quoting the sketches of the candidates as seen by the *Knoxville Register; Senate Journal* (1863), pp. 42, 109-11.

28. Floyd King to Georgia King Smith, March 22, April 29, 1864; Cuyler King to Georgia King Smith, March 23, May 1, 1864; Mallery King to Georgia King Smith, May 21, 1864; Georgia King Smith to [Floyd King?], April 19, 1864; Georgia King Smith to Floyd King, June 7, 1864, King Papers.

29. J. L. Locke to Virginia King, May 17, 1864, King Papers.

Bibliographical Note

THE VOLUMINOUS King Papers in the Southern Historical Collection, University of North Carolina, constitute the principal source for the investigator who wishes to unearth details of the life of Thomas Butler King. Political, personal, and business letters to King, together with drafts of his speeches and reports, give a measure of his varied interests and activities. If he kept copies of his outgoing correspondence, the letter books have not been preserved; the collection contains only occasional drafts of letters written by King, except to members of his family. In those of his letters which are available, it is noticeable that he seldom dwelt on the past; rather, he gave detailed accounts of what was happening, what he was doing, or what he intended to do in the near future. He was not a reflective man, nor was he much given to humor. His speeches as well as his letters indicate that he was content to take his political philosophy from others and to adopt the prevailing economic views of a burgeoning entrepreneurial society. The family letters reveal him to have been a Victorian paterfamilias, dominating, but occasionally indulgent.

Other collections of papers in the Southern Historical Collection that supplement the King Papers include the William Page Papers, which are concerned with Retreat before King took over the management, the John McPherson Berrien Papers, the Thomas Jefferson Green Papers, and the Iverson Louis Harris Papers.

For local material, it was the writer's good fortune to have access to the many records and maps and to the extensive knowledge of the late Mrs. Margaret Davis Cate of Sea Island, Georgia. Among her records was the photostatic copy of a domestic account book of Anna Page King. Mrs. Cate also paved the way for two interviews with Buford King (Mrs. Frank D.) Aiken of Saint Simons Island, the last surviving member of the King family who had lived at Retreat. She was able to locate paths, gardens, trees, outbuildings, and other features of the plantation house and grounds, and to relate traditional family lore.

The excellent state of preservation and the maintenance of the Glynn County records in the courthouse at Brunswick, Georgia, make it possible to follow the often complex legal transactions to which King was a party. The records of Wayne County in the courthouse at Jesup, Georgia, also supply legal data. The manuscript history of Glynn County by William Wigg Hazzard in the Library of the University of Georgia gives a contemporary view of the area by one of King's personal friends.

For King's political career in Georgia and nationally, aside from his own papers, U. B. Phillips' printed collection of the letters of Robert Toombs, Howell Cobb, and Alexander H. Stephens is invaluable. In addition, the John McPherson Berrien Papers in the Manuscript Division of the Library of Congress, besides those already mentioned in the Southern Historical Collection, furnish minor sidelights. More valuable Library of Congress holdings are the John Middleton Clayton Papers, the Thomas Corwin Papers, and the John Jordan Crittenden Papers, all of which throw light on the leadership of the Whig party and furnish direct references to King. The manuscript calendar of the papers of President Millard Fillmore gives a key to letters concerning California while King was Collector of San Francisco, and when the transcripts of these letters (kindly supplied by the Secretary of the Buffalo Historical Society, Buffalo, New York) are read in conjunction with letters from the Corwin Papers, they illuminate the party difficulties in early California politics.

Other manuscript records in Washington include the Confederate States of America, Miscellany, and the Confederate States of America, State Department Papers, Division of Manuscripts, Library of Congress. The National Archives contain (in Judicial Records, Admiralty, 1862) some personal papers of King which were captured when he attempted to run the blockade. This file is not complete, and some letters from it were apparently released to the *Washington National Intelligencer* to be printed to stimulate the Union war effort. At the National Archives also is preserved (in Judicial Records, Files of the Solicitor of the Treasury, Case of U.S. *v.* King) the prosecution's record of a case that was never adjudicated. The Treasury Department Records contain the reports and letters of King and other Treasury Department officials on the West Coast, together with the corresponding orders and instructions in the letter books of the Secretary of the Treasury. The Assistant Marshals' Returns, Seventh and Eighth Censuses, Slave Inhabitants, Georgia, Volume III (Glynn County), give precise figures on the number of slaves at Retreat in 1850 and 1860. More information on Retreat can be derived from the Assistant Marshals' Returns, Seventh and Eighth Censuses, Agriculture, Georgia, in the Duke University Library, Durham, North Carolina.

All of the foregoing manuscript sources serve to flesh out the official record in printed governmental documents, such as the constitutional and legislative journals, the records of debates, and the committee reports of the States of California, Georgia, and Texas, and of the United States Congress. Whenever possible, at least one of the principal newspapers of the area where King resided was gleaned for references to his public activities.

For additional specific and general information the writer used numerous magazine articles and books, most of which are cited in the Notes. The select list which follows contains the most frequently consulted monographic studies, biographies, unpublished works, and fugitive imprints.

SELECT LIST OF WORKS CONSULTED

Adams, Ephraim Douglass. *Great Britain and the American Civil War*, 2 vols. New York: Longmans, Green and Co., 1925.

Avery, Isaac Wheeler. *The History of the State of Georgia From 1850 to 1881, Embracing the Three Important Epochs: The Decade Before the War of 1861-5; The War; The Period of Reconstruction, with Portraits of the Leading Public Men of this Era*. New York: Brown and Derby, 1881.

Carpenter, Jesse Thomas. *The South as a Conscious Minority, 1789-1861: A Study in Political Thought*. New York: New York University Press, 1930.

Cate, Margaret Davis. *Our Todays and Yesterdays: A Story of Brunswick and the Coastal Islands*. Revised edition. Brunswick: Glover Bros., 1930.

Charter of the Texas Western Railroad Company, and Extracts from the Reports of Col. A. B. Gray and Secretary of War, on the Survey of Route, From Eastern Borders of Texas to California. Nature of Country and Climate, Mineral and Agricultural Resources, etc., etc. Cincinnati: Porter, Thrall and Chapman, 1855.

Chitwood, Oliver Perry. *John Tyler, Champion of the Old South*. New York: D. Appleton-Century Co., 1939.

Circular to the Stockholders of the Atlantic and Pacific Railroad Company. New York: G. F. Nesbit and Co., 1855.

Circular to the Stockholders of the Texas Western Railroad Company. Issued by Authority of the Executive Committee, New York, June, 1856. New York: W. H. Arthur and Co., 1856.

Cole, Arthur Charles. *The Whig Party in the South*. Washington: American Historical Association, 1913.

Coulter, Ellis Merton. *A Short History of Georgia.* Chapel Hill: University of North Carolina Press, 1933.

Ellison, Joseph. "The Struggle for Civil Government in California, 1846-1850," *California Historical Society Quarterly,* X (1931), 3-26, 129-64, 220-44.

Fortune, Porter Lee, Jr. "George M. Troup: Leading State Rights Advocate." Unpublished doctoral dissertation, University of North Carolina, 1949.

Goodwin, Cardinal Leonidas. *The Establishment of State Government in California.* New York: The Macmillan Co., 1914.

Gray, Andrew B. *Texas Western Railroad. Survey of Route, Its Cost and Probable Revenue, in Connection with the Pacific Railway; Nature of Country, Climate, Mineral and Agricultural Resources, etc.* Cincinnati: Porter, Thrall and Chapman, 1855.

Gray, Lewis Cecil. *History of Agriculture in the Southern United States to 1860,* 2 vols. Washington: The Carnegie Institution, 1933.

Green, Fletcher Melvin. *Constitutional Development in the South Atlantic States, 1776-1860. A Study in the Evolution of Democracy.* Chapel Hill: University of North Carolina Press, 1930.

Greene, Helen Ione. "Politics in Georgia, 1830-1854." Unpublished doctoral dissertation, University of Chicago, 1946.

Hamilton, Holman. *Zachary Taylor, Soldier in the White House.* Indianapolis: The Bobbs-Merrill Co., 1951.

_____. *Zachary Taylor, Soldier of the Republic.* Indianapolis: The Bobbs-Merrill Co., 1941.

Hammond, Matthew Brown. *The Cotton Industry: An Essay in American Economic History: Part I, The Cotton Culture and the Cotton Trade.* Ithaca: [n.p.], 1897.

Haney, Lewis Henry. *A Congressional History of Railways in the United States to 1850.* Madison: University of Wisconsin, 1908.

_____. *A Congressional History of Railways in the United States, 1850-1887.* Madison: University of Wisconsin, 1910.

Heath, Milton Sidney. *Constructive Liberalism: The Role of the State in Economic Development in Georgia to 1860.* Cambridge: Harvard University Press, 1954.

Kemble, John Haskell. *The Panama Route, 1848-1869.* Berkeley: University of California Press, 1943.

King, Thomas Butler. *Address to the People of the First Congressional District, May, 1859.* Savannah: [n.p.], 1859.

_____. *Address to the People of the First Congressional District of Georgia.* [July 23, 1863] [No facts of publication].

_____. *California: The Wonder of the Age. A Book for Everyone Going to or Having an Interest in that Golden Region; Being the*

Report of Thomas Butler King, United States Government Agent in and for California. New York: W. Gowans, 1850.

————————. Correspondence on the Subject of Appraisements, &c., Between T. Butler King, Collector, and J. Vincent Browne, Appraiser, Custom House, San Francisco, California. With the Opinion Thereon of one of the General Appraisers, and the Secretary of the Treasury. Washington: [n.p.], 1852.

————————. A Letter to the Right Hon. Lord John Russell. London: [n.p.], 1861.

————————. Lettre à son Excellence, M. le Ministre du Commerce. Paris: Dubuisson et Cie., 1861.

————————. Speech of the Hon. T. Butler King, Delivered in the Hall of the House of Representatives, at Milledgeville, Ga., November 10, 1863. Milledgeville: Boughton, Nisbet, Barnes and Moore, 1863.

————————. Speech on the Memorial of the Society of Friends. [No facts of publication.]

————————. Speech on the Resolution of Mr. Clay. Washington: [n.p.], 1834.

Kirwan, Albert Dennis. John J. Crittenden: The Struggle for the Union. Lexington: University of Kentucky Press, 1962.

McGrane, Reginald Charles. The Panic of 1837: Some Financial Problems of the Jacksonian Era. Chicago: University of Chicago Press, 1924.

Meyer, Balthasar Henry, ed. History of Transportation in the United States before 1860. Washington: The Carnegie Institution, 1917.

Montgomery, Horace. Cracker Parties. Baton Rouge: Louisiana State University Press, 1950.

Muir, Andrew F. "The Thirty-Second Parallel Pacific Railroad in Texas to 1872." Unpublished doctoral dissertation, University of Texas, 1949.

Murray, Paul. The Whig Party in Georgia, 1825-1853. Chapel Hill: University of North Carolina Press, 1948.

Nevins, Allan. Ordeal of the Union, 2 vols. New York: Charles Scribner's Sons, 1947.

New Policy of the Southern Pacific Railroad Company. [April 12, 1859.] [No facts of publication.]

Nichols, Roy Franklin. The Disruption of American Democracy. New York: The Macmillan Co., 1948.

Owsley, Frank Lawrence. King Cotton Diplomacy: Foreign Relations of the Confederate States of America. 2nd edition, revised by Harriet Chappell Owsley. Chicago: University of Chicago Press, 1959.

Papers Relative to the Mission of the Hon. T. Butler King, to Europe. Milledgeville: Confederate Union Power Press, 1863.

Peebles, Cornelius Glen. Exposé of the Atlantic and Pacific Railroad Company. (Extraordinary Developments). New York: [n.p.], 1854.

Phillips, Ulrich Bonnell. *American Negro Slavery: A Survey of the Supply, Employment and Control of Negro Labor as Determined by the Plantation Regime.* New York: D. Appleton and Co., 1918.

Phillips, Ulrich Bonnell, ed. *The Correspondence of Robert Toombs, Alexander H. Stephens, and Howell Cobb.* (*Annual Report of the American Historical Association, 1911,* Volume II.) Washington: Government Printing Office, 1913.

Phillips, Ulrich Bonnell. *Georgia and State Rights: A Study of the Political History of Georgia from the Revolution to the Civil War, with Particular Regard to Federal Relations.* Washington: Government Printing Office, 1902.

——————. *A History of Transportation in the Eastern Cotton Belt to 1860.* New York: Columbia University Press, 1908.

——————. *Life and Labor in the Old South.* Boston: Little, Brown and Co., 1929.

——————. *The Life of Robert Toombs.* New York: The Macmillan Co., 1913.

Poage, George Rawlings. *Henry Clay and the Whig Party.* Chapel Hill: University of North Carolina Press, 1936.

Quaife, Milo Milton, ed. *The Diary of James K. Polk During His Presidency, 1845-1849,* 4 vols. Chicago: A. C. McClurg & Co., 1910.

Russel, Robert Royal. *Economic Aspects of Southern Sectionalism, 1840-1861.* Urbana: University of Illinois, 1924.

——————. *Improvement of Communication with the Pacific Coast as an Issue in American Politics, 1783-1864.* Cedar Rapids: Torch Press, 1948.

Shenton, James P. *Robert John Walker: A Politician from Jackson to Lincoln.* New York: Columbia University Press, 1961.

Shryock, Richard Harrison. *Georgia and the Union in 1850.* Durham: Duke University Press, 1926.

Taylor, George Rogers. *The Transportation Revolution, 1815-1860.* New York: Rinehart and Co., 1951.

Van Deusen, Glyndon Garlock. *The Life of Henry Clay.* Boston: Little, Brown and Co., 1937.

——————. *Thurlow Weed, Wizard of the Lobby.* Boston: Little, Brown and Co., 1947.

Wheeler, Henry G. *History of Congress, Biographical and Political: Comprising Memoirs of Members of the Congress of the United States, Drawn from Authentic Sources; Embracing the Prominent Events of Their Lives, and Their Connection with the Political History of the Times,* 2 vols. New York: Harper and Bros., 1848.

White, Leonard D. *The Jacksonians: A Study in Administrative History, 1829-1861.* New York: The Macmillan Co., 1954.

Wiltse, Charles Maurice. *John C. Calhoun,* 3 vols. Indianapolis: The Bobbs-Merrill Co., c. 1944-1951.

Index

DATE DUE
